Green Digital Transformation

How to Sustainably Close the Digital Divide and Harness Digital Tools for Climate Action

Climate Change and Development Series

Green Digital Transformation

How to Sustainably Close the Digital Divide and Harness Digital Tools for Climate Action

WORLD BANK GROUP

Cover design: Bill Pragluski, Critical Stages, LLC.

Library of Congress Control Number: 2023919982

Climate Change and Development

The Climate Change and Development Series was created in 2015 to showcase economic and scientific research that explores the interactions between climate change, climate policies, and development. The series aims to promote debate and broaden understanding of current and emerging questions about the climate–development nexus through evidence-based analysis.

TITLES IN THIS SERIES

Green Digital Transformation: How to Sustainably Close the Digital Divide and Harness Digital Tools for Climate Action (2024) by the World Bank

Within Reach: Navigating the Political Economy of Decarbonization (2024) by Stéphane Hallegatte, Catrina Godinho, Jun Rentschler, Paolo Avner, Ira Irina Dorband, Camilla Knudsen, Jana Lemke, and Penny Mealy

Reality Check: Lessons from 25 Policies Advancing a Low-Carbon Future (2023) by World Bank

Diversification and Cooperation in a Decarbonizing World: Climate Strategies for Fossil Fuel-Dependent Countries (2020) by Gregorz Peszko, Dominique van der Mensbrugghe, Alexander Golub, John Ward, Dimitri Zenghelis, Cor Marijs, Anne Schopp, John A. Rogers, and Amelia Midgley

Unbreakable: Building the Resilience of the Poor in the Face of Natural Disasters (2017) by Stephane Hallegatte, Adrien Vogt-Schilb, Mook Bangalore, and Julie Rozenberg

Shock Waves: Managing the Impacts of Climate Change on Poverty (2016) by Stephane Hallegatte, Mook Bangalore, Laura Bonzanigo, Marianne Fay, Tamaro Kane, Ulf Narloch, Julie Rozenberg, David Treguer, and Adrien Vogt-Schilb

Decarbonizing Development: Three Steps to a Zero-Carbon Future (2015) by Marianne Fay, Stephane Hallegatte, Adrien Vogt-Schilb, Julie Rozenberg, Ulf Narloch, and Tom Kerr

Contents

Boxes

Figures

Maps

Tables

Acknowledgments

Green Digital Transformation: How to Sustainably Close the Digital Divide and Harness Digital Tools for Climate Action was prepared by the World Bank's Digital Development Global Practice. Members of other World Bank Global Practices—Agriculture; Climate Change; Energy; Transport; and Urban, Disaster Risk, Resilience, and Land—contributed to its preparation. Colleagues from Information Technology Solutions (ITS); the Trade, Investment and Competitiveness Global Practice; and the International Finance Corporation, as well as external experts, development partners, international organizations, and companies, provided valuable comments.

The core team members are Tania Begazo, Senior Economist; Rong Chen, Economist; and Sara Ballan, Senior Digital Development Specialist. The foundational work led by Astrid Jacobsen, former Senior Digital Development Specialist, is gratefully acknowledged.

Members of the extended team at the World Bank who provided inputs for specific chapters are Edward Anderson, Senior Technology and Resilience Specialist; Xavier Decoster, Senior Digital Development Specialist; Amol Gupta, Senior Energy Specialist; Rachel Alexandra Halsema, Information Technology (IT) Officer; Nagaraja Rao Harshadeep, Lead Environmental Specialist; Marie-Agnès Jouanjean, Agricultural Economist; Tala Khanji, Digital Development Consultant; Jia Li, Senior Economist; Stela Mocan, Manager, ITS Technology and Innovation Lab; Jeongjin Oh, Junior Professional Officer; Wenxin Qiao, Senior Transport Specialist; Prema Shrikrishna, IT Officer; and Gayatri Singh, Senior Urban Development Specialist.

Background analyses and inputs were provided at the World Bank by Rami Amin, Digital Development Extended Consultant; Joseph Ashraf El-Cassabgui, Digital Development Consultant; Andrea Carugati, Senior Digital Development Consultant; Aldy Darwili, Climate Change Consultant; Sandeep Goel, Energy Consultant; Michael Minges, Senior Digital Development Consultant; Shailendra Mudgal, Senior Digital Development Consultant; Afua Owusua Oguah, Climate Change Consultant; Shuvam Sarkar Roy, Energy Consultant; Tiffany Minh Tran, Urban Consultant; and Dimitri Zenghelis, Senior Digital Development Consultant. Edward Oughton, Assistant Professor of Data Analytics, George Mason University, and Shanjiang Zhu, Associate Professor of Civil Engineering, George Mason University, provided inputs as well. The preparation of this report also benefited from insights and guidance on World Bank project design and implementation under the Green Digital Development program led by Sara Ballan and Seth Ayers.

The developmental editing of the report was carried out by Steven B. Kennedy and Stephen Spector. Sabra Ledent edited the final draft, and Mary C. Fisk oversaw production of the report. Digital Development Consultants Nadina Alexandra Iacob, Linda Kirigi, Nino Lazariia, and Maria Jose Vidal Roman provided support for its preparation. Administrative support was lent by Program Assistants Marga O. De Loayza, Hadiza Nyelong Eneche, and Shegufta Shahriar. The comments and inputs from the following stakeholders are greatly appreciated: Deutsche Gesellschaft für Internationale Zusammenarbeit (GIZ), GSMA, International Telecommunication Union, Orange, Telefónica, and Vodafone.

The team is grateful to the following peer reviewers at the World Bank for their valuable comments: Vivien Foster, former Chief Economist, Infrastructure Vice-Presidency; Stephane Hallegatte, Senior Climate Change Adviser; Penelope Mealy, Economist; Kwawu Mensan Gaba, Practice Manager; Parmesh Shaw, Lead Rural Development Specialist; and Rajendra Singh, Senior Regulatory Specialist. It is also grateful to Felix Creutzig, Mercator Research Institute on Global Commons and Climate Change, and Björn-Sören Gigler, Deputy Head of Digital Transformation Cluster, GIZ.

In addition, at the World Bank, the team is grateful for guidance from former Chief Economist of the Infrastructure Vice-Presidency Vivien Foster; Christine Zhenwei Qiang, Director, Digital Development; Pablo Fajnzylber, former Director of Strategy and Operations, Infrastructure Practice Group; Economic Adviser Roumeen Islam; and Acting Chief Economist Maria Vagliasindi. The report benefited from guidance provided by Casey Torgusson, Program Manager, Global Knowledge and Expertise; Isabel Neto, Practice Manager, East and Southern Africa; and Mark Williams, former Practice Manager, Global Knowledge and Expertise. Young Professional Devvart Poddar and Digital Development Consultants Nadina Alexandra Iacob, Linda Kirigi, Nino Lazariia, and Maria Jose Vidal Roman provided support for its preparation.

Financial support from the Digital Development Partnership administered by the World Bank made this report possible and is gratefully acknowledged. The Korea Green Growth Trust Fund (KGGTF) supported the preparation of underlying analysis for the report.

Main Messages

Climate change is unfolding amid a digital revolution. From digital identification to e-commerce to precision farming, digital technologies have emerged in all facets of economic and social life. Digital technologies are also increasingly shaping responses to climate change: early warning systems are alerting populations when storms are looming, and apps are helping farmers choose drought-resistant seeds. The growing array of digital tools, however, is beyond the reach of many of the people and countries who need them most. Nearly 3 billion people remain digitally unconnected, with the overwhelming majority concentrated in low- and middle-income countries (LMICs). Investing in inclusive digitalization and climate action is intertwined. Climate-relevant applications and services are needed, as are universal digital foundations such as connectivity, data infrastructure, and digital skills.

Digital technologies are necessary to accelerate climate action. Digital technologies, for example, have an important role to play in reducing greenhouse gas (GHG) emissions in high-emitting sectors, such as energy, transportation, and materials. The targets of the 2015 Paris Agreement on climate change will not be reached at the present level of effort and investment. Accelerating the pace of climate action will depend, among other things, on technological innovation, much of which will be powered by digital solutions. LMICs recognize the power of digital technologies for climate action. Two-thirds of developing countries include technology as part of their climate action plans (Nationally Determined Contributions) to help adapt to or mitigate the impacts of climate change.

The digital sector needs to be greener and more resilient. The digital sector itself is being affected by climate change—and is contributing to GHG emissions. Digital infrastructure is susceptible to climate hazards. As countries become digitalized, weather-related digital infrastructure failures can have significant economywide consequences. Climate proofing digital infrastructure is important and can be part of wider efforts to protect critical infrastructure. Digital infrastructure and technologies are also part of the climate change problem, as they consume substantial energy. Increasing energy efficiency and transitioning to renewable energy for connectivity, equipment, and data processing will be important to ensure that digital emissions dwarf climate dividends from the digital sector.

Achieving a green digital transformation needs a push from industry and a pull from government. Globally, multinational digital firms are the biggest consumers of renewable energy and are investing in more energy-efficient digital infrastructure. This *push* from industry is critical. In parallel, countries can create enabling environments that incentivize, and *pull,* the greening of the digital sector, for example, by providing access to cleaner energy sources and partnering with operators. Some governments have embarked on this journey, but in many countries digital and climate ambitions are siloed. There is a need to create a bridge between the digital and green transitions. Doing this entails mainstreaming climate considerations in digital policies, closing the digital divide in a sustainable way, and strategically integrating digital technologies in climate change efforts.

Executive Summary

Governments across the world are looking for solutions that match the urgency and scale of the climate crisis—digital technologies are a key tool in this effort. Advances in digital technology are changing the way people interact, work, and live. They are also creating new ways to manage climate change. At the country level, digital technologies are increasingly powering adaptation efforts and supporting low carbon development pathways. A more strategic approach is needed, however, to develop, enable, and scale solutions and ensure they reach the most climate vulnerable populations.

From drought to floods, climate change is affecting populations across the world. Although no country is spared, climate change disproportionately affects the poorest and most vulnerable populations, threatening to push as many as 130 million people into poverty by 2030 and 200 million into migrating by 2050. Unchecked, climate change poses huge risks to countries' long-term development, growth, and stability.

A green and digital twin transition is imperative. Digitalization can help nations fight climate change by enabling novel solutions and greater efficiency in a wide range of practices, processes, and services. Digital technologies, however, carry climate costs as well as benefits stemming from the use of energy and resources to build, power, and dispose of digital infrastructure, devices, and components. A twin transition approach seeks to pair digital transformation with climate action. This means ensuring inclusive and sustainable digital foundations and applications are in place to accelerate mitigation and adaptation efforts while reaping wider benefits of digital transformation for growth, job creation, and better lives.

This report proposes a path toward low-emission applications of digital technologies to help countries mitigate and adapt to climate change, while simultaneously meeting their digital transformation goals. It examines how to increase the synergies among socioeconomic development goals, climate change policies, and digital technologies, offering guidance on how government institutions and private organizations in the digital field can catalyze green digitalization. The guidance includes strategies for greening the digital sector[1] itself, as well as leveraging digital technologies for climate action across sectors (figure ES.1).

FIGURE ES.1 The Green–Digital Nexus

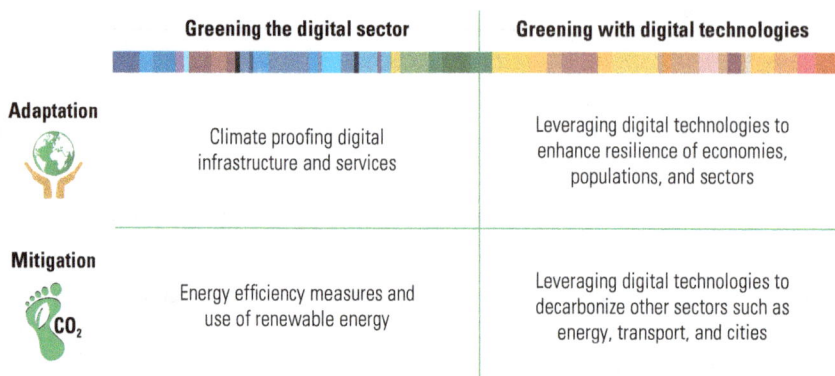

	Greening the digital sector	Greening with digital technologies
Adaptation	Climate proofing digital infrastructure and services	Leveraging digital technologies to enhance resilience of economies, populations, and sectors
Mitigation	Energy efficiency measures and use of renewable energy	Leveraging digital technologies to decarbonize other sectors such as energy, transport, and cities

Source: World Bank.

The Digital–Climate Change Nexus

The links between the digital sector and climate change are less well understood than those with other sectors. This report proposes a conceptual framework with two channels—direct and indirect—to illustrate how digitalization interacts with climate change:

- *Direct channel.* The production, use, and disposal of digital technology contribute directly to GHG emissions. Digital infrastructure is also directly exposed to significant climate change–induced risks, including rising temperatures and sea levels; water scarcity; and extreme events such as drought, cyclones, and flooding.
- *Indirect channel.* As digital technologies become pervasive in social and economic activities, they also have an indirect impact on climate change at the macroeconomic level and across sectors. At the macro level, digital technologies increase productivity, thereby increasing total consumption and increasing emissions. Decoupling economic growth from emissions—that is, ensuring that the growth rate of GHG emissions is less than that of its economic driving forces—becomes essential to achieving a sustainable growth trajectory. The fact that both production and consumption across sectors are being "dematerialized" thanks to the rapid development of digital technologies provides opportunities to achieve decoupling.

Climate action and digital transformation are core policy priorities for many governments, but most often these efforts are carried out in isolation. There are, however, modest signs of convergence. Many LMICs are already incorporating technology—including digital technology—into their plans to combat and adapt to climate change. Overall, 84 percent of countries mention "technology" in the mitigation provisions and 63 percent mention it in the adaptation provisions of their Nationally Determined Contributions (NDCs). NDCs reflect the efforts by each country to reduce national emissions and adapt to the impacts of climate change (figure ES.2). Although the role of technology is often mentioned, it is rarely addressed strategically in the NDCs, and the proposed applications are narrow (mainly disaster risk management technology and smart consumption solutions), indicating a need for a greater awareness of digital technologies for climate action.

At the policy level, integration of green and digital policies cuts across governments and stakeholders, calling for a whole-of-government approach. Digital ministries need to understand how to integrate climate considerations into their sector policies, such as through strategies that promote climate-resilient digital infrastructure, and encourage investments in low-carbon digital infrastructure. Digital ministries also need to ensure that the digital fundamentals such as connectivity and data infrastructure are in place to enable use for climate action. Other ministries, institutions, and organizations that grapple with climate change should focus on identifying digital applications for combating climate change, weighing the factors that may limit the scale and scope of implementation.

FIGURE ES.2 **Mentions of Technology in Mitigation and Adaptation Provisions of Nationally Determined Contributions (NDCs)**

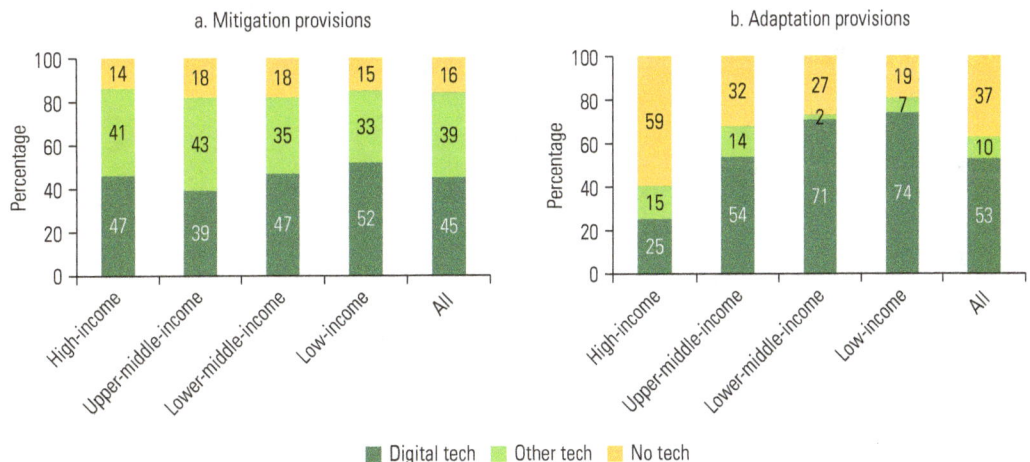

Source: World Bank analysis based on Nationally Determined Contributions Registry, United Nations, New York (accessed September 2022), https://unfccc.int/NDCREG.

Note: Digital tech: a country mentioned one or more technological initiatives heavily underpinned by digital technologies; other tech: a country mentioned one or more technological initiatives that do not necessarily involve digital technologies for connectivity or analytics; no tech: a country did not explicitly mention technology in their NDCs. The analysis covered 197 countries, including 138 low- and middle-income economies.

Decarbonizing the Digital Sector

Current estimates of the sector's share of global carbon dioxide (CO$_2$) emissions range from 1.5 to 4 percent—or roughly equal to the footprints of commercial aviation or maritime transportation. The booming digital economy relies on devices and networks that consume energy and electricity, creating carbon footprints. Country-level emissions vary considerably and depend on a country's level of digitalization, patterns in the consumption of digital technologies, and sources of the energy used.

Data centers are a large source of emissions, but so are digital devices and telecom networks. Although much attention has been paid to the energy consumption—and, thus, the emissions—of data centers, emissions from digital devices and networks are similar (figure ES.3). It is heartening that as data consumption has skyrocketed in recent years, data centers' energy consumption and emissions have not grown apace, a result traceable to efficiency gains and greater use of renewable energy. Overall, however, without a sharper change in direction, expansion of the information and communication technology (ICT) sector will continue to increase emissions, calling for substantially greater investments in innovation, energy-efficient technology, and renewable energy as digitalization increases. Technologies tailored to low- and middle-income economies must not be overlooked in the process.

FIGURE ES.3 **Emissions from Subsectors of the ICT Sector**

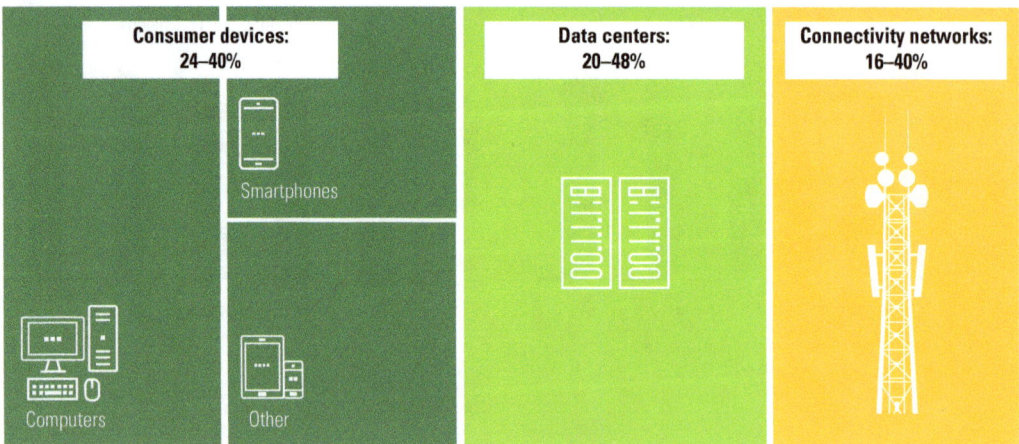

Consumer devices: 24–40%
Smartphones
Computers
Other

Data centers: 20–48%

Connectivity networks: 16–40%

Source: Adapted from WIK-Consult and Ramboll (2021) to include estimates by Minges, Mudgal, and Decoster (forthcoming) based on analysis of reported emissions by more than 150 international digital companies.

Note: The midpoint of the range of the subsector's contribution to total emissions in the sector is reflected in the size of the boxes. Televisions (including smart TVs) are excluded from the sector breakdown. "Other" includes routers and connected devices. Mobile network operations account for more than 50 percent of the emissions of connectivity network operations. Deployment and decommissioning account for 10 percent of total connectivity network emissions. ICT = information and communication technology.

The sphere of influence for governments will depend on their country's position in the digital value chain. For example, devices, which emit most during manufacture, are manufactured in a small number of countries. Similarly, hyperscale data centers serving global markets are located in relatively few countries. In these countries, corporate climate commitments, effective government policies, and use of renewable energy can have a strong effect on global digital emissions. With shifts to edge infrastructure, data center emissions may be become more dispersed globally.

Multinational digital firms lead in the use of renewable energy. In line with corporate commitments, the ICT sector is the largest purchaser of renewable energy globally. This sector is therefore an important and potentially underestimated part of the overall transition to renewable energy, with multinational corporations emerging as significant drivers of demand for renewable power in some LMICs. Governments play a critical role through renewable energy policies, investments, and the enabling of direct power purchase agreements by firms.

From artificial intelligence (AI) to emails, it is the sum that counts. New technologies can expand the use of digital and data infrastructure, generating ever more emissions such as from blockchain, fifth-generation (5G) technology, and AI. Although AI algorithms can be energy intensive to run, the same is true of the millions of emails, video calls, and bytes of stored data. Greening digital requires big and small actions across multiple use cases and stakeholders, including individual users. As the ICT sector grows across countries at all income levels, every country and every sector will have to consider how the digital transformation can be made more sustainable.

Making the Digital Sector More Resilient

Digital infrastructure is increasingly susceptible to climate risks. Digital disruption means social and economic disruption. Among these hazards are floods (both coastal and riverine), landslides, tsunamis, cyclones, powerful storms and winds, water scarcity, and extreme heat. Damage to digital infrastructure disrupts connectivity and access to linked data and digital systems. Even localized damage can affect entire networks. Because of economywide digitalization, interruptions can cause failures of the associated critical infrastructure, such as communication services, banking, power grids, railways, and government services. Digital infrastructure is, therefore, critical infrastructure that must be climate proofed.

Digital Technologies for Mitigation

Digital technologies are creating new opportunities to cut emissions and fight climate change across sectors. In this report, energy, transportation, agrifood systems, and urban centers are identified as high-emitting sectors in which digital technologies can be leveraged for mitigation:

- In the energy sector, digital technologies can advance the transition to renewable energy. Examples range from pay-as-you-go solutions for solar devices to satellite imagery that helps identify the best locations for geothermal and hydro sites. Digital solutions can also enhance energy efficiency and enable demand-side flexibility (smart grids, meters, and devices/appliances/machines) as well as support implementation of decentralized distributed energy systems powered by renewables.
- In the transportation sector, digital technologies can accelerate the transition to electric vehicles and to modal shifts in passenger transport, public transport, and shared mobility. They can also optimize traffic flows and contribute to digitally enabled logistics systems that enhance freight management and reduce transport needs.
- In the agrifood system, digital technologies can lower emissions systemwide (energy, fertilizer, transportation, processing, and sales) through direct, enabling, and behavioral effects that improve food production, reduce waste, and lead to better use of natural resources.
- In the urban sector, digital technologies can mitigate climate change in urban planning and waste management. They can also improve the carbon footprint and energy efficiency of buildings. Applications can be deployed as well to precisely identify, measure, and manage key sources of pollution (air, waste, water, and noise) in urban areas.

Achieving mitigation at scale will require building digital foundations and promoting widespread adoption. Many climate technologies are never scaled up. The cost of adoption, the lack of adoption incentives, and the failure to tailor solutions to local contexts too often limit demand. On the supply side, the need for digital foundations as prerequisites and enablers of climate action is often underestimated. These foundations include investments in universal broadband coverage and uptake; digital literacy and advanced digital/data skills; and public digital infrastructure to allow governments to generate, share, analyze, and utilize data. Early consideration of cyber resilience and data protection in the design of digitally enabled systems is also vital to minimize risks.

Digital technologies are not a panacea for climate action. Digitalization does not by default shrink the carbon footprint of any sector. Some solutions may reduce unit-level emissions while boosting overall usage, producing a rebound effect. For example, although 5G technology—which can be used for Internet of Things solutions—is more energy efficient per unit of data, increases in data volume and in use of the underlying network infrastructure can result in higher total emissions. Because these effects are not always foreseeable at the outset, constant attention should be paid to measuring and balancing the climate-friendly effects of an innovation and its possible rebound effects. Substantial research is needed to clarify these relationships and guide climate action. In the meantime, the transition to renewable energy is the surest way to minimize the adverse effects of any digital advance.

Digital Technologies for Resilience

Countries must cope with climate shocks as well as the gradual effects of climate change. Eight of the 10 countries most affected by extreme weather events in 2019 were low- and middle-income economies. Half were in the least-developed category. Geographically, many of these countries are exposed to direct effects from rising temperatures and flooding because they lie at low elevations and have densely populated coastlines or riverine zones.

Digital technologies can contribute to resilience to both long-term climate risks and climate shocks. At the macro level, development of the digital sector and economywide digitalization can strengthen the resilience of an economy, for example, by diversification to less climate vulnerable sectors and jobs and virtualization of transactions and communications. Digital technologies can also help policy makers adapt to climate change by providing the tools and data needed to sharpen predictions, enhance decision-making, and better prepare for disasters. Digital infrastructure and applications can enhance resilience before, during, and after climate shocks:

- Before climate shocks, digital solutions can enhance disaster preparedness by identifying high-risk areas and informing investments in, for example, flood protection measures. Digital financial and insurance services can also serve as a safety net against potential income losses.
- During climate shocks, early warning solutions can be critical to protecting vulnerable populations. Advanced technologies using AI and satellites are pushing the boundaries of disaster risk management, while simple technologies such as WhatsApp-based early warning systems are proving equally important.
- After a climate shock, the availability of digital identification systems and digital financial services can allow rapid, targeted, and effective outreach to affected populations through cash transfers, remote access to services, and information. As countries mounted a response, those that used digital databases and data sharing platforms reached more than three times the beneficiaries with social protection payments and services than countries that had to collect new recipient information.

Both strong digital foundations and advanced digital applications are needed for resilience. Areas for investment include connectivity, digital skills, and safeguards (cybersecurity and data protection). Global and local investments are needed as well in digital public goods requiring data access, management, and governance. A key concern is whether solutions and digital investments are able to reach the most climate vulnerable people, regions, and countries. Rural areas are a particular challenge because population density and connectivity costs can reduce commercial viability.

Policy Recommendations

Governments, private companies, the broad community of nongovernmental and scientific organizations, and the public at large share the burden and challenge of taking action to combat climate change. Governments, in particular, have a stake in clearing the way for and actively encouraging the ICT sector and other actors to use the full power of digital technology to advance mitigation and adaptation while mitigating the climate impacts of increased digitalization.

Key principles to inform green digitalization strategies include the following:

- **Complete a risk and emissions profile.** Each country must determine its green digitalization priorities around its climate risk profile and carbon footprint. LMICs are particularly exposed to climate change and need to find cost-effective ways to adapt. High- and low-tech solutions alike can play a key role, but both require investments in digital foundations. Governments must also encourage the ICT sector to build its own climate resilience and set a good example by climate proofing public digital infrastructure to ensure continuity of critical operations, communications, and services.
- **Decouple digitalization from emissions.** Growth of the ICT sector is going one way: up. With nearly 3 billion people remaining offline across the globe, fostering digital inclusion is of great importance. The climate change impact cannot be neglected during digital transformation, however. According to International Telecommunication Union estimates, to contribute proportionally to the reduction of global warming, emissions from the sector must be cut in half by 2030. Doing so will require all countries to accelerate the adoption of smarter, more energy-efficient equipment, devices, and processes; expand the use of renewable energy in the digital sector; and apply digital technologies effectively to reduce GHG emissions from other sectors. Policies are needed across the digital value chain. Some examples include the following:
  - *Telecom networks:* policies to promote infrastructure sharing as well as incentives and investments to promote renewable energy across the value chain (including off-grid, last-mile connectivity).
  - *Data infrastructure:* data infrastructure strategies that factor in energy and water resources, including the reuse of heat; regulations to limit the use of problematic refrigerants; and investments in technological innovation and capacity building of the workforce (sustainable data center planning and operations).
  - *Devices:* policies and investments to promote durable and repairable devices, e-waste management, and the circular economy; and a push for global standards, as well as regulation and incentives in countries that manufacture devices.

   ○ *Data:* investments in climate data platforms and data policies for the trustworthy collection, use, and reuse of data as well as a focus on interoperability, data standards, digital skills, safeguards, and open data access.

- **Ensure resilience of critical digital infrastructure.** Climate events inevitably have an impact on digital infrastructure. Nevertheless, governments can improve the resilience of digital infrastructure by incentivizing adoption of resilient technology choices; requiring consideration of climate risks in the design, deployment, and upgrade processes; and ensuring adequate redundancy while maximizing infrastructure sharing.

- **Calculate costs and benefits in a local context.** Most energy efficiency measures and green technology choices are cost-effective over the life of the asset. However, costs and benefits should be assessed considering a country's development profile and weighed against other development priorities such as digital inclusion. For resiliency investments, a paradigm shift is needed to move from corrective to preventive measures that are much cheaper and more effective.

- **Leverage position in the value chain.** Because of the global nature of the ICT sector, emissions from some parts of the value chain are concentrated in a few countries (such as those where digital manufacturing takes place or where large data centers operate). Governments in these countries have an opportunity and a responsibility to engage internationally to set enhanced standards—and to apply those standards at home.

- **Break policy silos.** Green digitalization calls for whole-of-government approaches. Digital ministries must consider national climate risks and ambitions and engage with stakeholders to leverage digital technologies effectively. Other sector ministries and implementing agencies may require capacity building to apply digital technologies effectively to climate action and to recognize digital risks.

- **Engage multiple stakeholders.** Private companies play a key role in green digitalization. They have a natural interest in reducing energy consumption and its associated costs, as demonstrated by changes in the telecommunication value chain and data center industry. Meanwhile, multinationals in the ICT sector have set the bar higher by embarking on net zero carbon strategies. Governments should create a strong enabling environment for these efforts and partner with the private sector in, for example, encouraging renewable energy power purchase agreements to power digital infrastructure and leverage the sector to drive demand for the local renewable energy sector.

- **Apply agile regulation principles.** The green–digital policy nexus is uncharted territory for most governments. Agile policy principles can help governments create a responsive enabling environment for green digitalization. So-called regulatory sandboxes and support for innovation test beds can enable novel approaches to data use and testing of climate-friendly digital technologies.

For the global community, important tasks are at hand:

- **Improve research, standards, and innovation.** The ICT sector lags other sectors when it comes to understanding its links with climate change. Despite digitalizing rapidly, very few countries are able to report emissions from the ICT sector. Stronger methodologies and country-level capacity are needed. In the data center industry, efforts toward greening are common, but internationally recognized standards are lacking. The country-level or regional codes of conduct that are emerging are important for setting a common direction. For cross-sectoral technologies, the focus is moving from uncritical optimism to tough but necessary exploration of the positive and negative drivers of emissions. The multistakeholder partnerships leading the way will be critical in determining which solutions and approaches deserve to be scaled up through investments.

- **Introduce digital climate financing.** The adoption of digital technologies to fight climate change requires investment in digital foundations: networks, devices, applications, capabilities, and services. This investment calls for a new mindset when allocating climate financing. Currently, the ICT sector and digital foundations are largely ignored in climate financing. To unleash the power of digital solutions across sectors, financing should not be limited to sector-specific interventions. Similarly, digital technologies can help solve some of the fundamental challenges of wider climate financing, for example, by improving data collection, verification, and aggregation to create a more transparent and accountable carbon marketplace. The international community, including development banks, has a role to play on both fronts.

The Next Steps to Using and Greening Digitalization to Combat Climate Change

This report aims to provide policy makers in low- and middle-income countries with information about the opportunities and risks digitalization can bring to combating climate change. Climate action and digitalization are already policy priorities across many governments, providing the underpinnings for the transition to green digitalization. For the digital development community, two main challenges remain: (1) closing the digital divide in a sustainable way and (2) developing and scaling digital solutions in a way that ensures that climate dividends dwarf digital emissions.

As the climate and digital transformation agenda evolves, more research is needed to monitor and quantify the enabling effects of digital technologies and the carbon footprint of the ICT sector at both the country and global levels. The World Bank welcomes cross-sectoral collaboration and partnerships in moving this important agenda forward. This effort includes developing the guidance needed to help countries translate green digital ambitions into policies, investments, and innovations as well as to leverage climate finance to catalyze digital technologies for climate action.

Note

1. Also called the information and communication technology (ICT) sector in this report.

References

Minges, Michael, Shailendra Mudgal, and Xavier Decoster. Forthcoming. "Information and Communication Technology (ICT) and Climate Change. Direct Greenhouse Gas Emissions of the ICT Sector." World Bank, Washington, DC.

WIK-Consult and Ramboll. 2021. "Environmental Impacts of Electronic Communications." WIK-Consult, Bad Honnef, Germany.

Abbreviations

ACRE	Agriculture and Climate Risk Enterprise
AF	Adaptation Fund
API	application programming interface
BEREC	Body of European Regulators for Electronic Communications
BESS	battery energy storage system
BIM	building information modeling
CAD	computer-aided design
CCDR	Country Climate and Development Report (World Bank)
CDM	Clean Development Mechanism
CER	Certified Emission Reduction
CIF	Climate Investment Funds
CO_2	carbon dioxide
CO_2e	carbon dioxide equivalent
CUE	carbon usage effectiveness
EAP	East Asia and Pacific
ECA	Europe and Central Asia
EO	Earth observation
ESG	environmental, social, and governance
ETSI	European Telecommunications Standards Institute
EU	European Union
g	gram
G	generation (as in 5G)
GB	gigabyte
GCF	Green Climate Fund
gCO_2/kWh	grams of carbon dioxide per kilowatt-hour
GEF	Global Environment Facility
GeSI	Global e-Sustainability Initiative
GHG	greenhouse gas
GIS	geographic information system
GPS	global positioning system
GRID	Green, Resilient and Inclusive Development (World Bank)
Gt	gigatonne
GWh	gigawatt-hour
ICT	information and communication technology

IDC	International Data Corporation
IEA	International Energy Agency
IETA	International Emissions Trading Association
IGBC	Indian Green Building Council
IoT	Internet of Things
IPCC	Intergovernmental Panel on Climate Change
ISIC	International Standard Classification of All Economic Activities
IT	information technology
ITU	International Telecommunication Union
kg	kilogram
$kgCO_2e$	kilograms of carbon dioxide equivalent
kgoe/$	kilograms of oil equivalent per dollar
LAC	Latin America and the Caribbean
LMICs	low- and middle-income countries
LTD	long-term evolution
MaaS	mobility as a service
MENA	Middle East and North Africa
MNO	mobile network operator
Mt	megatonne (million tonnes)
$MtCO_2e$	megatonnes of carbon dioxide equivalent
MTSFB	Malaysian Technical Standards Forum Bhd
MW	megawatt
MWh	megawatt-hour
NAP	national adaptation plan
NATF	National Academy of Technologies of France
NDC	Nationally Determined Contribution
OECD	Organisation for Economic Co-operation and Development
OMEA	Orange Middle East and Africa
PaaS	product as a service
PAYG	pay-as-you-go
PUE	power usage effectiveness
R&D	research and development
RAN	radio access network
RISE	Regulatory Indicators for Sustainable Energy
SAR	special administrative region
SBTi	Science Based Targets initiative
SDG	Sustainable Development Goal
SSA	Sub-Saharan Africa
Tbps	terabits per second
tCO_2e	tonnes of carbon dioxide equivalent
TEG	Thermo Electric Generator
TESCO	telecom energy services company

TRAI	Telecom Regulatory Authority of India
TV	television
TWh	terawatt-hour
UNFCCC	United Nations Framework Convention on Climate Change
V2G	vehicle-to-grid
VAT	value added tax
VMT	vehicle miles traveled
VPN	virtual private network

1. The Digital–Climate Nexus

Introduction

Climate change, the defining challenge of these times, is taking place amid the greatest information and communication technology revolution in human history. Unchecked, climate change poses huge risks to countries' long-term development, growth, and stability. It will disproportionately affect the poorest and most vulnerable populations, especially in low- and middle-income countries (LMICs), pushing as many as 130 million people into poverty by 2030 and 200 million into migrating by 2050 (Clement et al. 2021). Climate change also poses growing risks of famine and death from extreme weather events, drought, and the loss of reliable water supplies, especially in Sub-Saharan Africa and Asia. The heat waves, fires, floods, and droughts of 2022 are a preview of what lies ahead.

The 2015 Paris Agreement sets out global commitments to combat climate change.[1] At the current rate of progress, however, the Paris Agreement goals will not be reached. Accelerating the pace will depend on, among other things, technological innovations, many powered by digital technologies. These technologies—already available, in development, or foreseeable—could help nations fight climate change by enabling greater efficiency in a wide range of practices, processes, and services. Examples of those technologies follow:

- Digital communications and data access technologies (fixed/mobile telecommunication infrastructure, handheld devices, and computers) to enable use of digital solutions for mitigation and adaptation
- The Internet of Things (IoT), comprising devices, resource-efficient appliances, and components embedded in industrial equipment and vehicles to allow for machine-to-machine communication
- Information services, big data analytics, and artificial intelligence for more efficient use and reuse of resources
- Information services, data collection, data analytics, and blockchain to track emissions and monitor climate commitments
- Digital technologies to collect and assess the data used to track how, where, and in what form climate change is occurring.

The application of digital technology spans both climate change mitigation and adaptation efforts. *Mitigation*[2] efforts are aimed at reducing greenhouse gas (GHG) emissions to limit the increase in the average global temperature to 1.5 degrees Celsius above preindustrial levels. Mitigation strategies are characterized by measures that reduce GHG emissions. Digital solutions are at the core of technologies for mitigation actions. However, their increased use, in turn, has implications for emissions from digital infrastructure. The growing use of digital technologies carries climate costs as well as benefits. Costs—in the form of emissions—stem from the use of energy and resources to build, power, and dispose of digital infrastructure, devices, and components.[3] To support the 1.5 degrees Celsius goal, GHG emissions from the information and communication technology (ICT) sector would have to be reduced by half by 2030 (ITU 2020b).

Climate strategies also require *adaptation*.[4] Adaptation efforts are aimed at reducing vulnerability and exposure to climate variability, building adaptive capacity, and lowering the costs and damage from climate-related impacts and natural disasters. In addition to meeting urgent present needs, implementation of adaptation strategies will help countries prepare for the long-term effects of climate change. Digital solutions have an important role to play in monitoring, predicting, planning for, and responding to climate change and extreme events, and in protecting critical infrastructure and vulnerable populations. For digital infrastructure, this also means planning and designing connectivity and data infrastructure that is more resilient to current and future climate change events.

Adaptation and mitigation are complementary strategies for reducing and managing the risks of climate change, but they need to be linked to other societal objectives. The impacts of and responses to climate change are closely linked to sustainable development, which balances social well-being, economic prosperity, and environmental protection. The United Nations' Sustainable Development Goals (SDGs) provide a framework for assessing the links between global warming and development goals, which include eradicating poverty, reducing inequalities, and combating climate change. Digital technologies can contribute to achieving the SDGs. Meanwhile, considerations of ethics and equity should underpin efforts to address the uneven distribution of adverse impacts associated with higher levels of global warming, as well as those from mitigation and adaptation, particularly for poor and disadvantaged populations in all societies. Therefore, closing the digital divide is critical to ensuring that these populations can enjoy the benefits of digital technologies for adaptation.

Digitalization has been a major global trend in recent decades. Nine out of 10 people across the globe are now covered by third-generation (3G) networks. More than half of the global population is using the internet. From e-commerce to social media to smart manufacturing and precision farming, digital technologies have emerged in all facets of economic and social life, changing the way production and consumption take place. However, the challenge of unequal access persists. The opportunity to leverage climate technologies hinges on digital inclusion. Three billion people remain digitally unconnected, with the vast majority concentrated in low- and middle-income economies. To reap broader development gains from digitalization, governments and the development community must, as noted, close the digital divide. In addition, a shared understanding of and a common strategy for the use of digital technologies in the fight against climate change are critical to achieving climate targets.

This report looks at opportunities to bridge the digital divide in a sustainable way and leverage digital technologies effectively for climate action by asking the following questions:

- Chapter 1: What is the relationship between digitalization and climate change?
- Chapter 2: What are the present GHG emissions of digital technologies, and how can they be reduced even as use of those technologies continues to grow?
- Chapter 3: How can digital infrastructure be made more resilient to the risks arising from climate change?
- Chapter 4: What roles can digital technologies play in designing and implementing mitigation strategies in key sectors?
- Chapter 5: How can digital technologies be leveraged to make economies and people more resilient to climate change?
- Chapter 6: What policy options are available to the LMICs seeking to ensure that digital technologies provide the right foundations for their national strategies to combat climate change and promote economic and social development?

To reap the digital opportunities for accelerated climate action, countries need to better understand how digital technologies affect climate change and how they can help address the challenges it poses. This chapter explores the relationship between digitalization and climate change. It begins by looking at the current extent of digital considerations in national climate commitments and policies. It then explores the links among digitalization, economic development, and climate change. The chapter concludes with a conceptual framework that summarizes the digital–climate nexus and sets the stage for the rest of the report.

The Digital–Climate Policy Nexus

The Role of Digital Technologies in National Climate Commitments

Governments' commitments to achieving the goals of the 2015 Paris Agreement on climate change are captured by their Nationally Determined Contributions (NDCs). NDCs are national plans detailing current and planned climate actions, including emissions reduction targets, policies, and implementation measures. The United

Nations Framework Convention on Climate Change (UNFCCC) maintains the registry of NDCs, a public record of all countries' commitments under the Paris Agreement.[5]

For adaptation specifically, the *Sendai Framework for Disaster Risk Reduction 2015–2030* seeks to reduce disaster risks and losses in livelihoods and assets. It functions as a United Nations–endorsed international agreement to protect countries' development gains from disasters. The framework outlines a set of global targets and priorities to both guide and assess progress and highlights the use of digital technologies and tools that support information platforms and dissemination, online monitoring and reporting tools, provision of hazard data, risk assessments and data analytics, and facilitation of public participation and social inclusion (UNDRR 2015).

In addition to the Paris Agreement's requirement that parties to it develop NDCs, the agreement also calls for countries to develop long-term development strategies and targets for low GHG emissions.[6] Some countries have pledged to achieve net zero emissions in their NDCs across various target years, but many will converge at net zero by 2050 (figure 1.1). Setting specific targets ensures a clearer path for mitigation efforts.

As indicated by the NDCs, many low- and middle-income countries are already incorporating technology—including digital technology—into their plans to combat and adapt to climate change. Overall, 84 percent of countries mention "technology" in the mitigation provisions of their NDCs and 63 percent mention it in the adaptation provisions (figure 1.2). Digital technologies underpin various mitigation and adaption actions, with 45 percent of all countries mentioning these technologies for mitigation (mostly for monitoring and smart sectoral solutions) and 53 percent mentioning them for adaptation (mostly early warning systems and monitoring).[7] The limited use of digital technologies demonstrates the need for increased awareness and sharing of knowledge about the use of these technologies for climate action.

A growing number of LMICs are integrating digital technologies in their climate commitments. For example, as described in boxes 1.1 and 1.2, respectively, Rwanda and Maldives strategically consider digital technologies in both their mitigation and adaptation actions. Hydroinformatics and early warning systems are examples of solutions mentioned by many countries. According to its NDC, Sudan plans to scale up Smart IT used in the Nile to all major catchments, create a national map for potential water resource use and a recharging zone, and introduce sustainable irrigation systems for vulnerable farmers and livestock. Nicaragua not only plans to modernize the country's hydrometeorological monitoring services to provide accurate forecasts and build early warning systems, but also is emphasizing the importance of receiving access to new sensors and technologies and training staff. Moreover, Honduras plans to improve its hydrometeorological stations and provide better access to quality data, as well as enhance its forestry monitoring and management system.

FIGURE 1.1   National Pledges to Reduce Emissions, by Target Year

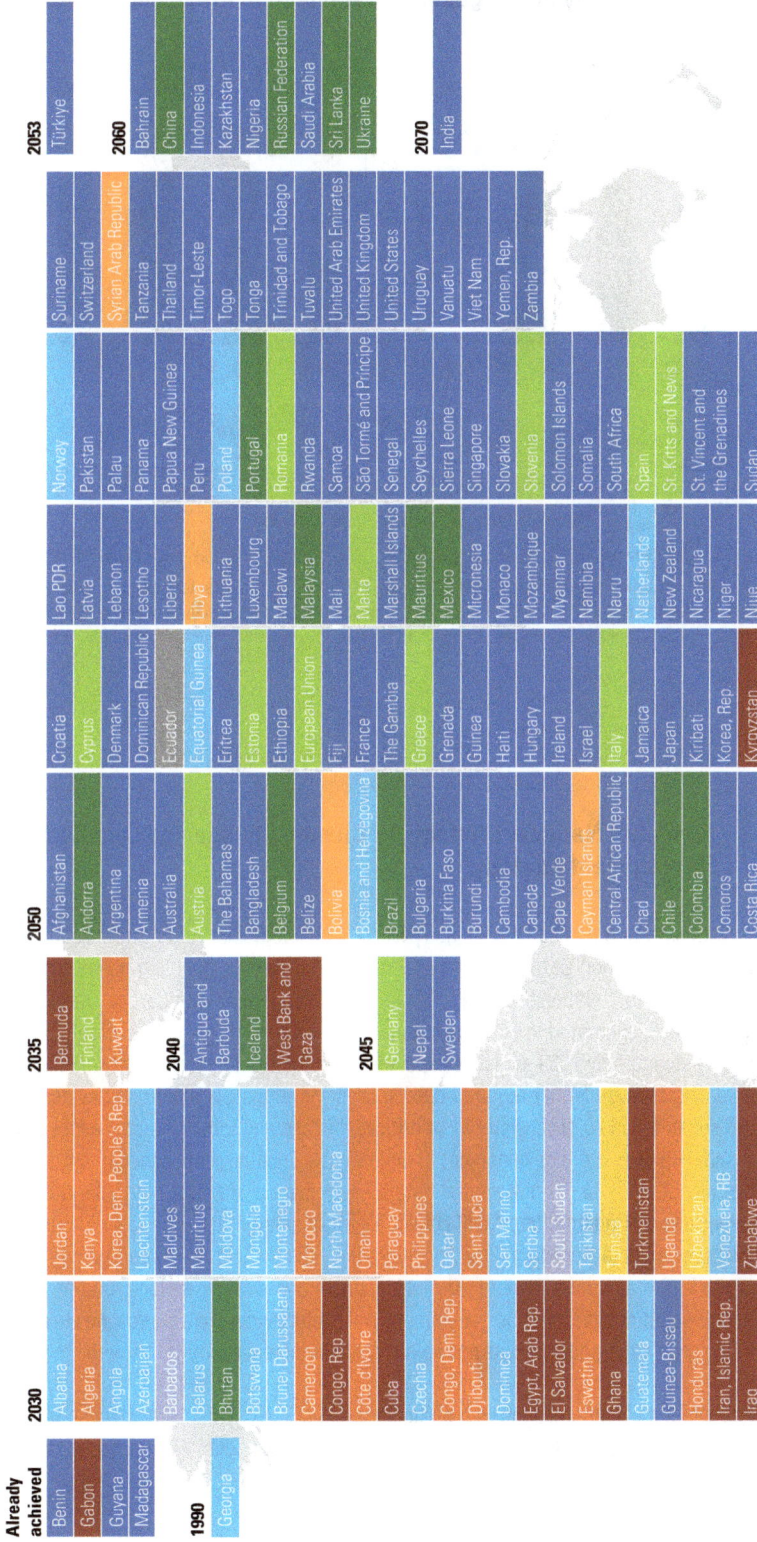

Already achieved: Benin, Gabon, Guyana, Madagascar

1990: Georgia

2030: Albania, Algeria, Angola, Azerbaijan, Barbados, Belarus, Bhutan, Botswana, Brunei Darussalam, Cameroon, Congo Rep., Côte d'Ivoire, Cuba, Czechia, Congo Dem. Rep., Djibouti, Dominica, Egypt Arab Rep., El Salvador, Eswatini, Ghana, Guatemala, Guinea-Bissau, Honduras, Iran Islamic Rep., Iraq, Jordan, Kenya, Korea Dem. People's Rep., Liechtenstein, Maldives, Mauritius, Moldova, Mongolia, Montenegro, Morocco, North Macedonia, Oman, Paraguay, Philippines, Qatar, Saint Lucia, San Marino, Serbia, South Sudan, Tajikistan, Tunisia, Turkmenistan, Uganda, Uzbekistan, Venezuela, RB, Zimbabwe

2035: Bermuda, Finland, Kuwait

2040: Antigua and Barbuda, Iceland, West Bank and Gaza

2045: Germany, Nepal, Sweden

2050: Afghanistan, Andorra, Argentina, Armenia, Australia, Austria, The Bahamas, Bangladesh, Belgium, Belize, Bolivia, Bosnia and Herzegovina, Brazil, Bulgaria, Burkina Faso, Burundi, Cambodia, Canada, Cape Verde, Cayman Islands, Central African Republic, Chad, Chile, Colombia, Comoros, Costa Rica, Croatia, Cyprus, Denmark, Dominican Republic, Ecuador, Equatorial Guinea, Eritrea, Estonia, Ethiopia, European Union, Fiji, France, The Gambia, Greece, Grenada, Guinea, Haiti, Hungary, Ireland, Israel, Italy, Jamaica, Japan, Kiribati, Korea, Rep., Kyrgyzstan, Lao PDR, Latvia, Lebanon, Lesotho, Liberia, Libya, Lithuania, Luxembourg, Malawi, Malaysia, Mali, Malta, Marshall Islands, Mauritius, Mexico, Micronesia, Monaco, Mozambique, Myanmar, Namibia, Nauru, Netherlands, New Zealand, Nicaragua, Niger, Niue, Norway, Pakistan, Palau, Panama, Papua New Guinea, Peru, Poland, Portugal, Romania, Rwanda, Samoa, São Tomé and Príncipe, Senegal, Seychelles, Sierra Leone, Singapore, Slovakia, Slovenia, Solomon Islands, Somalia, South Africa, Spain, St. Kitts and Nevis, St. Vincent and the Grenadines, Sudan, Suriname, Switzerland, Syrian Arab Republic, Tanzania, Thailand, Timor-Leste, Togo, Tonga, Trinidad and Tobago, Tuvalu, United Arab Emirates, United Kingdom, United States, Uruguay, Vanuatu, Viet Nam, Yemen, Rep., Zambia

2053: Türkiye

2060: Bahrain, China, Indonesia, Kazakhstan, Nigeria, Russian Federation, Saudi Arabia, Sri Lanka, Ukraine

2070: India

Legend:
- Carbon neutral
- Climate neutral
- Emissions intensity target
- Emissions reduction target
- Net zero
- No target
- 1.5°C target
- Other
- Reduction v. BAU
- Zero carbon

Source: Elaborated by World Bank's KIDS (Knowledge, Information & Data Science) Helpdesk based on https://zerotracker.net/ (as of September 2022).

Note: BAU = business as usual; carbon neutral = removal of carbon emissions, including through compensation; climate neutral = removal of greenhouse (GHG) emissions; net zero = removal of all GHGs; zero carbon = abatement of carbon emissions.

FIGURE 1.2 Mentions of Technology in Mitigation and Adaptation Provisions of NDCs, by Country Income Group

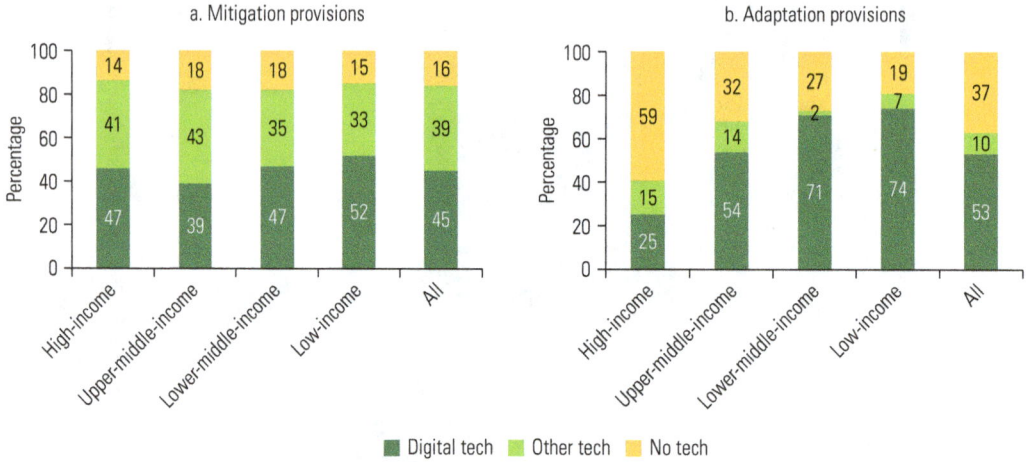

a. Mitigation provisions

Income group	Digital tech	Other tech	No tech
High-income	47	41	14
Upper-middle-income	39	43	18
Lower-middle-income	47	35	18
Low-income	52	33	15
All	45	39	16

b. Adaptation provisions

Income group	Digital tech	Other tech	No tech
High-income	25	15	59
Upper-middle-income	54	14	32
Lower-middle-income	71	2	27
Low-income	74	7	19
All	53	10	37

■ Digital tech   ■ Other tech   ■ No tech

Source: World Bank analysis based on Nationally Determined Contributions Registry, United Nations, New York, https://unfccc.int/NDCREG.

Note: Digital tech: a country mentioned one or more technological initiatives heavily underpinned by digital technologies; other tech: a country mentioned one or more technological initiatives that do not necessarily involve digital technologies for connectivity or analytics; no tech: a country did not explicitly mention technology in their Nationally Determined Contributions (NDCs). The analysis covered 197 countries, including 138 low- and middle-income economies.

BOX 1.1   Rwanda's National Strategy for Climate Change and Low Carbon Development Strategy

In Rwanda's Nationally Determined Contribution (NDC), "Technology, Innovation and Infrastructure" and "Integrated Planning and Data Management" are two of the five enabling pillars for implementation of the country's National Strategy for Climate Change and Low Carbon Development Strategy. Its first NDC, submitted in 2015, mentions the government's plan to develop a national spatial data infrastructure by 2030, which is expected to help the country efficiently manage land information resources and identify required data sets for developing a monitoring system.[a] The updated NDC submitted in 2020 consistently prioritizes the land and forestry sector, especially for adaptation, and emphasizes the development of an integrated spatial data management system.

The government plans to use the spatial data management system for both adaptation and mitigation measures. For adaptation, it will collect accurate data on the exposure of households and infrastructure to climate vulnerability. For mitigation, the system will help Rwanda reduce greenhouse gas emissions through more efficient land use and a larger surface area for carbon sink. In another mitigation measure, the government will explore innovative approaches to agriculture such as vertical farming technologies to help the sector increase crop yields within a smaller land area.

In adaptation, the country recognizes a particular need to build and further develop its monitoring and evaluation capacity. Acknowledging the country's lack of climate adaptation data and

(Box continues on the following page)

> **BOX 1.1** **Rwanda's National Strategy for Climate Change and Low Carbon Development Strategy** *(continued)*
>
> the need to enhance data quality and reliability, the government plans to improve monitoring and evaluation systems by leveraging information technology tools and processes. For example, the NDC mentions the health sector's use of drone technology for data collection, as well as the use of smartphones to mine and process health statistics to acquire quality data for reliable data management systems for climate adaptation. To continue the effort, the country cites the imperative for global financing and technology transfer (such as the application of web-based tools) for capacity building.[b]
>
> a. Nationally Determined Contributions Registry, United Nations, New York, https://www4.unfccc.int/sites/ndcstaging /PublishedDocuments/Rwanda%20First/INDC_Rwanda_Nov.2015.pdf.
> b. Nationally Determined Contributions Registry, United Nations, New York, https://www4.unfccc.int/sites/ndcstaging /PublishedDocuments/Rwanda%20First/Rwanda_Updated_NDC_May_2020.pdf.

> **BOX 1.2** **Maldives's Plans to Incorporate Digital Technologies in Adaptation and Mitigation**
>
> The Nationally Determined Contribution (NDC) of Maldives emphasizes the role of technologies in adaptation and mitigation. For example, the transformational changes needed to address climate change adaptation and mitigation will require proper knowledge transfer, human resource capacity building, and greater public awareness in addition to the financial and technological enhancements. Developing and promoting appropriate technologies to address climate change impacts with support from the international community are a priority for good climate governance.
>
> Early warning and systematic observation are other areas requiring data and analytics. Information and data availability on climatology, hydrology, and geophysics are scarce in Maldives. The wide geographic spread of the islands as well as capacity constraints and inadequate resources have posed challenges for expansion of the observation networks. Better data collection, management, and forecasts remain critical areas for early warning dissemination. Key measures include collecting the data needed to understand past and future climate trends and their associated impacts, strengthening and expanding the meteorological network and early warning systems to cover the entire archipelago, and improving the climate and weather forecasting tools for decision-making.[a]
>
> a. Ministry of Environment, Maldives, 2020.

The Intersection of Climate and Digital Technologies at the Policy Level

Climate action and digital development are core policy priorities for many governments, but they are often conducted in silos with limited links among the responsible government entities. Despite the wide recognition in NDCs of the role of technologies—including digital ones—systematic integration of climate change and digital development is still largely missing at the policy level. For example, mapping of policies for digital and green transitions in the Nordic and Baltic countries reveals limited policy integration (box 1.3).

Some countries are, however, including digital considerations in climate policies and integrating climate considerations in digital policies (table 1.1). Both are needed to green the ICT sector and create strong digital enablers for climate action. As table 1.1 indicates, empirical examples are emerging in the ICT sector, whereas strategic integration of digital considerations in climate-related policies at the national level is less prevalent.

At a regional level, there are also efforts to strategically link digitalization and climate change strategies. The European Union (EU) has in recent years adopted policy initiatives such as "Digitalization for the Benefit of the Environment" that address the twin societal challenges of digital transformation and green transition (box 1.4). In a related move, the Council of the European Union adopted Conclusions underlining the potential of the transition to the new green and digital jobs needed for economic recovery after the COVID-19 (coronavirus) pandemic. The "conclusions" state that digitalization is an excellent lever to accelerate the transition to a climate-neutral, circular, and more resilient economy and that an appropriate policy framework is needed to avoid adverse effects of digitalization on the environment. The Council encouraged the European Commission to develop an ambitious policy agenda for using digital solutions to achieve zero pollution and called on the Commission to propose regulatory or nonregulatory measures to reduce the environmental footprint of data centers and communication networks (Council of the European Union 2020).

Overcoming the challenges of linking digitalization and climate change will require policy coherence and close cooperation between policy areas. The digital component will be key in reaching the goals of the European Green Deal and the

---

| BOX 1.3 | **Integration of Policies for Digital and Green Transition in Nordic and Baltic Countries** |

A study commissioned by the Nordic Council of Ministers analyzed the level of policy integration between digital and climate policies in the Nordic-Baltic region (figure B1.3.1). The study found that very few policies across the Nordic-Baltic countries display a thorough and dedicated integration of digital technologies and climate mitigation. The result is likely to be low or insufficient impacts related to the digital and green transitions. The policy areas energy and utilities, climate, digitalization, and industry have the highest number of relevant policy initiatives. The study recommends promotion of policy innovation and an integrated approach to policy making moving forward.

(Box continues on the following page)

BOX 1.3   Overview of National Policies by Policy Area and Degree of Digital and Green Integration *(continued)*

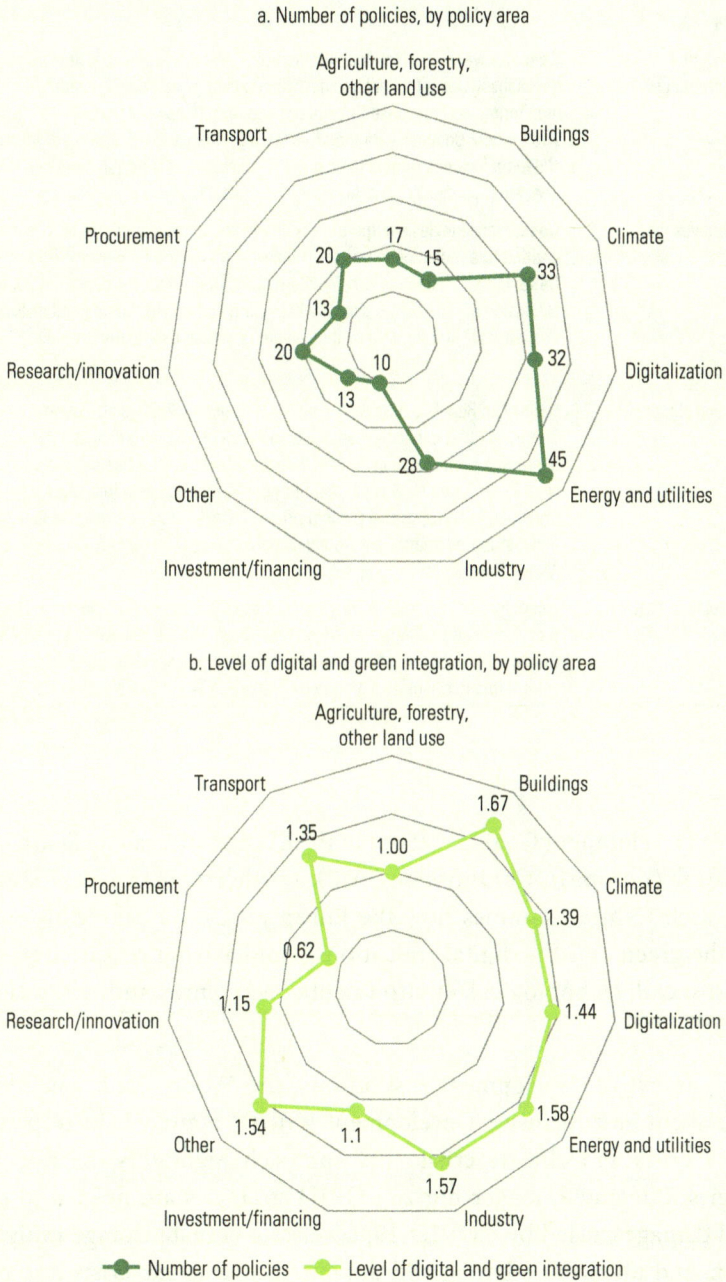

FIGURE B1.3.1   Overview of National Policies, by Policy Area and Degree of Digital and Green Integration

a. Number of policies, by policy area

b. Level of digital and green integration, by policy area

Number of policies   Level of digital and green integration

Source: Nordic Council of Ministers 2021.

TABLE 1.1   Examples of Green Digital Policy Types (Nonexhaustive)

Digitalizing climate policy	
Including digital infrastructure or enablers in climate commitments or action plans	**Case:** The National Adaptation Plan of the Democratic Republic of Congo recognizes that the inaccessibility of local communities to communication channels could be a major negative impact of climate change, and it identifies improvement of access to communication, including information and communication technology (ICT) infrastructure, as a planned action (DRC 2021).
"Greening" digital policy	
Including climate targets in digital transformation policies or strategies	**Case:** Kenya's 2019 National Information, Communications and Technology (ICT) Policy envisions ICT as a tool enhancing "climate change modelling, adaptation, mitigation, monitoring, and response through the appropriate use of relevant ICTs" (Ministry of Information, Communication and Technology, Kenya, 2019. Kenya's *Digital Economy Blueprint* includes targets to ensure the efficiency of ICT equipment and minimize e-waste (Communications Authority of Kenya, 2019).
Plans, regulations, and incentives that green the ICT sector	**Case:** France levies a corporate tax on electricity consumption. Data centers are entitled to a reduction in this tax if they live up to certain energy efficiency criteria. **Case:** China's "Eastern Data, Western Computing" plan, introduced in 2020, targets the expansion of data center capacity in eastern and western China and includes energy efficiency criteria for data centers—that is, power usage effectiveness (PUE) levels.
Cross-cutting policies	
Policies that bridge digital and climate policies	**Case:** The Republic of Korea's New Deal from July 2020 is an example of a policy framework that explicitly leverages digital technologies for climate action and also addresses climate action in the ICT sector. New Deal 1.0 has three pillars: Digital New Deal, Green New Deal, and Stronger Safety Net with initiatives such as green transition in cities/spatial planning/living infrastructure, diffusion of low-carbon and distributed energy, and establishment of innovative green industry ecosystems (World Bank 2022).
Cross-sector policies or regulation that enable green digitalization	**Case:** In Jordan, the Electricity Regulations Commission introduced a wheeling regime that allows large enterprises to generate electricity via renewable energy sources for their use. The ICT industry played a role in this process and subsequently invested in solar farms to offset its high energy costs (GSMA 2019; also see box 2.5).

Source: World Bank.

Sustainable Development Goals as set out in the EU digital strategy *Shaping Europe's Digital Future* (European Commission 2020). Furthermore, a recent study by the Joint Research Centre examines how the European Union can reinforce the link between the green and the digital transitions, emphasizing requirements on various fronts: social, technological, environmental, economic, and political (Muench et al. 2022).

In the context of development institutions, the World Bank has adopted the Green, Resilient and Inclusive Development (GRID) approach in response to the COVID-19 crisis and climate crisis. The approach highlights the role of digital technologies. Integrated, longer-horizon GRID strategies are needed to repair the structural damage caused by COVID-19, accelerate climate change mitigation and adaptation, and underpin a strong and durable recovery. The crisis responses offer

BOX 1.4   **Ministerial Declaration on a Green and Digital Transformation of the EU**

In 2021, 26 member states of the European Union (EU), as well as Norway and Iceland, signed a declaration to accelerate the use of green digital technologies for the benefit of the environment. The signatories of the Ministerial Declaration on a Green and Digital Transformation of the EU will take action at the national level in the following areas:

- Set up a digital twin of Earth to help monitor climate change.
- Make data available in common European data spaces.
- Support the deployment of green digital solutions that accelerate the decarbonization of energy networks, enable precision farming, reduce pollution, combat the loss of biodiversity, and optimize resource efficiency.
- Lead on energy-efficient artificial intelligence solutions.
- Help cities become greener and more digital.
- Use technologies to make buildings more energy-efficient.
- Support smart and sustainable mobility systems.
- Use digital product passports to track and trace products to improve circularity and sustainability.
- Promote ecodesigned products and accessible digital public services.
- Contribute to the use of a climate-neutral, sustainable, energy-efficient European cloud and blockchain infrastructure.
- Propose permits for the deployment of networks and data centers that comply with the highest environmental sustainability standards.
- Make green public procurement the default option overall.
- Develop low-power hardware technologies.
- Use EU funding programs and private equity to support European green tech start-ups and small and medium enterprises.

multiple opportunities to build stronger, greener, and more equitable systems and institutions (World Bank 2021).

The Country Climate and Development Reports (CCDRs) being completed across World Bank client countries integrate climate change and development considerations to inform policy and investments. A key finding across the first batch of 25 reports is that "the transition to more resilient and lower-carbon development requires managing political economy obstacles, strengthening institutional capacity, accelerating diffusion of new technologies, and the careful management of negative distributional outcomes."[8] The reports also find that reducing emissions can be achieved without compromising development: CCDR low-carbon development strategies could reduce emissions by 70 percent without a significant impact on growth, provided that policies are well-designed and financing is available (World Bank 2022).

Digitalization, Economic Development, and Climate Change

Economic development, digital transformation, emissions, and socioeconomic resilience to climate change are intertwined. Over the last decade, the development of digital technology has been a catalyst for economic growth. Although the increase in production and consumption from economic growth is often associated with higher carbon dioxide (CO_2) emissions, the growth-enhancing effect of digitalization does not mean that it inevitably results in higher emissions. A cross-country multivariate analysis confirms that there is no significant relationship between digitalization and GHG emissions after controlling for growth of the gross domestic product (GDP). Furthermore, climate policy (measured by NDC commitments related to technology) is found to be associated with lower emissions, suggesting that emissions from digital development can be curbed with the right policy that considers both climate change and digital development.

Meanwhile, economic development improves income, services, education, and health, and it builds socioeconomic resilience to climate shocks. Cross-country multivariate analysis suggests that digital development is positively correlated with a country's socioeconomic resilience and negatively correlated with vulnerability indicators (measured by risks to well-being and to physical assets and by the economic costs of climate change for households and firms). The results are robust across alternative indicators of vulnerability and resilience and digital indicators—such as the digital

MAP 1.1   Areas Susceptible to Flood Hazards

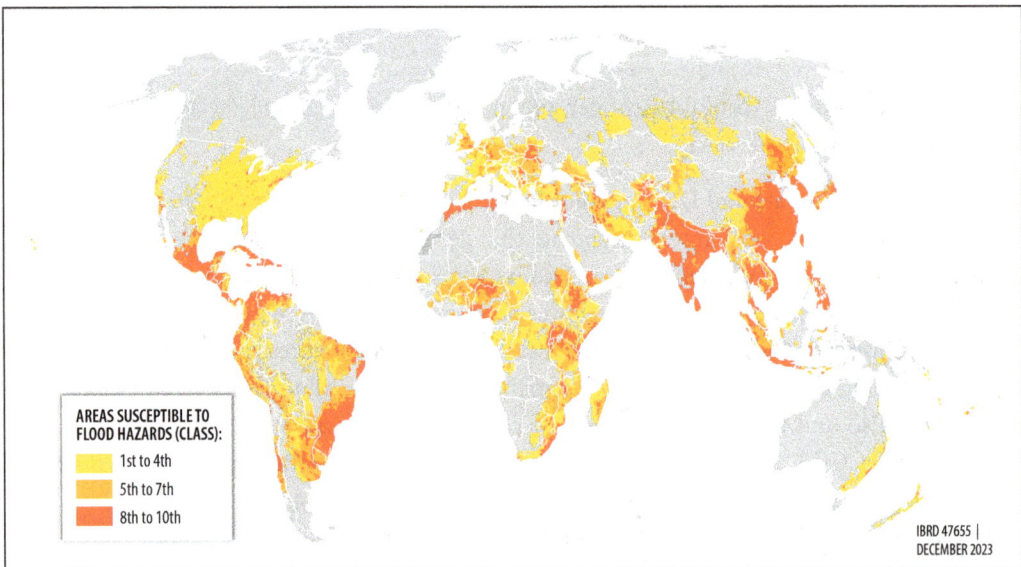

AREAS SUSCEPTIBLE TO
FLOOD HAZARDS (CLASS):

- 1st to 4th
- 5th to 7th
- 8th to 10th

IBRD 47655 |
DECEMBER 2023

Source: https://maps.worldbank.org/datasets/flood_main?viewMore=Disaster%20Risk%20Management.

adoption index, third-generation/fourth-generation (3G/4G) coverage, and mobile broadband subscription—and when controlling for GDP per capita, suggesting that digital development can play a significant role in building climate resilience and reducing the economic costs of climate change.

Digital technologies and data are important because climate disasters are occurring more frequently. For example, analysis of the correlation between climate events and deaths finds that disaster-related deaths have declined substantially over time thanks to better early warning systems (WMO 2022). However, there are digital coverage gaps in certain areas vulnerable to climate hazards. Correlating geospatial information on second-generation (2G) coverage and areas prone to flooding demonstrates that investments in digital infrastructure and services are still needed to support early warning systems to prevent loss of life from flooding in some areas of South America (such as Peru and the Amazon), Africa (such as Ethiopia), and inner Asia (see maps 1.1 and 1.2). However, the generally wide mobile data coverage globally serves as a good platform for mobile digital innovations for early warning in low-lying flood-prone areas with high levels of population, such as in Bangladesh and in east and northeast India. These opportunities need to materialize.

Government policies on digital development and climate change would therefore need to carefully consider countries' development contexts to achieve a twin digital and green transition.

MAP 1.2 **Mobile Network Coverage**

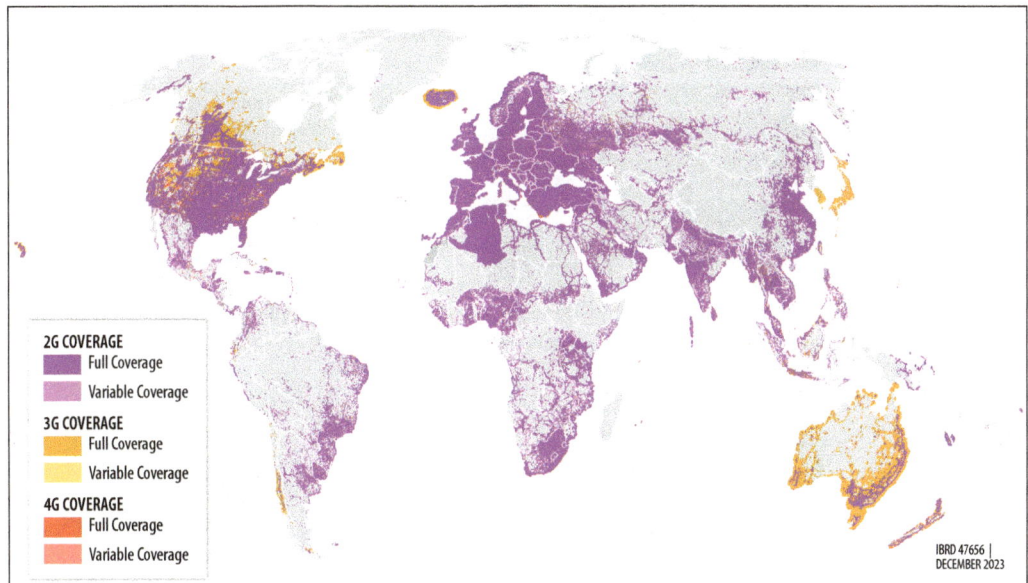

Source: Global System for Mobile Communications Association and Collins Bartholomew 2023.

Conceptual Framework: Untangling the Relationship between Digitalization and Climate Change

Digitalization creates both challenges and opportunities for the climate change agenda. The conceptual framework presented in figure 1.3 summarizes two channels—direct and indirect—through which digitalization interacts with climate change.

Direct Channel

The production, use, and disposal of ICT contribute directly to GHG emissions. Digital infrastructure is directly exposed to significant risks from rising temperatures, mounting sea levels, water scarcity, and extreme events such as droughts, hurricanes, and

FIGURE 1.3   Conceptual Framework for Relationship between Digitalization and Climate Change

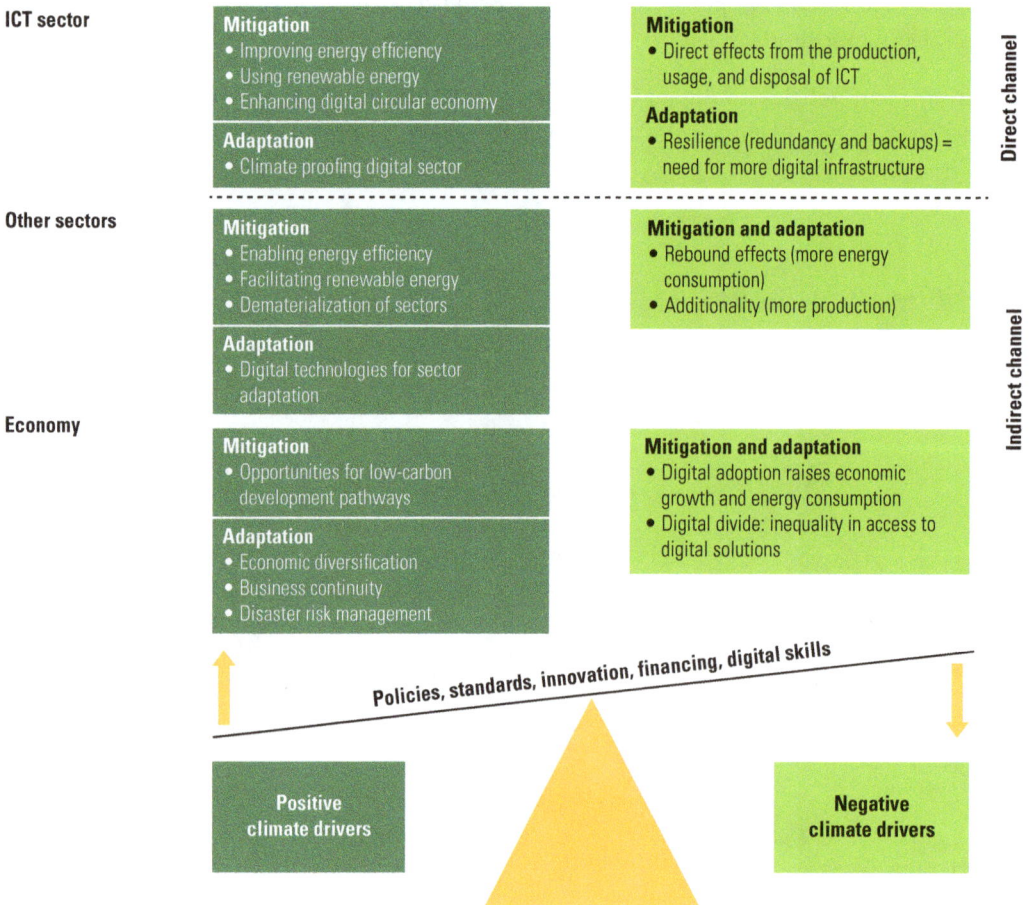

ICT sector	**Mitigation** • Improving energy efficiency • Using renewable energy • Enhancing digital circular economy **Adaptation** • Climate proofing digital sector	**Mitigation** • Direct effects from the production, usage, and disposal of ICT **Adaptation** • Resilience (redundancy and backups) = need for more digital infrastructure	Direct channel
Other sectors	**Mitigation** • Enabling energy efficiency • Facilitating renewable energy • Dematerialization of sectors **Adaptation** • Digital technologies for sector adaptation	**Mitigation and adaptation** • Rebound effects (more energy consumption) • Additionality (more production)	Indirect channel
Economy	**Mitigation** • Opportunities for low-carbon development pathways **Adaptation** • Economic diversification • Business continuity • Disaster risk management	**Mitigation and adaptation** • Digital adoption raises economic growth and energy consumption • Digital divide: inequality in access to digital solutions	

Policies, standards, innovation, financing, digital skills

Positive climate drivers   **Negative climate drivers**

Source: World Bank.

Note: ICT = information and communication technology.

flooding. Current estimates of the ICT sector's share of global CO_2 emissions vary, ranging from 1.5 percent to 4 percent.[9] A decarbonization pathway for the digital sector is needed through a combination of expanded use of renewable energy and energy efficiency measures (see chapter 2).

As various systems such as electricity, water, and digital connectivity become more and more interdependent and interconnected, disruptions of digital connectivity and the data infrastructure by climate change and natural hazard shocks will have ripple effects across a span of services vital to livelihoods. Climate and disaster risks must therefore be taken into account throughout the planning, construction. and operation phases of digital infrastructure (see chapter 3).

Indirect Channel

As digital technologies become pervasive in social and economic activities, they have an impact on climate change indirectly at the macroeconomic level and across sectors.

First, as shown earlier, at the macro level digital technologies increase productivity, thereby potentially increasing total consumption, which increases emissions. Low- and middle-income countries, especially upper-middle-income, have achieved significant productivity gains from foundational ICT investment in recent years (Dedrick, Kraemer, and Shih 2013). Such productivity gains are reflected in economic growth—for example, all the non-Annex I countries (developing countries under the Kyoto Protocol) experienced, on average, economic growth of 1.9 percent from 2000 to 2017. However, GHG emissions in those countries have been increasing at an even faster rate, 3.3 percent, since 2000, leading to growing carbon intensity.[10]

Decoupling of economic growth and emissions—that is, ensuring that the growth rate of GHG emissions is less than that of its economic driving force—becomes essential in achieving a sustainable growth trajectory. Since 2010, more than 40 percent of countries have grown their economies faster than the increase in carbon emissions, and 16 percent have grown without increasing carbon emissions.[11] However, among those that realized the decoupling, only 5 percent are low-income countries. Decoupling can be attributed to factors such as changes in a country's economic structure, a shift in energy mix toward renewable sources, and improvements in energy efficiency. Digital technologies provide opportunities to change a country's economic structure, efficiency, and energy consumption patterns to support low-carbon development pathways.

Second, at the sectoral level digital technologies could potentially reshape the structure of an economy and the size of each sector. Because the emission profiles of each sector differ, changes in the sectoral structure would also change the overall emissions. The worldwide energy intensity in industrial production is 0.12 kilograms of oil equivalent per dollar (kgoe/$); agriculture, 0.036 kgoe/$; and services, 0.016 kgoe/$.[12] Further tertiarization enabled by increasing the penetration of digitally supplied services helps to reduce emission intensity. However, for LMICs climbing the ladder to reap the development benefits of the manufacturing sector instead of rushing resources to the service sector (which could result in premature deindustrialization), leveraging digital solutions to help reduce emissions across all sectors is more viable to achieve a sustainable growth path.

A dematerialization pattern across sectors in production and consumption is emerging thanks to the rapid development of digital technologies. The development of the product as a service (PaaS) model, such as servicification of manufacturing, is a case in point, showing how digital technologies can enable using a product without purchasing it, thereby reducing the carbon emissions associated with the production of new products. The digitally enabled "mobility as a service" also helps achieve better integration and operation of various low-carbon transportation modes (Wadud and Namala 2022). Similarly, the online-enabled sharing economy helps optimize the utilization of existing assets, thereby reducing carbon footprints from new production. For example, Hello Tractor, an asset and service sharing platform in Nigeria, establishes a network of tractor owners, offering the equipment as well as services if needed to those who cannot afford to buy one for farming activities.[13]

However, further digitalization in production activities involves intensive use of ICT products and services, which could potentially shift carbon footprints back to the ICT sector itself, as reflected in the direct channel for the impact of digital technologies on climate change. For example, mobility as a service often involves the use of big data analytics that rely on data centers, which results in energy consumption in the ICT sector. This factor strengthens the importance of introducing renewable energies and improving energy efficiency of the ICT sector. Statistics reveal that substantial progress has been made in this regard; the carbon footprint per gigabyte (GB) in networks fell from 7 kilograms of carbon dioxide equivalent per gigabyte (kgCO$_2$e/GB) in 2007 to 0.8 kgCO$_2$e/GB in 2015 (Malmodin and Lundén 2018).

Third, within each sector digital technologies help shape emission profiles. Estimates reveal that the adoption of digital technology solutions in different sectors could help reduce global GHG emissions by 6–20 percent by 2030, depending on modeling scenarios and the sectors taken into account.[14] Most of the reduction is attributed to solutions applied in sectors such as transport, manufacturing, agriculture, building, and energy. For example, in the agriculture sector, precision agriculture—the digitally enabled precise application of water, seeds, fertilizers, and pesticides, depending on the needs of plants and soil quality—is thought to play a crucial role in making agricultural production more sustainable (Gebbers and Adamchuk 2010; Mendes et al. 2020). In the energy sector, linking real-time data on location-specific climatic conditions and gauging heating and cooling demands with smart thermostats show significant potential for greater energy efficiency and optimized energy management (WBGU 2019)—see chapter 4.

Sectoral digitalization does not, however, guarantee a smaller carbon footprint. Additionality versus substitution and energy efficiency versus rebound effects are two dimensions that merit special attention when analyzing the impacts of digital technologies within each sector. Technologies can reduce emissions when they produce the same thing, but they can increase emissions when they produce new (additional) services. The effects of shared mobility modes on carbon footprints depend on which transport mode is replaced. For example, the net effect of ride hailing services is an increase in urban traffic in New York and San Francisco from the additional trips generated. But carpooling could help reduce CO_2 emissions by attracting users that would have traveled with private cars (Butt d'Espous and Wagner 2019). In a similar vein, it is important to take into consideration the rebound effect, which covers additional energy consumption triggered by energy savings, when hailing improvements in energy efficiency stemming from digitalization.

Finally, besides enabling mitigation efforts, digital technologies also play an important role in climate change adaptation and monitoring. This role includes, for example, facilitating access to weather and disaster information (Aréstegui 2018); coordinating response, relief, and recovery efforts (Kalas and Finlay 2009); and strengthening the voices of those most affected by climate change in decision-making processes to bring about combined actions (Hilty, Lohmann, and Huang 2011; Melville 2010; Ospina and Heeks 2010). Sensors, drones, and satellite-based technological systems allow the collection of large amounts of data on climate change dynamics. The Global Observing System and Global Data Processing and Forecasting System are also widely used to monitor the global environment/ecosystem (Dickerson et al. 2010; Ilčev 2018)—also see chapter 5.

Forces That Shape Effects on Climate Change: Policy, Financing, and Market Forces

In both the direct and indirect channels, policy and regulatory environment, availability of financing, and market forces would shape the final impacts of digitalization on climate change. In the meantime, effects depend on the country context, including configuration of the digital value chain and its development, socioeconomic context, maturity of the digital ecosystems, institutional capacity, and capabilities. Policy interventions can play an important role in guiding market players developing and adopting digitally enabled low-carbon solutions. Incorporating climate change goals in the design of ICT policy as well as other sectoral policies ensures synergies across the policy spectrum.

Governments can also support digital transformation in general to exploit the potential of various digital solutions to address climate change challenges. Huge digital divides in terms of connectivity, data, technologies, and capabilities in LMICs could prevent countries from enjoying the benefits of using digital technologies for climate action (figure 1.4). Policy interventions to narrow the digital divide and improve digital literacy help ensure that vulnerable and marginal groups can also reap the benefits of digital technologies in combating climate change. On the one hand, robust data

FIGURE 1.4 Levels of Digitalization, by Country Income Group and Region

a. Share of households with internet access at home, 2005–20

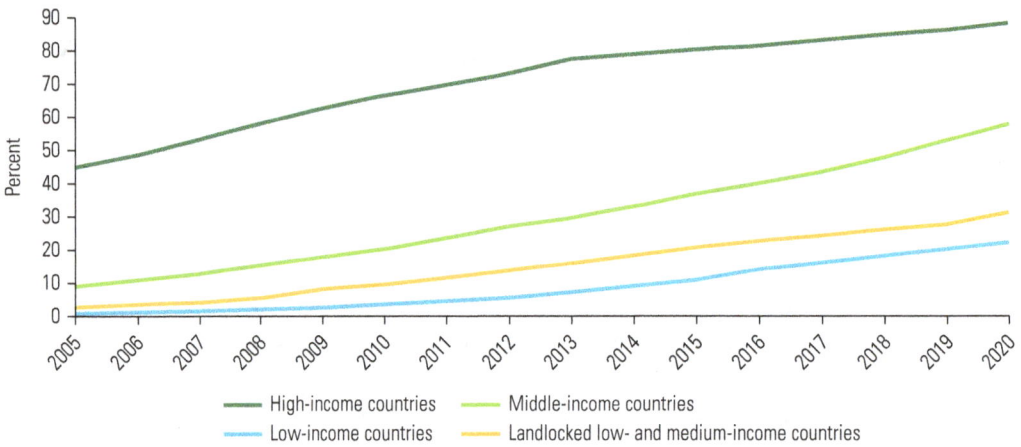

Source: International Telecommunication Union (ITU), time series, ICT data, https://www.itu.int/en/ITU-D/Statistics/Pages/stat/default.aspx.

b. Connectivity, coverage, and usage gaps across regions, 2020

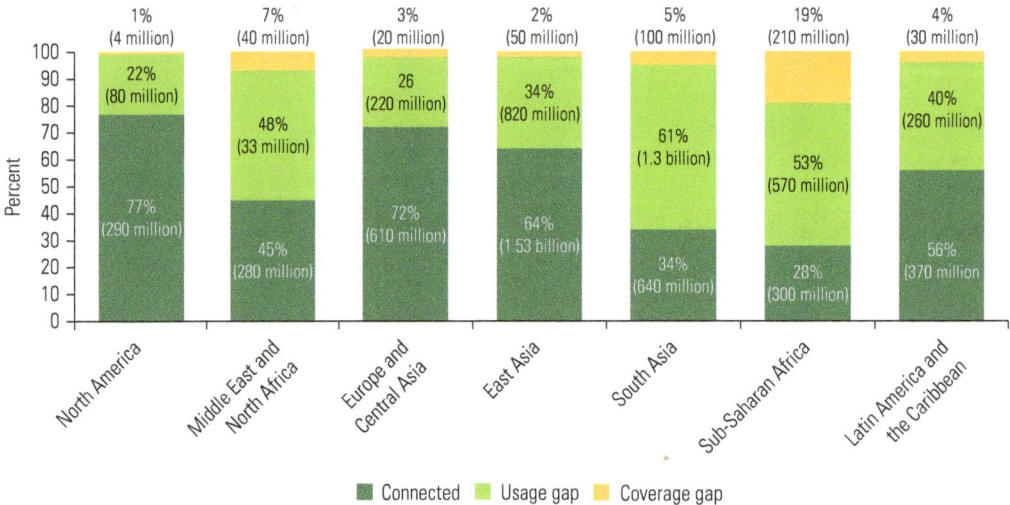

Source: GSMA 2021.

Note: Figure shows population in millions.

governance frameworks that enable data use and reuse, as well as safeguards protecting the rights of data subjects, create trust in the adoption of digital solutions. On the other hand, lack of cybersecurity measures could deter people from using digital technologies, thereby missing the opportunities they offer in climate change mitigation or adaptation.

Adoption of digital technologies for climate change strategies requires investments in networks, devices, applications, capabilities, and services. This approach calls for a new mindset when allocating climate change–related resources. Financial support should not be limited to sector-specific climate change interventions. Investments in foundational digital economy components also warrant attention because of their important role in supporting climate change mitigation, adaptation, and monitoring efforts across the board.

The investment needed to provide global universal coverage of a minimum quality level of broadband is estimated at US$428 billion (ITU 2020a). In addition to investments in digital infrastructure, financing is needed to promote take-up of digital services from the demand side. Investments in education and training are needed as well to strengthen the capacities, know-how, and skills required by individuals, the private sector, and public sector organizations in leveraging digital solutions to tackle the climate change challenges. Although this report does not focus on climate financing, it is worth noting that both public and private sources are needed to close the financing gaps for mitigation and adaptation. It is estimated that the global gap for mitigation is about US$850 billion a year and between US$180 billion and US$300 billion a year for adaptation.

Multilateral climate funds are playing a key role in fostering climate financing in low- and middle-income countries. Among the largest multilateral climate funds are the Green Climate Fund (GCF), Global Environment Facility (GEF), Adaptation Fund (AF), and Climate Investment Funds (CIF). Although these funds invest in solutions that help achieve climate change adaptation and mitigation and that may have a digital component such as early warning systems, none of the funds invests directly in digital infrastructure. GCF has developed a climate information and early warning systems sectoral guide, acknowledging that investments in trustworthy climate information services and impact-based multihazard early warning systems are being driven by digital transformation to enable informed, scientific decision-making. GEF also recognizes that technologies, including digital technologies, are both a source of GHG emissions and an essential tool to achieve climate adaptation and mitigation. It therefore supports projects that include the accelerated transfer of low-emission technology innovation. But digital is not considered to be a standalone recipient sector of climate financing, and no direct investments in digital infrastructure have been identified through these multilateral climate funds.

Carbon credits are an important tool for climate financing, but they have been subject to criticism arising from issues of accountability and transparency. The Paris Agreement allows countries to design their own systems to manage and track climate action. This approach has benefits, but it also creates challenges on standardizing data, verifying data in a uniform way, and connecting registries. Cross-cutting platforms and digital technologies can play a role overcoming these barriers. Platforms are, for example, being developed to reduce the cost of accreditation and ensure more direct links between sellers and buyers of credits. So far, many small businesses in LMICs have been left out of the carbon markets because of the cost of verification and other transaction costs associated with carbon trading. Blockchain and tokenization are also being explored as ways to improve trust and efficiency. For example, the World Bank, the government of Singapore, and the International Emissions Trading Association (IETA) developed the Climate Warehouse program, which is building an open-source global platform that connects, aggregates, and harmonizes carbon credit data.

Policy and financial incentives reinforce one other in achieving the climate change agenda. Access to affordable finance helps accelerate and amplify the effectiveness of public policies. By enabling the policy and regulatory environment, it attracts stakeholders to invest in solutions that support sustainable development. Tax incentives for research and development, programs to support technology adoption and the development of pro-climate applications, and a fiscal strategy supporting public-private partnerships can help direct financial resources to support a climate agenda.

Overall, the combination of an enabling policy and regulatory environment, sufficient financing support, and a functioning market delivers impacts on climate change. Collaboration among stakeholders from governments, the private sector, academia, and civil society is needed to tackle the challenge. The private sector is the main provider or adopter of digital solutions in addressing climate change challenges. Policy incentives are among the key enablers for innovation at the firm level. Academic research provides the scientific foundation for development of digital applications. And civil society supports public outreach and awareness enhancement.

Notes

1. The Paris Agreement can be found at https://unfccc.int/sites/default/files/english_paris_agreement.pdf.

2. *Mitigation* refers to actions to manage the direct relationship between global average temperatures and the concentration of greenhouse gases in the atmosphere. Limiting global warming to 1.5 degrees Celsius depends on reducing both the emissions released into the atmosphere and the current concentration of carbon dioxide (CO_2) by enhancing and safeguarding "carbon sinks," such as forests that absorb CO_2 (United Nations Framework Convention on Climate Change, https://unfccc.int/topics/mitigation/the-big-picture/introduction-to-mitigation). Effective mitigation measures result in lower emissions and decarbonization.

3. Mining of materials for digital equipment, e-waste, as well as the effects of deploying digital infrastructure on biodiversity impose additional burdens on the environment.

4. *Adaptation* refers to the adjustments made in ecological, social, or economic systems in response to actual or expected climatic stimuli and their effects. It also refers to changes in processes, practices, and structures that moderate potential damage or exploit opportunities associated with climate change (United Nations Framework Convention on Climate Change, https://unfccc.int /topics/adaptation-and-resilience/the-big-picture/what-do-adaptation-to-climate-change-and -climate-resilience-mean). Effective adaptation measures support resilience outcomes.

5. For the Nationally Determined Contributions Registry, see https://www4.unfccc.int/sites /ndcstaging/Pages/Home.aspx.

6. Article 19: All Parties should strive to formulate and communicate long-term low greenhouse gas emission development strategies, mindful of Article 2 taking into account their common but differentiated responsibilities and respective capabilities, in the light of different national circumstances.

7. See appendix for details on actions related to general technology and digital technology.

8. CCDRs are available at https://www.worldbank.org/en/topic/climatechange/publication/climate -and-development-an-agenda-for-action. The report on Malawi (https://www.worldbank.org/en /publication/country-climate-development-reports) covers the issue of digital infrastructure and technologies in more detail.

9. Based on the United Nations' International Standard Classification of All Economic Activities (ISIC), the ICT sector includes manufacturing of ICT equipment and devices, telecommunications, IT software, and services. In this report, the analysis focuses on data management and transmission infrastructure (data centers and telecommunications networks) and on ICT equipment and end user devices. The terms *ICT sector* and *digital sector* can be used interchangeably.

10. Food and Agriculture Organization of the United Nations, Rome; Paris Reality Check: PRIMAP-hist, https://www.pik-potsdam.de/paris-reality-check/primap-hist/.

11. Global Carbon Atlas (dashboard), http://www.globalcarbonatlas.org/en/content/welcome -carbon-atlas.

12. EnerData (dashboard), https://www.enerdata.net/about-us/.

13. Hello Tractor (dashboard), http://hellotractor.com.

14. Global e-Sustainability Initiative (GeSI), SMARTer2030, https://smarter2030.gesi.org/; Malmodin and Bergmark (2015).

References

Aréstegui, Miguel. 2018. "Intermediate Climate Information Systems for Early Warning Systems." Practical Action, infoHub, https://infohub.practicalaction.org/handle/11283/620977.

Butt d'Espous, V., and L. Wagner. 2019. *Zero Empty Seats.* https://www.clasicosalvolante.com/wp -content/uploads/2019/03/EN_Environmental_Report.pdf.

Clement, Viviane, Kanta Kumari Rigaud, Alex de Sherbinin, Bryan Jones, Susana Adamo, Jacob Schewe, Nian Sadiq, et al. 2021. "Groundswell Part 2: Acting on Internal Climate Migration." Climatewatchdata, https://www.climatewatchdata.org/.

Communications Authority of Kenya. 2019. *The Digital Economy Blueprint.* Nairobi: Communications Authority of Kenya. https://www.ict.go.ke/wp-content/uploads/2019/05 /Kenya-Digital-Economy-2019.pdf.

Council of the European Union. 2020. "Digitalisation for the Benefit of the Environment: Council Approves Conclusions." Press release, December 17, 2020. https://www.consilium.europa.eu/en /press/press-releases/2020/12/17/digitalisation-for-the-benefit-of-the-environment-council -approves-conclusions/#:~:text=The%20Council%20underlines%20in%20its,should%20 leave%20no%20one%20behind.

Dedrick, Jason, Kenneth L. Kraemer, and Eric Shih. 2013. "Information Technology and Productivity in Developed and Developing Countries." *Journal of Management Information Systems* 30: 1, 97–122.

Dickerson, Keith, Daniela Torres, Jean-Manuel Canet, John Smiciklas, Dave Faulkner, Cristina Bueti, and Vassiliev Alexandre. 2010. "Using ICTs to Tackle Climate Change." https://www.itu.int/dms_pub/itu-t/oth/0B/11/T0B1100000A3301PDFE.pdf.

Dilley, M., R. S. Chen, U. Deichmann, A. L. Lerner-Lam, M. Arnold, J. Agwe, P. Buys, O. Kjekstad, B. Lyon, and G. Yetman. 2005. *Natural Disaster Hotspots: A Global Risk Analysis.* Disaster Risk Mangement Series. Washington, DC: World Bank. http://documents.worldbank.org/curated/en/621711468175150317/Natural-disaster-hotspots-A-global-risk-analysis.

DRC (Democratic Republic of Congo). 2021. National Adaptation Plan to Climate Change (2022–2026). Kinshasa: Deputy Prime Minister's Office, Ministry of the Environment and Sustainable Development. https://unfccc.int/sites/default/files/resource/DRC-NAP_EN.pdf.

European Commission. 2020. *Shaping Europe's Digital Future.* Brussels: European Commission. https://commission.europa.eu/strategy-and-policy/priorities-2019-2024/europe-fit-digital-age/shaping-europes-digital-future_en.

Gebbers, R., and V. I. Adamchuk. 2010. "Precision Agriculture and Food Security." *Science* 327 (5967): 828–31.

GSMA. 2019. "Case Study: Orange Jordan. Solar Farms in the Desert." https://www.gsma.com/futurenetworks/wiki/case-study-orange-jordan/.

GSMA. 2021. *The State of Mobile Internet Connectivity 2021.* London: GSMA.

Hilty, Lorenz, Wolfgang Lohmann, and Elaine M. Huang. 2011. "Sustainability and ICT: An Overview of the Field." *Notizie di Politeia* 27 (104): 13–28. https://www.zora.uzh.ch/id/eprint/55640/1/Hilty_et_al_Sustainability_and_ICT.pdf.

Ilčev, Stojče Dimov. 2018. *Global Satellite Meteorological Observation (GSMO) Applications.* New York: Springer International Publishing AG. https://www.akademika.no/teknologi/telekommunikasjon/global-satellite-meteorological-observation-gsmo-applications/9783319670461.

ITU (International Telecommunication Union). 2020a. *Connecting Humanity: Assessing Investment Needs of Connecting Humanity to the Internet by 2030.* Geneva: ITU. https://digitallibrary.un.org/record/3895170.

ITU (International Telecommunication Union). 2020b. "Greenhouse Gas Emissions Trajectories for the Information and Communication Technology Sector Compatible with the UNFCCC Paris Agreement." Recommendation ITU-T L.1470. https://www.itu.int/ITU-T/recommendations/rec.aspx?rec=14084.

Kalas, P. P., and A. Finlay. 2009. "Planting the Knowledge Seed: Adapting to Climate Change Using ICTs: Concepts, Current Knowledge and Innovative Examples." https://www.apc.org/sites/default/files/BCO_ClimateChange.pdf.

Malmodin, Jens, and Pernilla Bergmark. 2015. Exploring the Effect of ICT Solutions on GHG Emissions in 2030." In *Proceedings of EnviroInfo and ICT for Sustainability.* Dordrecht, the Netherlands: Atlantis Press. https://www.atlantis-press.com/proceedings/ict4s-env-15/25836149.

Malmodin, Jens, and Dag Lundén. 2018. "The Energy and Carbon Footprint of the Global ICT and E&M Sectors 2010–2015." *Sustainability* 10 (9): 3027. https://doi.org/10.3390/su10093027.

Melville, Nigel. 2010. "Information Systems Innovation for Environmental Sustainability." *MIS Quarterly* 34 (1): 1–21. https://aisel.aisnet.org/misq/vol34/iss1/3/.

Mendes, Jorge, Tatiana M. Pinho, Filipe Neves dos Santos, Joaquim J. Sousa, Emanuel Peres, José Boaventura-Cunha, Mário Cunha, and Raul Morais. 2020. "Smartphone Applications Targeting Precision Agriculture Practices—A Systematic Review." *Agronomy* 10 (6): 855. https://doi.org/10.3390/agronomy10060855.

Ministry of Environment, Maldives. 2020. "Update of Nationally Determined Contribution of Maldives." https://unfccc.int/sites/default/files/NDC/2022-06/Maldives%20Nationally%20 Determined%20Contribution%202020.pdf.

Ministry of Information, Communications and Technology, Kenya. 2019. *National Information, Communications and Technology (ICT) Policy.* Nairobi: Ministry of Information, Communications and Technology. https://www.ict.go.ke/wp-content/uploads/2019/12/NATIONAL-ICT-POLICY -2019.pdf.

Muench, S., E. Stoermer, K. Jensen, T. Asikainen, M. Salvi, and F. Scapolo. 2022. *Towards a Green and Digital Future.* EUR 31075 EN. Luxembourg: Publications Office of the European Union.

Nordic Council of Ministers. 2021. *Enabling the Digital Green Transition: A Study of Potentials, Challenges, and Strengths in the Nordic-Baltic Region.* Copenhagen: Nordic Council of Ministers. https://pub.norden.org/nord2021-044/.

Ospina, Angelica Valeria, and Richard Heeks. 2010. "Linking ICTs and Climate Change Adaptation: A Conceptual Framework for eResilience and eAdaptation." Centre for Development Informatics, Institute for Development Policy and Management (IDPM), University of Manchester, Manchester, UK.

UNDRR (United Nations Office for Disaster Risk Reduction). 2015. *Sendai Framework for Disaster Risk Reduction 2015–2030.* New York: United Nations.

Wadud, Zia, and Jeevan Namala. 2022. "The Effects of Ridesourcing Services on Vehicle Ownership in Large Indian Cities." *Transportation Research Interdisciplinary Perspectives* 15.

WBGU (German Advisory Council on Global Change). 2019. "Towards our Common Digital Future. Summary." WBGU, Berlin.

WMO (World Meteorological Organization). 2022. "Status of Mortality and Economic Losses: Status of Mortality and Economic Losses Due to Weather, Climate and Water Extremes (1970–2021)." https://public.wmo.int/en/resources/atlas-of-mortality.

World Bank. 2022. "Greening Digital in Korea: Korea Case Study for Greening the ICT Sector." Korea Office Innovation and Technology Note, World Bank, Washington, DC. http://hdl.handle.net /10986/37554.

World Bank Group. 2021. "From COVID-19 Crisis Response to Resilient Recovery: Saving Lives and Livelihoods while Supporting Green, Resilient and Inclusive Development (GRID)." Development Committee, World Bank Group, Washington, DC.

World Bank Group. 2022. *Climate and Development: An Agenda for Action. Emerging Insights from World Bank Group 2021–22 Country Climate and Development Reports.* Washington, DC: World Bank. https://openknowledge.worldbank.org/handle/10986/38220.

2. Decarbonizing the Digital Sector

Introduction

Ultimately, reducing greenhouse gas (GHG) emissions along the digital value chain will depend on greater use of renewable energy to generate the electricity that powers the information and communication technology (ICT) sector. It will also depend on greater energy efficiency stemming from new technologies, better processes, and better design of equipment. Issues related to shaping public, private, and citizen demand are also important, but they are beyond the scope of the report.

The ICT Sector's Contribution to Global Carbon Dioxide Emissions: Baseline and Forecasts

Measuring the Digital Carbon Footprint

As the uptake of digital technologies expands, including to enable the green transition and to mitigate climate change,[1] emissions by the digital sector are expected to rise unless measures to facilitate low-carbon technologies and processes are adopted. What should industry and policy makers do to combat the growing carbon footprint of ICT? They can begin by better understanding the sources of GHG emissions along the digital value chain—the subject of this section.

In the context of direct GHG emissions, the digital sector has three main components: (1) digital connectivity infrastructure (telecommunication networks), (2) data management infrastructure (data centers), and (3) end user devices (such as smartphones and computers).[2] GHG emissions in the ICT sector are generally limited to those generated by ICT equipment and infrastructure to avoid the risk of double counting. This approach is consistent with the definition of *ICT sector* set out by the International Telecommunication Union (ITU) in assessing the sector's environmental impact (ITU 2018). Estimations of the direct GHG emissions of the sector depend on which emission scope[3] is included. Scope 1 (direct emissions) and Scope 2 (indirect emissions from energy purchases) are the most directly relevant to digital connectivity providers and data centers. Scope 3 is particularly important for equipment and devices to account for emissions along the value chain (such as by suppliers and distributors). Furthermore, different methods are used to estimate emissions. Life-cycle assessment is the most commonly used. It "takes into consideration the spectrum of resource flows and environmental interventions associated with a product, service, or organization from a life-cycle perspective, including all phases from raw material acquisition through processing, distribution, use, and end-of-life processes."[4]

Over the past few years, numerous studies have measured and quantified the GHG emissions of the ICT sector, but their results have differed because of the lack of quality data and varying assumptions. Studies of the direct GHG emissions of the ICT sector focus on either the relative weight of the sector within the whole economic activity (relative approach) or calculation of total GHG emissions (absolute approach). Even though questions remain about the best methodologies to apply and the data sets to be used, the majority of the studies agree that the ICT sector will have an expanding footprint in absolute terms unless specific climate actions are taken (Belkhir and Elmeligi 2018; Corcoran and Andrae 2013; Malmodin and Lundén 2018).

The possibility of double counting scopes of emissions makes sector estimations more challenging. Although the division of GHG emissions into three different scopes makes sense from a firm's perspective, it is harder to put into practice when considering the ICT sector as a whole, especially when it comes to differentiating Scopes 1 and 2 from Scope 3 (box 2.1). For example, from the perspective of a data center, the transmission of a signal through a telecommunication network can be counted as an indirect downstream activity from the perspective of GHG emissions (Scope 3). However, the same task is clearly counted as part of Scope 1 from the perspective of the telecommunication network. In this respect, the ITU points out that there is a risk of double counting because "Scope 1 and 2 GHG emissions of one organization may be accounted for as Scope 3 GHG emissions by another organization" (ITU 2018).

| **BOX 2.1** | **Methodological Considerations for Assessing Greenhouse Gas Emissions of the ICT Sector** |

From the point of view of one company, greenhouse gas (GHG) emissions (usually aggregated as tonnes of carbon dioxide equivalent) can be measured considering three scopes: direct emissions (Scope 1), indirect energy consumption (Scope 2), and indirect derived from the use of other inputs (Scope 3)—see figure B2.1.1. At the sectoral level, aggregating Scope 3 emissions would lead to double counting because information and communication technology (ICT) services and equipment are essential inputs in other ICT products.

Furthermore, organizations can choose from several available methodologies in assessing the carbon footprint of their ICT activities (Scopes 1 and 2). A mapping of most of these methodologies is provided by the ICTFootprint.eu program, a European program to support action in the field of energy and environmental efficiency in ICT that is funded by the European Commission. All the methodologies rely on a life-cycle assessment.

(Box continues on the following page)

BOX 2.1 **Methodological Considerations for Assessing Greenhouse Gas Emissions of the ICT Sector** *(continued)*

FIGURE B2.1.1 **Overview of GHG Protocol Scopes and Emissions across the Value Chain**

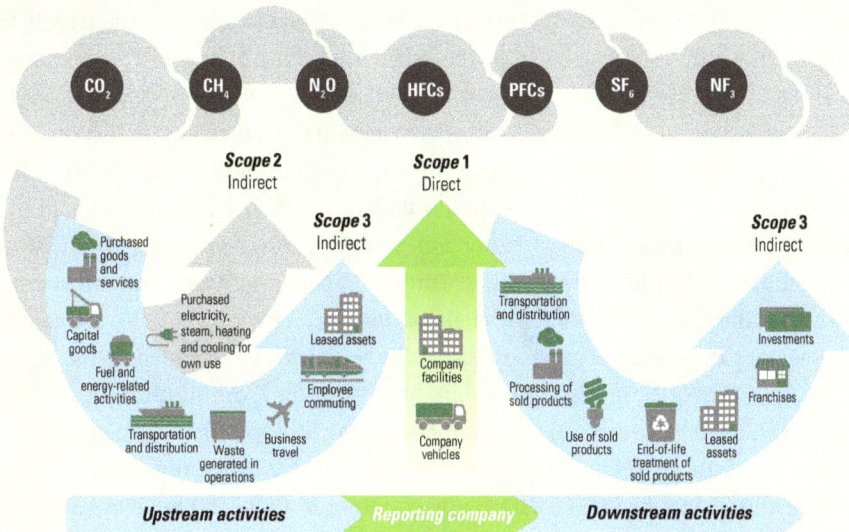

Source: WRI and WBCSD 2013.

Note: CH_4 = methane; CO_2 = carbon dioxide; GHG = greenhouse gas; HFCs = hydrofluorocarbons; NF_3 = nitrogen trifluoride; N_2O = nitrous oxide; PFCs = perfluorochemicals; SF_6 = sulfur hexafluoride.

Because they are limited to a subsegment of the ICT sector and are not harmonized between them, these methodologies are not suitable for assessing the global footprint of the ICT sector. In fact, most of the literature reviewed relies on some sort of "in-house" methodology, but little detail is provided on the methodological approach, assumptions, boundaries, and scope. According to Freitag et al. (2020), most of the studies rely on a bottom-up methodology—that is, based on a life-cycle assessment to gauge the energy required for the goods and services considered. That methodology is at times combined with some macro data (such as historical and forecasted traffic data consumption in the world).

As for the time boundaries, ICT is a fast-evolving sector because of the rapid pace of changes in technology. It is thus difficult to make long-term projections. Most studies limit projections to a maximum of 10–15 years. For past trends, however, studies often analyze all available historical data. For data centers and the mobile telecom aspects of the sector, most estimates cover the period from the early 2000s, from where one observes significant growth in these technologies, onward.

Direct GHG Emissions of the ICT Sector Worldwide

According to several studies in the literature, the ICT sector's current share of global GHG emissions ranges from 1.5 to 4 percent. In 2015, the National Academy of

Technologies of France (NATF)[5] calculated that in 2012 the ICT sector accounted for 4.7 percent of worldwide electricity consumption and a total carbon footprint of about 1.7 percent (including private, industry, and telecom hardware and infrastructure and data centers). In 2018, Malmodin and Lundén estimated that in 2020 the ICT sector would account for about 3.6 percent of global electricity demand and 1.4 percent of global GHG emissions.[6] The total emissions from networks, data centers, and user devices would amount to about 730 megatonnes of carbon dioxide equivalent ($MtCO_2e$) in 2020.[7] Some studies point out that the GHG emissions of the ICT sector may be overestimated because the rapid growth in data services and connected devices have been counterbalanced by equally rapid improvements in efficiency that have helped moderate the impact of the ICT sector on energy consumption.[8] On the other hand, Freitag et al. (2020) find that several studies *underestimate* the carbon footprint of the ICT sector, possibly by as much as 25 percent, by failing to account for all of the sector's supply chains and full life cycle (that is, emission Scopes 1, 2, and fully inclusive 3). Adjusting for the truncation of supply chain pathways, Freitag et al. (2020) estimate that the ICT sector's share of emissions could actually be as high as 2.1–3.9 percent. A recent study by the Body of European Regulators for Electronic Communications (BEREC) summarizes that the current carbon footprint of the sector is between 2 percent and 4 percent based on a review of the literature (BEREC 2022). Finally, an analysis conducted for this report based on data reported by more than 150 international digital companies[9] for 2020 estimated location-based emissions of 405 $MtCO_2e$ in 2020 (1.3 percent of the global total) and 467 $MtCO_2e$ (1.5 percent) when personal computer and smartphone use is added (Minges, Mudgal, and Decoster, forthcoming).[10]

Studies show a general rising trend of emissions in the sector, but estimated growth rates vary. Some studies find that emissions will remain generally stable in relative terms, while others point to a potential 14–24 percent of global emissions by 2030/40 (WIK-Consult and Ramboll 2021). Belkhir and Elmeligi (2018) estimate past (2007–17) and future (2018–20) GHG emissions from the ICT sector and conclude that the energy consumption of the sector represents about 400–500 $Mt\text{-}CO_2e$ in 2007 and nearly triples to reach 1,100–1,300 $MtCO_2e$ in 2020 (figure 2.1). A similar growth rate is also found for the contribution of the ICT sector to global GHG emissions, which grew from 1.06–1.6 percent in 2007 to more than double in 2020, reaching 3.06–3.6 percent in 2020. Furthermore, the International Telecommunication Union, in its Recommendation ITU-T L.1470 (ITU 2020), provides detailed trajectories of GHG emissions for the global ICT sector and subsectors that are quantified for the year 2015 and estimated for 2020 (figure 2.2). The results of the ITU study are similar to those by Malmodin and Lundén (2018) with total GHG emissions reaching 740 $MtCO_2e$ in 2020 and a low growth rate between 2020 and 2015. Finally, the metastudy by Freitag et al. (2020)—including both Belkhir and Elmeligi (2018) and Malmodin and Lundén (2018), complemented by the study by Andrae and Edler (2015)—highlights that even though all studies agree that the GHG emissions from the ICT sector have increased over the past decades, there are some significant disparities between the results.

FIGURE 2.1   Energy Consumption Estimates 2010–15 (left) and Carbon Footprint Estimates 2010–15 and Forecasts 2020 (right), ICT Sector

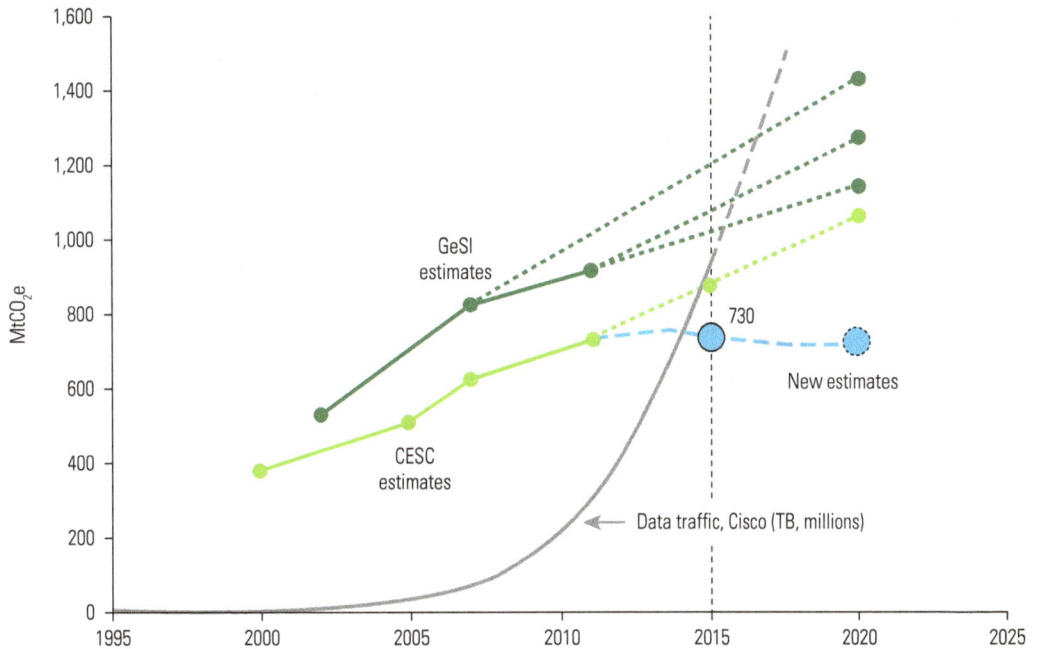

Source: Malmodin and Lundén 2018.

Note: Global e-Sustainability Initiative (GeSi) estimates: previous estimates by GeSi in SMART 2020 and SMARTer 2020. Center for Sustainable Communications (CESC) estimates: previous estimates by the authors and CESC. New estimates provided by Malmodin and Lundén (2018). $MtCO_2e$ = megatonnes of carbon dioxide equivalent; TB = terabytes.

The GHG emissions in 2020 estimated by Malmodin and Lundén (2018) are less than those estimated by Belkhir and Elmeligi (2018).

The analysis prepared for this report, based on data reported by more than 150 major digital companies accounting for about two-thirds of ICT emissions, reveals that although emissions continued to grow from 2017 to 2020, the rate of growth has been declining. Meanwhile, electricity use continues to increase (figure 2.3). A notable slow-down in emissions was evident in 2020, even as COVID-19 mobility restrictions led to higher use of digital services. On the other hand, electricity use increased in 2020 among these companies by 10 percent (60 percent between 2017 and 2020 for data centers), despite a 0.9 percent global drop in electricity generation. The drop in emissions growth but increase in electricity use suggests that the conversion to renewable energy by ICT companies is beginning to bear fruit. Scope 2 market-based emissions (considering actual electricity purchase contracts) reduced operational emissions for ICT networks and data centers by 32 megatonnes in 2020. Sixteen major digital companies reported being carbon-neutral in 2020 by using carbon credits (ITU and WBA 2022).

FIGURE 2.2 **Carbon Footprint Estimates (2007–17) and Forecasts (2018–20), ICT Sector**

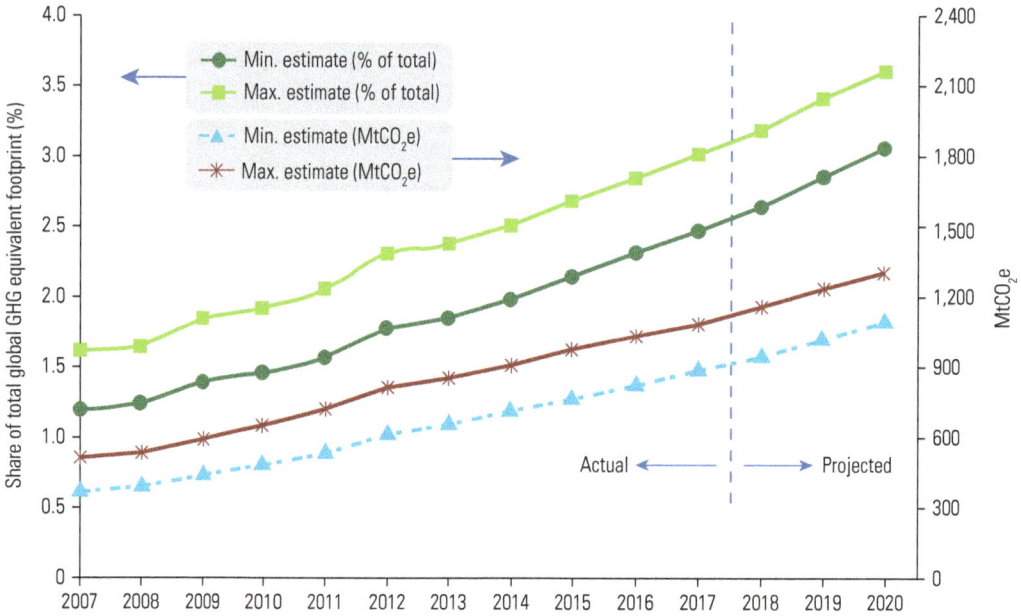

Source: Belkhir and Elmeligi 2018.

Note: $MtCO_2e$ = megatonnes of carbon dioxide equivalent.

FIGURE 2.3 **Changes in ICT Sector Scope 1 and 2 Emissions and Electricity Use, 2018–20**

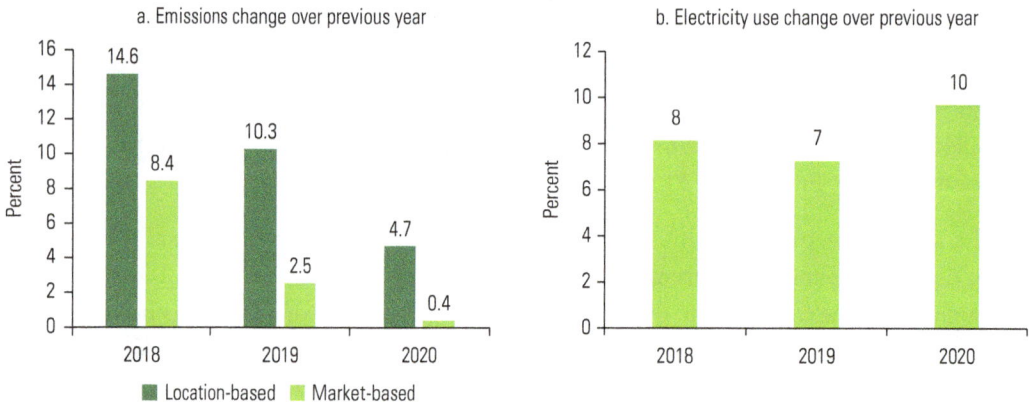

Source: Minges, Mudgal, and Decoster (forthcoming), based on data reported by more than 150 tech companies.

Note: Panel a: Location-based: considering the energy mix in the country; market-based: considering each digital company's actual electricity purchase contracts.

GHG emissions from the ICT sector are expected to increase in the coming years if mitigation actions are not taken, but forecasts depend on the expected improvements in energy efficiency and demand forecasts. Belkhir and Elmeligi (2018) predict that by 2040 the direct GHG emissions of the ICT sector could account for as much as 6–7 percent of total worldwide GHG emissions using a linear fit. Using an exponential fit, they predict that emissions could reach as much as 14 percent of the total worldwide, although this is less likely because of improvements in energy efficiency (figure 2.4). The ITU (2020) also provides some forecasts for 2025 and 2030 and a long-term goal for 2050 (figure 2.5). The consensus is that GHG emissions are not expected to grow at an exponential rate.

Although there is no consensus on estimates of the future carbon footprint of the ICT sector (Freitag et al. 2020), it is clear that government policies and private sector initiatives are needed to change the emissions path to reduce the sector's carbon footprint. On energy efficiency, some studies argue that improvements in efficiency will continue and will offset the increase in ICT demand, whereas others find that efficiency improvements will not keep pace. On the demand for ICT, some studies find that demand will increase less than energy efficiency improvements (for example, because of market saturation for end user devices), leading to a decline (or at least a stabilization of the total GHG emissions of the ICT sector), whereas others predict that the demand for ICT will continue to increase due to innovation and the rise of Internet of Things (IoT) devices, which, in turn, will lead to an increase in GHG emissions. In this context, the ITU stresses that to contribute proportionally to a reduction in global warming, GHG emissions from the ICT sector must be cut by half by 2030, to less than 400 $MtCO_2e$ (ITU 2020).[11] Achieving this goal will certainly require rapid action by governments and the private sector.

FIGURE 2.4   ICT Carbon Footprint as a Percentage of Total GHG Emissions Projected through 2040 Using Exponential and Linear Fits

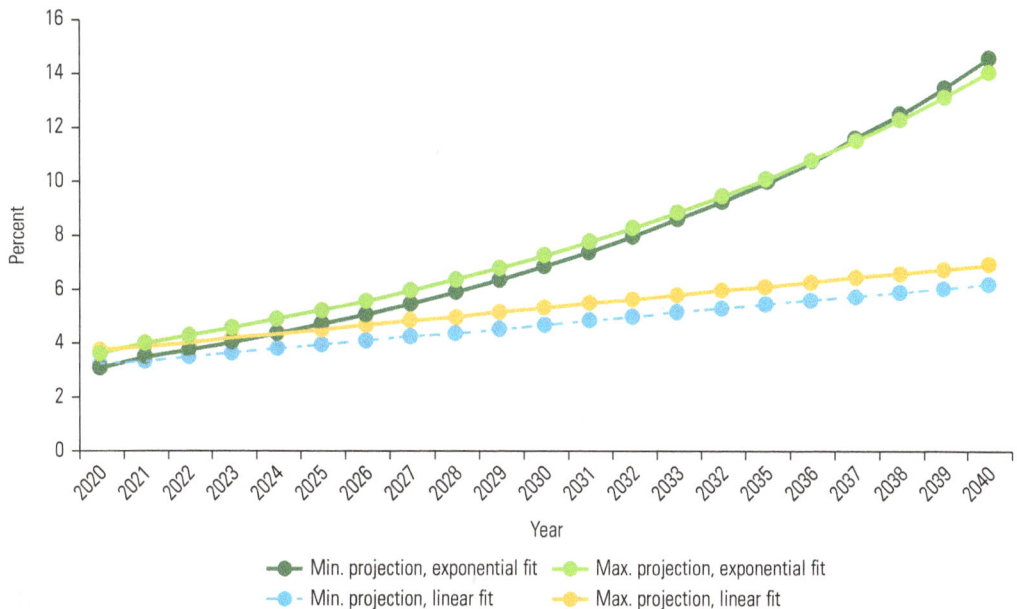

Source: Belkhir and Elmeligi 2018.

FIGURE 2.5 **ICT Sector Carbon Footprint Baseline, 2015–20, and Forecasts, 2025–30 (Including Electricity Supply Chain and Grid Losses)**

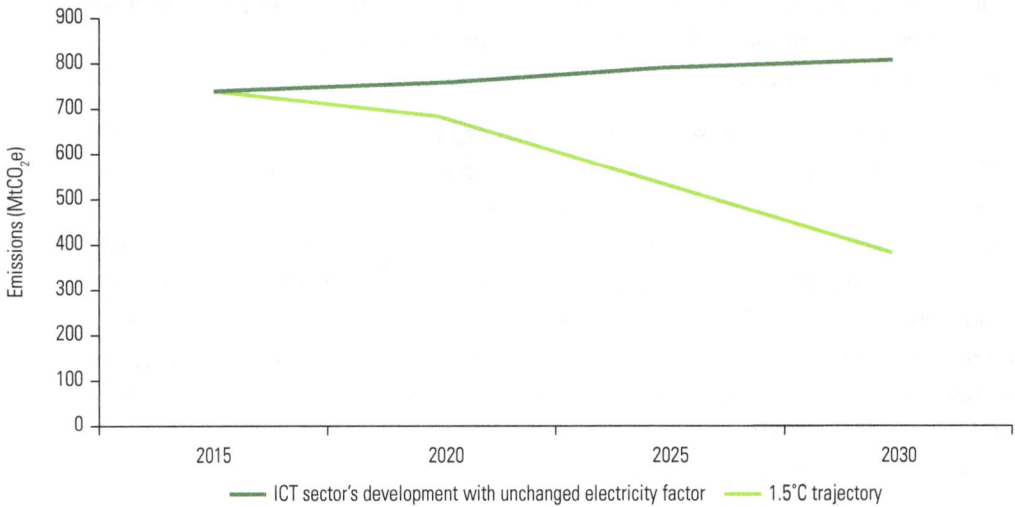

Source: ITU 2020.

Note: The trajectories, the long-term goals, and the 2015 baseline were derived in accordance with the International Telecommunication Union's Recommendation ITU-T L.1450 and through complementary methods in support of the 1.5 degrees Celsius objective described by the Intergovernmental Panel on Climate Change (IPCC) in its special report *Global Warming of 1.5°C* and in support of the Science Based Targets initiative. ICT = information and communication technology; MtCO$_2$e = megatonnes of carbon dioxide equivalent.

The relative weight of the three main components of the digital sector—digital connectivity networks, data infrastructure, and end user devices—is changing over time, with end user devices increasing in importance. Estimates of the composition of emissions vary based on methodologies and data sources. Data infrastructure, connectivity networks, and devices (excluding TVs and smartTVs) each account for around one-third of emissions (figure 2.6). According to a recent study by BEREC (2022) referencing a broad literature review, devices (terminal equipment, including TVs) are the largest source of emissions (60–80 percent). Networks and data centers have a more similar carbon footprint—12–24 percent and about 15 percent, respectively. Other studies find a larger footprint for data centers. The relative GHG emissions footprint contribution of smartphones has by far the largest increase, almost tripling over 10 years and by 2020 accounting for more than 50 percent of all other ICT devices combined (Belkhir and Elmeligi 2018).[12]

The second-largest increase in relative contribution is data centers (Belkhir and Elmeligi 2018), although estimates of their relative importance vary significantly. Belkhir and Elmeligi (2018) estimated that data centers emissions grew from 33 percent in 2010 to 45 percent of total ICT footprint by 2020 (figure 2.7), whereas Malmodin and Lundén (2018) estimate that only 20 percent can be attributed to data centers, similar to telecommunication networks. Freitag et al. (2020) highlight this discrepancy

FIGURE 2.6   Relative GHG Emissions of the ICT Sector, by Main Component

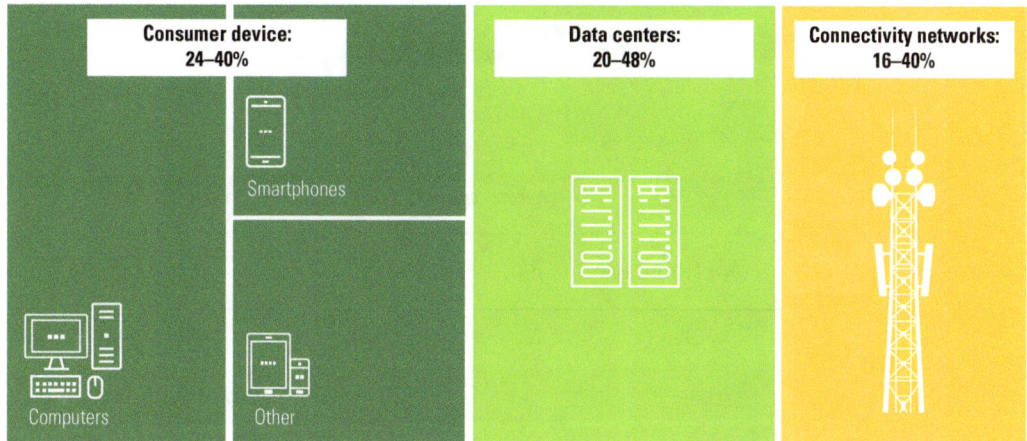

Source: Adapted from WIK-Consult and Ramboll (2021) to include estimates by Minges, Mudgal, and Decoster (forthcoming) based on analysis of reported emissions by more than 150 international digital companies.

Note: The midpoint of the range of the subsector's contribution to total emissions in the sector is reflected in the size of the boxes. "Other" includes routers and connected devices. Mobile network operations account for more than 50 percent of the emissions of connectivity network operations. Deployment and decommissioning account for 10 percent of the total emissions of connectivity network emissions. ICT = information and communication technology.

FIGURE 2.7   Relative Contributions of Components of ICT Sector, 2010 and 2020

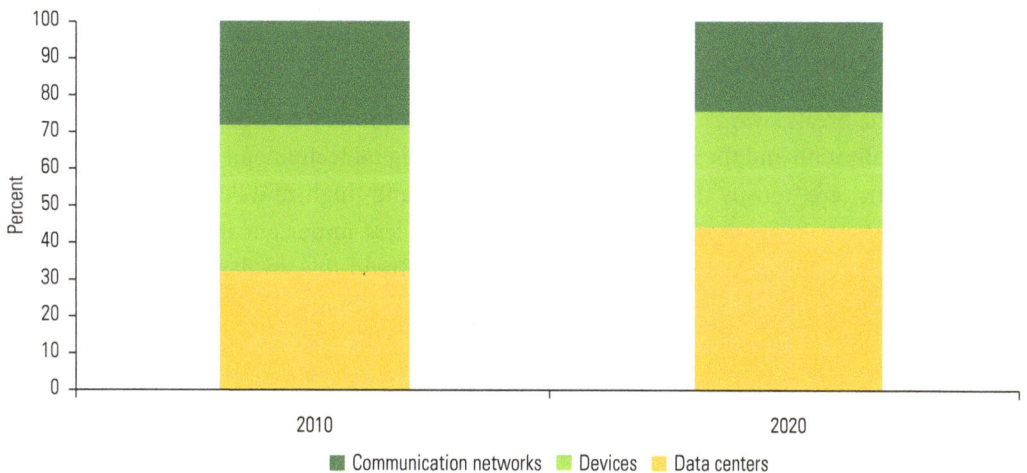

Source: Belkhir and Elmeligi 2018.

between both studies and explain it by the fact that Malmodin and Lundén (2018) use lower consumption estimates for networks and data centers (figure 2.8) than Belkhir and Elmeligi (2018).[13]

The next three sections of this chapter provide insights into the regional breakdown of electricity consumption for the three main segments of the ICT sector (data centers,

FIGURE 2.8   Relative Contributions of Components of ICT Sector

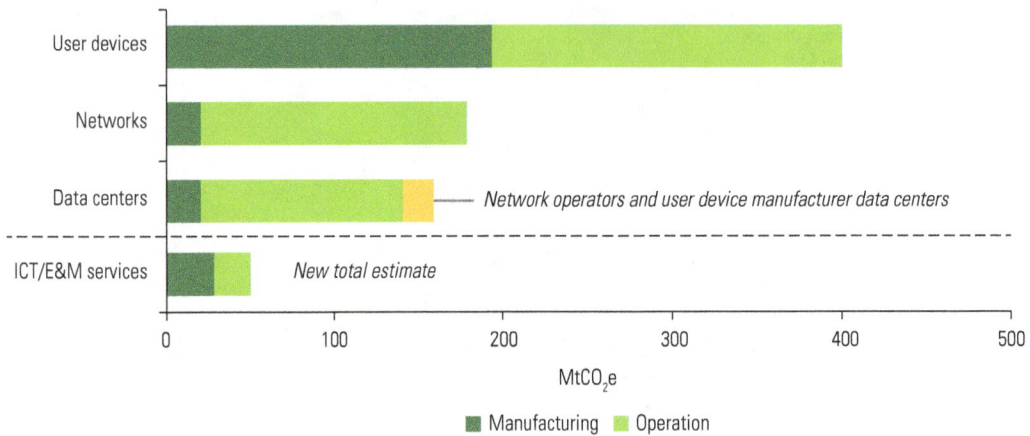

Source: Malmodin and Lundén 2018.

Note: E&M = entertainment and media; ICT = information and communication technology; $MtCO_2e$ = million tonnes of carbon dioxide equivalent.

telecommunication networks, and end user devices). Because of the lack of data on direct regional GHG emissions for each segment, proxy indicators for the regional "size" of each segment are used to approximate breakdowns of the sector's regional energy consumption. However, even though there is a direct relationship between energy consumption and GHG emissions, this relationship varies between regions—and even between countries—because it is highly dependent on the energy mix by country.

The breakdown of emissions by segment in a country will depend on the level of digitalization and the consumption patterns of digital technologies. For example, data centers are mostly located in high-income and high-middle-income countries. Therefore, emissions by data centers would be less important in low- and middle-income countries. However, there is a growing trend toward developing data center capacity in these countries. Devices in low-income countries are less energy-efficient per unit of data transmitted, but the use of multiple devices there is less prevalent, so the relative importance of devices is unclear. Networks in low-income countries are mostly based on wireless technologies and old generations (second, 2G, and third, 3G) that are less energy-efficient per unit of data, and base stations still use fossil fuels for off-grid and bad grid areas. Thus network operations could have a higher importance compared with the global composition.

Digital Connectivity Infrastructure

Mobile networks are an important component of digital connectivity emissions. According to the ITU (2020), about two-thirds of the total GHG emissions from digital connectivity networks are from mobile networks. According to BEREC (2022), more than half of GHG emissions stem from mobile networks. The overall share of mobile networks is expected to grow in the coming years because of an increase in the number of telecom towers as well as energy efficiency gains in the fixed broadband sector thanks to the transition from copper to fiber.[14]

Several industry sources have found that energy consumption is one of the highest operating costs for mobile network operators (MNOs), representing as much as a quarter of their total operating expenses (GSMA 2019). Most of this electricity is consumed by the link network (radio access network, RAN) made up of rooftops and towers because several equipment and cooling facilities are required to operate a mobile site and because much less energy is used in transporting data over the core network (Observatorio Nacional 5G 2021; Telecom Lead 2020). The size of the radio access network can also be significant, ranging from a few hundred mobile sites for small MNOs to tens of thousands of mobile sites (even several hundred thousand) for bigger MNOs. MNOs are enjoying positive trends in energy efficiency. Although network data traffic increased by 31 percent in 2021, total electricity use grew only by 5 percent (GSMA 2022a). Similarly, for European telecom network operators holding 36 percent of European subscriptions, the electricity consumption per subscription remained stable from 2010 to 2018 (about 30 kWh per subscription), although data traffic grew 12 times over the same period (Lundén et al. 2022).

Because of the importance of the energy consumption of (mobile) wireless networks compared with that of (fixed) wireline networks, one proxy indicator for assessing the regional breakdown of the GHG emissions of mobile networks is number of mobile sites deployed. Based on TowerXchange data compiled by the International Finance Corporation (IFC) and TowerXchange in 2019, there were about 4.8 million mobile sites worldwide (table 2.1).[15] With more than 2.4 million mobile sites, the East Asia and Pacific (EAP) region had 50 percent of the global total. With 1.96 million mobile sites, China accounted for more than 80 percent of EAP's total. South Asia, with some 700,000 sites (14 percent), held second place worldwide. North America and Western Europe collectively owned about 800,000 sites. Finally, Europe and Central Asia (ECA), Latin America and the Caribbean (LAC), the Middle East and North Africa (MENA), and Sub-Saharan Africa (SSA) account for the remaining 19 percent of the global number of mobile sites.

There are significant differences among countries in the quality of energy solutions provided to power mobile sites (table 2.1). At the global level, some 87 percent of mobile sites are connected to an electrical grid that is of acceptable quality (no or few power outages, and typical power outages last less than eight hours). An additional 9 percent are connected to a "bad" electrical grid (frequent power outages last eight hours or more). Finally, a remaining 3 percent of the global number of sites (about 165,000)—but 33 percent in Sub-Saharan Africa—are not connected to an electrical grid and rely on an off-grid power solution (usually a diesel generator). Even within

TABLE 2.1 Mobile Sites and Quality of Power Solutions: Global Distribution, 2019

Country/region	Total mobile sites (towers/rooftops, thousands)	Share of total (%)	Grid quality (%)		
			Good grid	Bad grid	Off-grid
EAP (China included)	2,420	50	93	6	2
China	1,968				
South Asia	698	14	68	26	6
North America	430	9	100	0	0
Western Europe	366	8	100	0	0
ECA	321	7	90	8	2
MENA	217	5	86	11	4
LAC	195	4	85	13	3
SSA	175	4	35	34	33
TOTAL	**4,822**	**100**	**87**	**9**	**3**

Source: International Finance Corporation mapping based on TowerXchange data: TowerXchange (dashboard), https://www.towerxchange.com/.

Note: EAP = East Asia and Pacific; ECA = Europe and Central Asia; LAC = Latin America and the Caribbean; MENA = Middle East and North Africa; SSA = Sub-Saharan Africa. For grid quality, some numbers may not sum to 100 because of rounding.

each region, the situation varies greatly between countries. For example, in Sub-Saharan Africa at least 80 percent of the sites in Côte d'Ivoire, Kenya, and South Africa are connected to a good grid, compared with less than 10 percent for Nigeria (figure 2.9).

Adding to the complexity, relying on bad grid or off-grid does not necessarily imply a larger GHG emission footprint because mobile sites can be connected to either a renewable source of energy (such as solar panels) or a fossil fuel source of energy (such as diesel generators). According to a recent study by the GSMA (2020b), about 88 percent of the off-grid and bad grid sites run on diesel generators, and the remaining sites—about 70,000 mobile towers—are powered by a renewable source of energy (mostly solar panels). The GSMA estimates that there was an increase of 45 percent in sites powered by a renewable source of energy between 2014 and 2019, with the bulk of the progress made by India. In total, the GSMA estimates that emissions from diesel generators at mobile towers are 7 $MtCO_2e$[16] (down from 9.2 $MtCO_2e$ in 2014), with some 27 percent of these emissions originating from Nigeria, followed by the MENA region and Sub-Saharan Africa (except Nigeria), each representing about 15 percent of the global GHG emissions from diesel generators for mobile towers (table 2.2). South and Southeast Asia (India excluded) account for 13 percent, and India accounts for 12 percent of the emissions by diesel-powered mobile towers.

The International Finance Corporation estimates that between 2019 and 2030 the total number of mobile sites will increase by about a third. Sub-Saharan Africa will likely show the greatest growth in sites, more than a doubling (from 175,000 mobile sites in 2019 to 369,000 in 2030), followed by the LAC region (a 69 percent rise),

FIGURE 2.9 Estimated Breakdown of Towers by Grid Condition: Sub-Saharan Africa, 2017

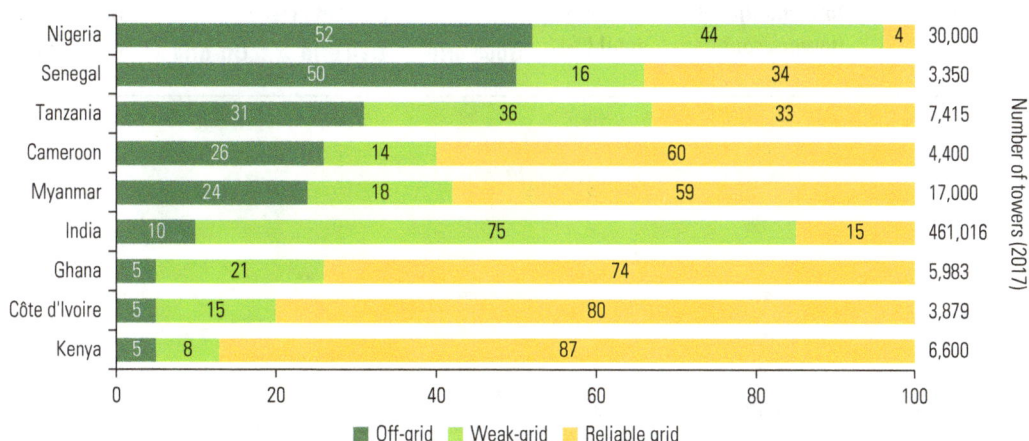

Source: BloombergNEF and Facebook 2018. BNEF estimates are compiled from various sources and company interviews.
Note: Total tower counts are shown (2017). Due to rounding, numbers may not total 100.

TABLE 2.2 Global Distribution of GHG Emissions from Diesel Generators Powering Mobile Sites, 2020

Country/region	GHG emissions (MtCO$_2$e)	Share of total (%)	Growth, 2014–20 (%)
Nigeria	1.90	27	9
MENA	1.07	15	−2
SSA (except Nigeria)	1.04	15	7
South and Southeast Asia (except India)	0.93	13	−18
India	0.84	12	−75
China	0.46	7	311
LAC	0.32	5	−21
Rest of the world	0.46	6	0
TOTAL	**7.02**	**100**	**−24**

Source: GSMA 2020b.
Note: GHG = greenhouse gas; LAC = Latin America and the Caribbean; MENA = Middle East and North Africa; MtCO$_2$e = megatonnes of carbon dioxide equivalent; SSA = Sub-Saharan Africa.

and the MENA region (a 65 percent rise). By 2030, the overall combined shares of the ECA, LAC, MENA, and SSA regions are forecast to rise from 19 percent in 2019 to 24 percent of total mobile sites (table 2.3). The breakdown of power solutions (between good, bad, and off-grid) within each region is expected to slightly improve, but with no major changes.

Although the data on the power solutions used by mobile network operators and the related GHG emissions are limited, analysis suggests that the EAP region dominates global energy consumption by mobile networks (using the total number of sites

TABLE 2.3 Mobile Sites and Power Solutions: Global Distribution by 2030

Country/region	Total mobile sites (towers/rooftops, thousands)	Share of total (%)	Grid quality (%)			Increase, 2019–30 (%)
			Good grid	Bad grid	Off-grid	
EAP (China included)	3,034	48	94	5	1	25
South Asia	857	13	71	26	3	23
North America	516	8	100	0	0	20
Western Europe	439	7	100	0	0	20
ECA	460	7	94	4	2	43
MENA	357	6	90	7	3	65
LAC	330	5	91	7	2	69
SSA	369	6	45	31	25	111
TOTAL	**6,362**	**100**	**88**	**8**	**2**	**32**

Source: International Finance Corporation estimates based on data from TowerXchange.

Note: The IFC and TowerXchange study does not cover North America and Western Europe (shown in italics). EAP = East Asia and Pacific; ECA = Europe and Central Asia; LAC = Latin America and the Caribbean; MENA = Middle East and North Africa; SSA = Sub-Saharan Africa. Due to rounding, numbers may not total 100.

per region as an indicator). The EAP region has about half of the mobile towers deployed worldwide. South Asia, North America, and Western Europe account for about 30 percent of total energy consumption. Finally, energy consumption by mobile networks attributed to the ECA, LAC, MENA, and SSA regions represents about a 20 percent share worldwide. Advances in off-grid energy and battery technology for transmission infrastructure may have a significant impact on reducing GHG emissions.

The introduction and expansion of new generations of mobile network systems that are more energy-efficient could reduce emissions as well. Upgrading (shutting down) 2G and 3G networks would reduce the energy consumption per bit of data, but the final effects on emissions will depend on the volume of data as well. It is unclear whether the introduction of fifth-generation (5G) mobile networks may also increase the direct GHG emissions of digital infrastructure (Polytechnique Insights 2022). On the one hand, 5G is hailed as a technology that is more energy-efficient than previous generations such 4G (fourth-generation). On the other hand, the multiplication of 5G devices (such as Internet of Things devices) could, in turn, increase data consumption and thus overall energy consumption. Moreover, because 5G promises to greatly increase bandwidth per user, there may also be a rebound effect with the additional use of data thanks to the better quality of service. Finally, extra GHG emissions could stem from the decommissioning of previous mobile systems and the production and installation of the new equipment required for 5G.

It is too early to have a clear idea of the impacts of 5G, but several studies point to growing emissions and possible enabling effects to reduce emissions in other sectors.

In France, for example, the Haut Conseil pour le Climate (High Council on Climate, HCC), an independent body tasked with issuing advice and recommendations to the government to reduce France's greenhouse gas emissions, studied different scenarios, all of which suggested that the deployment of 5G will result in a significant increase in the direct GHG emissions by the ICT sector. Specifically, 5G would increase GHG emissions by 2.7–6.7 $MtCO_2e$ in 2030, up from 15 $MtCO_2e$ in 2020, mainly because of the increase in the number of objects connected to the network (Haut Conseil pour le Climat 2020). Zain, the Kuwait-based telecommunication group, found that 5G increased energy and emissions in its countries of operation (Bahrain, Kuwait, and Saudi Arabia) where the technology has been deployed (Zain 2021). In Jordan, Orange has been accelerating use of solar energy as it anticipates that electricity consumption will increase by three times upon the introduction of 5G (Orange 2021). Although the evidence points to increased electricity use from 5G networks, there is also the potential for 5G to enable other sectors to reduce emissions through smart electricity networks and intelligent transportation systems (see chapter 4). According to Ericsson research, 5G and other network solutions can enable a reduction of global carbon emissions by up to 15 percent by 2030 (MIT Technology Review Insights 2021).

The choice of data transmission technology seems to affect the level of emissions. Copper cabling in fixed networks typically consumes more energy than its fiber counterparts (Huawei 2022). According to analysis by the Germany's Federal Ministry for the Environment, Nature Conservation and Nuclear Safety (2020), high definition (HD)–quality video streaming generates different levels of emissions, depending on the transmission technology. HD video streamed over a fiber-optic connection produces the lowest emissions: only 2 grams (g) of CO_2 per hour of video streaming for the data center and data transmission, excluding electricity used by the end user device. A copper cable (VDSL) generates 4 g per hour, while 3G mobile networks generate 90 g of CO_2 per hour. For the German study, 5G generates only about 5 g of CO_2 per hour. Low-income economies, because of the higher prevalence of 2G/3G subscriptions than fiber, copper cable, or newer generations of mobile networks, have higher emissions per subscription compared with high-income economies. However, upgrading to the latest digital technology will influence cost, thereby limiting affordability and uptake.

Finally, companies' decisions on sources of energy affect emissions as well. Some operators have committed to specific targets for renewable energy. Vodafone, for example, reached the milestone of 100 percent renewable electricity in Europe, including Turkey (now Türkiye) in 2021 (Vodafone 2021). Telefónica has done the same in Europe, Brazil, and Peru.[17] Orange is aiming for 50 percent renewable electricity by 2025. Furthermore, some network communication equipment suppliers of telecommunication companies use renewable energy significantly—for example, Cisco, 76 percent, and Ericsson, 52 percent—contributing to lower emissions.

Data Management Infrastructure (Data Centers)

A data center is a physical facility that any public or private organization can use to house its online applications and data. It hosts all the digital equipment required to store, share, and process data and applications such as servers, routers, and switches. A typical data center is about 10,000 square meters (m²) in size, and the largest data center in the world is about 600,000 m² (equivalent to the area occupied by the Pentagon or nearly 85 soccer fields).[18]

Data centers consume massive amounts of energy to run servers, network equipment, lighting, air distribution fans, and cooling systems. They typically operate 24/7. Except for servers, the useful life of their equipment exceeds 10 years, making energy consumption the main source of emissions in this segment (figure 2.10). [19]

With the evolution of cloud computing and the expansion of data-intensive applications (such as video streaming, cloud gaming, and blockchain for crypto assets), the number and capacity of data centers have grown exponentially. The International Energy Agency (IEA) estimates that data center workloads increased by more than 260 percent between 2015 and 2021 and that energy use, including for cryptocurrency mining,[20] rose by more than 50 percent (IEA 2022). In fact, data centers use more energy than entire countries (figure 2.10, panel b).

Despite the expanded use of data centers, energy use has grown moderately, and emissions have grown even less or have declined in some countries because of the use of renewable energy. Masanet et al. (2020) find that, despite sixfold growth in global workloads, the electricity consumption of data centers remained stable at about 205 TWh a year in 2020 (figure 2.10). This apparently surprising result is explained by greater server efficiencies, more server virtualization, the transition of traditional data centers to the cloud, and overall declines in power usage effectiveness (PUE) with improvements in

FIGURE 2.10 Data Center Energy Use, Magnitude and Trends

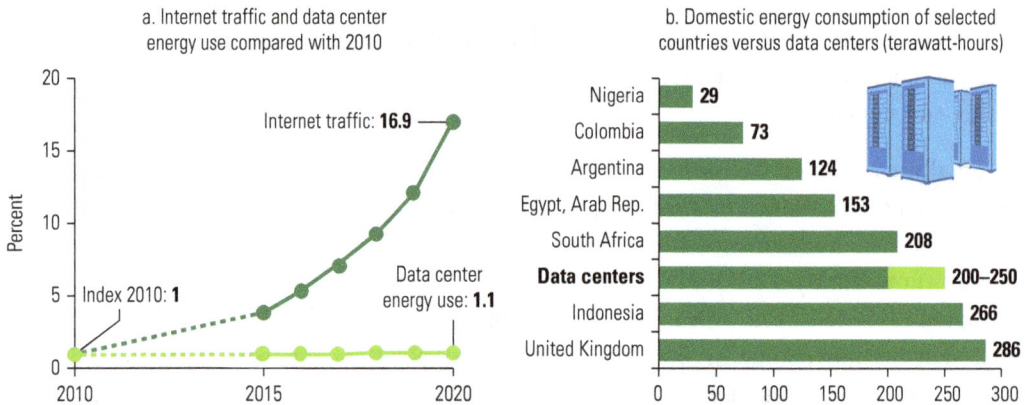

a. Internet traffic and data center energy use compared with 2010

b. Domestic energy consumption of selected countries versus data centers (terawatt-hours)

Source: IEA 2020.

cooling and power supply systems. Similarly, the *World Development Report 2021: Data for Better Lives* estimates that, although the global data traffic doubled between 2015 and 2018, the associated electricity consumption for data centers increased by only 16 percent over the same period, reaching 231 TWh a year in 2018 (World Bank 2021). The report explains this decoupling by citing huge gains in energy efficiency, and also by a technical shift from smaller data centers to more efficient larger ones, particularly among some of the bigger players in China, Japan, and the United States (World Bank 2021). The IEA (2022) also highlights the slow growth of energy use by data centers in general, except for cryptocurrency mining. Use went from 4 TWh in 2015 to 100–140 TWh in 2021, and for small economies hosting new data center capacity such as Denmark and Ireland, data center consumption represents 7 percent and 14 percent, respectively, of the country's electricity use. Several tech companies, including data centers and cloud service providers, are members of RE100, a global initiative of companies committed to 100 percent renewable electricity.[21] By means of direct energy purchases from renewable energy sources, compensation for emissions, and location in countries with a cleaner energy mix, data centers have further limited their impact on emissions.

To perform regional breakdowns, analysts approximate GHG emissions by looking at data centers' electricity consumption (figure 2.11, panel b). However, it is difficult to estimate regional breakdowns of GHG emissions based on electricity consumption. The exercise depends on various factors, including the energy mix of the power supply systems used locally by data centers and their related GHG emissions. As for the regional distribution, there has been no major shift in the regional breakdown of electricity consumption by data centers, with North America accounting for about 40 percent, followed by Asia (about 30 percent) and Western Europe (about 20 percent). Meanwhile, the location of data centers and thus the site of energy consumption do not overlap neatly with the location of users.

FIGURE 2.11 Data Centers Compute Instances and Energy Usage, by Region

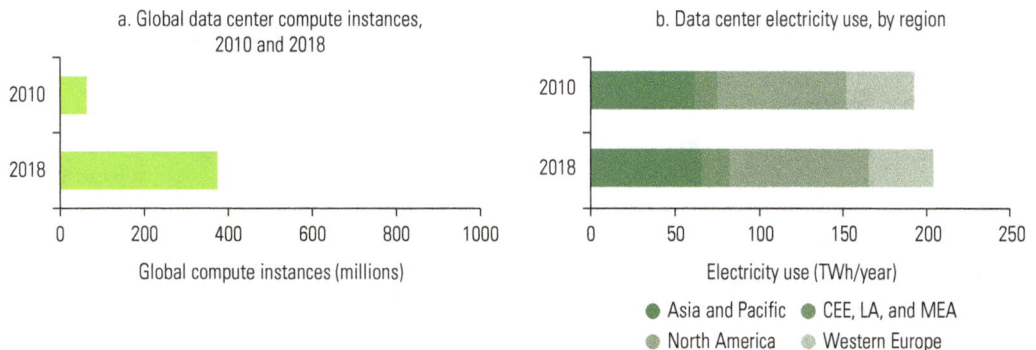

a. Global data center compute instances, 2010 and 2018

Global compute instances (millions)

b. Data center electricity use, by region

Electricity use (TWh/year)

● Asia and Pacific ● CEE, LA, and MEA
● North America ● Western Europe

Source: Masanet et al. 2020.

Note: Compute instance is a virtual server in a cloud computing environment. CEE = Central and Eastern Europe; LA = Latin America; MEA = Middle East and Africa; TWh = terawatt-hour.

Because the regional breakdowns of GHG emissions of data centers are likely highly aligned with electricity consumption, North America, Asia and Pacific, and Western Europe will continue to account for the majority of emissions by data centers (figure 2.11, panel b). According to the International Energy Agency, the overall electricity consumption of data centers is not expected to increase significantly in the next two years thanks to the ongoing improvements in energy efficiency and increased use of renewable energy sources.[22] Other indicators confirm these breakdowns and trends. The United States, China, Japan, and a handful of countries in the Organisation for Economic Co-operation and Development (OECD) still own the majority of the "large data centers,"[23] and these countries represent the bulk of data center IT investments (figure 2.12). In addition, a forecast of data center revenues up to 2023 shows that no major regional changes are expected at the global level (figure 2.13).[24]

Data are lacking on cross-border access to data center services—that is, when the demand for data center services in one country originates from outside of that country. However, analysis of the global internet bandwidth used from region to region (table 2.4) indicates that the wealthiest regions capture the bulk of the global data exchanges. The biggest international region-to-region internet routes are the intra-European, which represented about 1,100 terabits per second (Tbps) in 2020, or half of the total international routes (about 2,100 Tbps).[25] Those routes were followed by the Europe to North America route (355 Tbps, or 17 percent of the total international routes) and the intra-Asia to Asia route (153 Tbps). For comparison, the total international internet routes originating from Africa (including the intra-Africa to Africa routes) accounted for only 26 Tbps in 2020 (the majority of which were Africa to Europe routes). For 2027, it is estimated that the total bandwidth for internet routes will increase by nearly tenfold to reach 17,400 Tbps. However, no major changes are

FIGURE 2.12 **Global Distribution of Large Data Centers and Data Centers' Investment in Information Technology (IT), 2019**

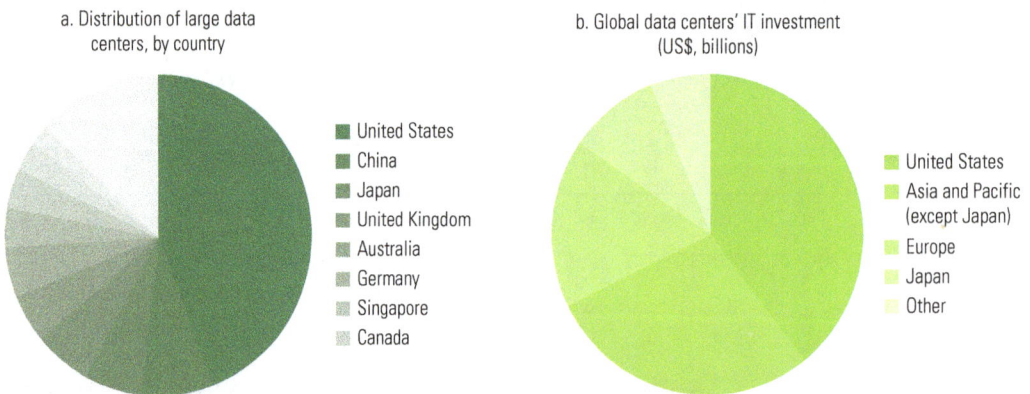

a. Distribution of large data centers, by country

- United States
- China
- Japan
- United Kingdom
- Australia
- Germany
- Singapore
- Canada

b. Global data centers' IT investment (US$, billions)

- United States
- Asia and Pacific (except Japan)
- Europe
- Japan
- Other

Source: Sai Industrial, Global and China Data Center Market, https://www.saiindustrial.com/global-and-china-data-center-market/, 2020.

FIGURE 2.13 Forecast of Revenue Market Share of Regional Data Centers, 2023

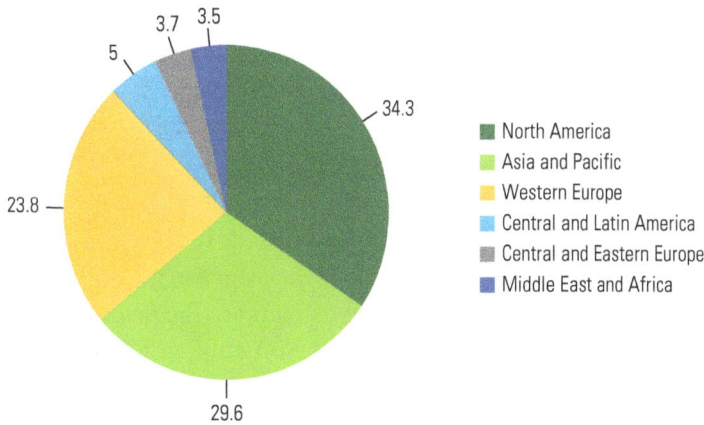

- North America
- Asia and Pacific
- Western Europe
- Central and Latin America
- Central and Eastern Europe
- Middle East and Africa

Source: GlobalData 2019.

TABLE 2.4   Top 10 Region-to-Region International Bandwidth Routes, 2020 and 2027

Route	Bandwidth (Tbps)	
	2020	2027
Europe–Europe	1,102	8,706
Europe–United States and Canada	355	2,697
Asia–Asia	197	1,741
Asia–United States and Canada	153	1,871
Latin America–United States and Canada	87	732
Europe–Middle East	44	318
Asia–Europe	40	395
United States and Canada–United States and Canada	31	216
Africa–Europe	21	334
Latin America–Latin America	17	139
All other region-to-region routes	31	328

Source: TeleGeography, https://www2.telegeography.com/.

Note: Tbps = terabits per second.

expected in the regional breakdown. Meanwhile, the higher demand for low-latency (small delay time) computing will boost the demand for edge data centers (those located close to the edge of a network—closer to end users and devices) and smartphones with greater computing capabilities, potentially affecting the importance of international data transmission.

End User Devices

Globally, more than 50 percent of emissions in the ICT sector are attributed to end user devices. The electricity consumption of devices is only a subset of GHG emissions;

the manufacture of end user devices can account for more than half of total GHG emissions by the devices (Malmodin and Lundén 2018).[26]

Devices such as computers and mobile phones are essential for using the services produced by the ICT sector. Understanding the emissions of these devices is thus important for seeing a more complete picture of the ICT sector's carbon footprint. Most of the largest device manufacturers publish GHG emissions as well as detailed life-cycle assessments. For example, Apple calculates emissions for each of its products. Life-cycle emissions for the company's iPhone declined by 19 percent between 2017 and 2021 (figure 2.14, panel a). An iPhone 13 (128 GB of storage) generates 79 kilograms of carbon dioxide equivalent ($kgCO_2e$) during its lifetime. The production phase generates over 80 percent of the emissions (51.84 $kgCO_2e$) of an iPhone, whereas its use generates 10.24 $kgCO_2e$ (16 percent) of emissions over its lifetime (figure 2.14, panel b).

The emissions from companies producing the two key user devices in the ICT sector, computers and smartphones, are concentrated in a few enterprises. Among companies accounting for over four-fifths of computer sales in 2020 (IDC 2022a) and about half of smartphone sales (IDC 2022b), Samsung and Apple stand out, as well as Dell, Hewlett-Packard (HP), and Lenovo (table 2.5). Six companies in the personal computer industry account for 83 percent of total shipments. All provide a complete GHG inventory, including supply chain emissions (Scope 3, Category 1, Purchase of Goods and Services). For 2020, Scope 1 and 2 location-based emissions are estimated at 1.2 million tCO_2e and electricity use at 2.5 TWh for the companies in this industry. For smartphones, supply chain emissions are estimated at 44.6 million tCO_2e. For 2020,

FIGURE 2.14 Life-Cycle GHG Emissions of an Apple iPhone

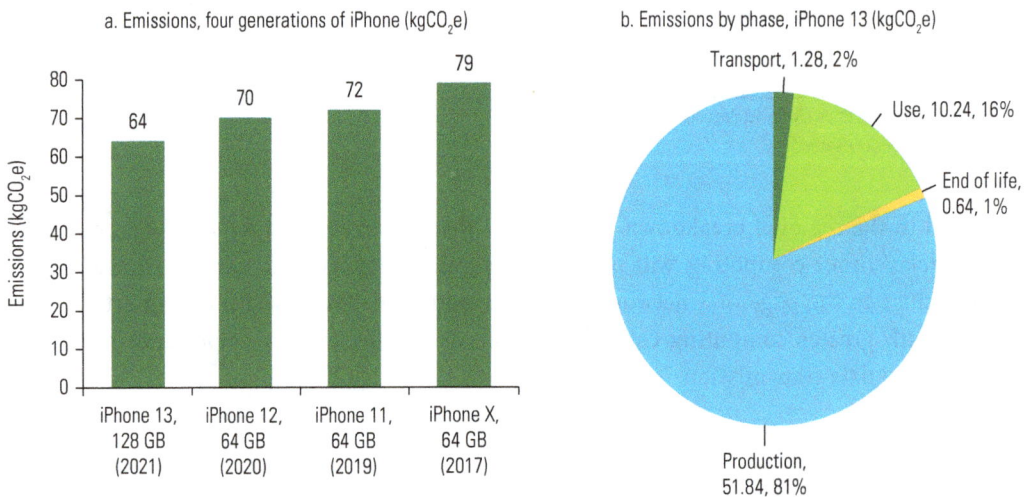

a. Emissions, four generations of iPhone ($kgCO_2e$)

b. Emissions by phase, iPhone 13 ($kgCO_2e$)

Source: Apple Product Environmental Reports, https://www.apple.com/environment.

Note: Panel a: iPhone storage is expressed in gigabytes (GB). GHG = greenhouse gas; $kgCO_2e$ = kilograms of carbon dioxide equivalent.

TABLE 2.5 **GHG Emissions, Consumer Device Hardware Companies, 2020**

Company	Headquarters	Shipments (millions)	Scopes 1 and 2				Scope 3, Category 1 (tCO$_2$e, millions)
			Emissions		Energy		
			Location-based (tCO$_2$e, millions)	Market-based (tCO$_2$e, millions)	Electricity (TWh)	Renewable energy (%)	
Computers							
Lenovo	Hong Kong SAR, China	72	0.18	0.03	0.30	11	2.28
HP	United States	68	0.25	0.17	0.50	40	26.40
Dell	United States	50	0.41	0.22	1.00	54	3.75
Apple	United States	23	0.09	0.05	0.20	100	3.41
Acer	Taiwan, China	21	0.02	0.01	0.03	54	0.04
ASUS	Taiwan, China	18	0.02	0.02	0.04	0	0.86
Subtotal		**251**	**0.97**	**0.50**	**2.04**	**49**	**36.75**
Other		52	0.20		0.43		7.86
Total		**304**	**1.17**		**2.47**		**44.61**
Smartphones							
Samsung	Korea, Rep.	257	0.89		1.61	18	14.01
Apple	United States	203	0.85	0.05	2.34	100	11.11
Xiaomi	China	148	0.03	0.03	0.05		8.56
Subtotal		**608**	**1.78**	**0.08**	**3.99**		**33.68**
Other		673	1.97		4.43		37.16
Total		**1,281**	**3.74**		**8.42**		**70.84**

Sources: Digital Inclusion Benchmark (dashboard), World Benchmarking Alliance, https://www.worldbenchmarkingalliance.org/digital-inclusion-benchmark/; World Bank estimates.

Note: This group falls in the International Standard Classification of All Economic Activities (ISIC) under 2620 Manufacture of computers and peripheral equipment and 2640 Manufacture of consumer electronics. The group averages for emissions per shipment for those reporting data have been applied to establish the overall estimates. Samsung and Apple estimates are based on smartphone shipments relying on life-cycle emissions reported by Apple, which is a higher estimate than Samsung's. GHG = greenhouse gas; tCO$_2$e = tonnes of carbon dioxide equivalent; TWh = terawatt-hours.

Scope 1 and 2 location-based emissions are estimated at 3.7 million tCO$_2$e and electricity use at 8.4 TWh for the companies in this industry. Supply chain emissions are estimated at 70.8 million tCO$_2$e (Minges, Mudgal, and Decoster, forthcoming).[27]

The distribution of emissions derived from the use of devices by region can be approximated by the number of devices, with the caveat that more recent models are expected to be more energy-efficient than older ones (most prevalent in low-income economies). According to the industry association GSMA, there are currently about 8 billion active mobile phones in the world, with many individuals owning more than one mobile phone due to the multi-SIM (subscriber identity module) phenomenon[28] (table 2.6). More than half of the total number of mobile phones is concentrated in Asia, with 4.3 billion phones in 2020, followed by Africa with more than 1.1 billion

TABLE 2.6 Mobile Phones and Smartphones: Global Distribution, 2020 and 2025

a. Mobile phones

Region	Total mobile phones (millions)		Share of total (%)	
	2020	**2025**	**Five-year increase (millions)**	**Five-year increase (%)**
Asia (including China)	4,320	4,715	395	9
Africa	1,152	1,381	229	20
Europe	971	983	12	1
LAC	663	751	88	13
MENA	525	580	55	11
North America	382	404	23	6
Oceania	45	48	4	8
(China)	1,599	1,688	89	6
TOTAL	**8,057**	**8,863**	**806**	**10**

Region	Total mobile phones (breakdown)	
	2020	**2025**
Asia (including China)	54	53
Africa	14	16
Europe	12	11
LAC	8	8
MENA	7	7
North America	5	5
Oceania	1	1
TOTAL	**100**	**100**

b. Smartphones

Region	Total smartphones (millions)		Share of total (%)	
	2020	**2025**	**Five-year increase (millions)**	**Five-year increase (%)**
Asia (including China)	3,015	4,023	1,008	33
Africa	576	899	323	56
Europe	743	830	87	12
LAC	476	605	130	27
MENA	350	471	121	35
North America	311	347	35	11
Oceania	35	43	8	23
(China)	1,156	1,501	345	30
TOTAL	**5,505**	**7,218**	**1,713**	**31**

Region	Total smartphones (breakdown)	
	2020	**2025**
Asia (including China)	55	56
Africa	10	12
Europe	13	11
LAC	9	8
MENA	6	7
North America	6	5
Oceania	1	1
TOTAL	**100**	**100**

Source: GSMA Intelligence.

Note: LAC = Latin America and the Caribbean; MENA = Middle East and North Africa. Numbers may not total 100 due to rounding errors.

phones and Europe with more than 970 million phones. The remaining regions—LAC, MENA, North America, and Oceania—collectively have around 1.6 billion active phones, which represent approximately 20 percent of the total.

The GSMA also forecasts that the total number of phones will increase globally by about 10 percent between 2020 and 2025. Looking *solely* at smartphones reveals some differences. An estimated 5.5 billion smartphones are currently being used worldwide and will likely reach 7.2 billion by 2025—a 31 percent increase over the period. This increase reflects the replacement of basic phones by smartphones in mature markets, as well as the growth of new users in developing markets such as in several parts of Asia and Africa.

Considerations for the Future

Several factors will affect GHG emissions from the ICT sector in the future. In addition to the greater energy efficiency of devices, equipment, and digital infrastructure, the use of new technologies that generate bigger volumes of data or need to use multiple devices will affect emissions as well.

Several new technologies being deployed or under development will have an influence on future GHG emissions of the digital economy. Although these technologies have important enabling effects on climate mitigation and adaptation across the global economy, they can also boost emissions in the ICT sector:

- *Increased connectivity*. More and more products are appearing on the market with interconnectivity features (such as the Internet of Things) that will increase the amount of data transfer in networks (even though there has been rising decoupling between energy consumption and data consumption over the last few years) and energy consumption during active and standby modes. In industrial setups, digital twin technology is increasingly being used to digitally simulate the real-time operation of a process, relying on a growing number of sensors. Its higher communications with servers for continuous simulations produces higher data traffic. As machine-to-machine (M2M) communications increase, data transfers will as well.
- *5G mobile network technology*. Progressively, telecom operators are moving from 4G to 5G technology. Although this latest technology is more energy-efficient per unit of data, a higher volume of data and use of the underlying network infrastructure and data centers—a rebound effect—could result in higher emissions. For example, in France it could increase the current GHG emissions by 1–2 percent (Haut Conseil pour le Climat 2020).
- *Blockchain technology*. Energy consumption and thus the GHG emissions of blockchain technology applications such as cryptocurrency is a hot topic in academic and policy circles. As a decentralized algorithm, blockchain generates high levels of replication and redundant computation, especially when based

on "proof of work." In fact, a single cryptocurrency transaction can generate 473 $kgCO_2e$ in emissions, or about the same emissions produced by 23 households in one day (Freitag et al. 2020). The use of energy for cryptocurrency has increased significantly, although providers claim that the transition to "proof of stake" is expected to cut it by 99 percent (Beekhuizen 2021).

- *Artificial intelligence (AI) and big data.* AI and data science drive growth in data storage and processing. Training algorithms and deep learning require more computational capacity because of their complexity, and higher model accuracy implies more energy use (Kaack et al. 2022).[29] Estimations vary widely, from 4.5 kg of CO_2 for a typical case of model training to as much as 284,019 kg for one natural language processing algorithm (Freitag et al. 2020). As AI is applied across sectors, such as for autonomous driving, it will affect the GHG emission trends from the ICT sector. On the one hand, AI/big data/machine learning could bring efficiency to computing. However, it could also lead to increases in data transfer.

Consumer behavior and the patterns of use of digital technologies are evolving. During the latter years of the COVID-19 pandemic, the world saw the growing use of digital tools because of mobility restrictions. Teleworking has also led to greater use of VPNs (Virtual Private Networks), which leads to increases in data transfers. In addition to the increase in working from home, this period has seen a significant shift in user behavior, such as the surge in online activities, including shopping, leisure, and learning. A shift from enterprise to home networks and heavier use of broadband internet have also been observed. With the greater dependency on digital devices and the arrival of newer technologies such as 5G and IoT, faster replacement of end user devices is also occurring, leading to an overall increase in the GHG emissions of the sector.

Conclusion

Although precise estimates of emissions by the sector are elusive, further digitalization is expected to boost emissions at a rate that is not enough to contribute to the Paris Agreement's goal. Both digital connectivity infrastructure and data infrastructure are equally important to reduce emissions and green the digital economy. Furthermore, devices are even more important as a share of emissions, calling for action, including greater energy efficiency and circularity for devices. Increased use of digital solutions acts as an enabler in reducing GHG emissions in several sectors. However, the direct emissions of the ICT sector are still a concern as digitalization deepens and digital divides close. The relationship between segments of the sector is complex, and the uptake of several new technologies adds further to the difficulty of precisely projecting the emissions pathways. That will require public policies that take into account the technological and behavioral elements in a specific country context to ensure sustainable and inclusive development of the digital sector.

Expanding the Use of Renewable Energy and Using Energy More Efficiently

Emissions from the digital economy can be mitigated through greater energy efficiency and the use of renewable energy for the provision of digital connectivity, applications, and devices (supply side), coupled with adjusted consumer behavior that limits rebound effects (demand side).[30] Ultimately, reducing emissions along the digital value chain will depend on making greater use of renewable energy to generate the electricity that powers the ICT sector and on improving energy efficiency through new technologies, better processes, and better design of equipment. Both the public and private sectors have important roles to play in achieving green goals. Interventions can occur at the policy and regulatory levels (including self-regulation), at the technical and engineering levels for the provision of services, and at the consumption level (user practices). This section describes examples of interventions along the value chain, although the effectiveness of those interventions has not yet been evaluated. Because of the differences in digitalization, digital infrastructure characteristics, electricity system characteristics, and consumption of digital services, certain policies may be more relevant to developing economies. This section provides guidance on key elements to consider for greening digital in low- and middle-income countries along various elements of the value chain.

Shrinking the Carbon Footprint of Digital Connectivity Infrastructure (Telecommunication Networks)

Reduction of emissions along the digital connectivity value chain, from first mile to last mile, should consider both energy efficiency and the use of renewable energy. Studies such as that by BEREC (2022) have found that network operations account for about 90 percent of emissions, mostly generated by the access network (70–80 percent). In high-income economies, mobile and fixed networks have a similar contribution to emissions. However, because of the prevalence of mobile data connections in low- and middle-income economies, actions to green mobile networks may be more relevant in the short term.

Operators can take various actions to limit their carbon footprint during infrastructure deployment, operation, and decommissioning along the value chain (first, middle, and last mile). During network deployment, sharing existing physical infrastructure (duct, poles, and masts) and microtrenching[31] for fiber deployment, as well as recycling or reusing customer premise equipment, would reduce the carbon footprint. In the operations phase, measures might include replacing less efficient technology (for example, copper with fiber or using new generations of mobile networks), optimizing energy efficiency for networks (such as energy switch-off, sleep and wake cycles, and optimal routing), and using more energy-efficient cooling techniques for servers.

For decommissioning, recycling, reuse, or resale of equipment would also reduce lifetime emissions of equipment. As a study of European countries shows, these techniques are used to different degrees across operators (figure 2.15). Mobile operators are using artificial intelligence, machine learning, and virtualization to optimize power use (GSMA 2022b). The impact of spectrum-related factors on energy consumption have not yet been studied, such as the effects of the frequency used (which has implications on the number of base station sites and possibility of sharing), the use of small cells, and antenna configuration and modulation. To green submarine cables, the introduction of high-efficiency fiber-optic cables, optimized used of existing cables, and improved maintenance and installation practices are also being explored. In general, energy-efficiency solutions are a win-win for the sector because they can limit emissions while contributing to operational savings in the medium term, but there are some trade-offs.

Decisions on greening digital networks come with some trade-offs (WIK-Consult and Ramboll 2021) that should be evaluated at the country level, especially about any socioeconomic effects that might affect inclusion. For example, in one trade-off some technologies can be more efficient per bit of data, but encouraging these technologies

FIGURE 2.15 Sustainable Initiatives Noted by Mobile Operators in Europe

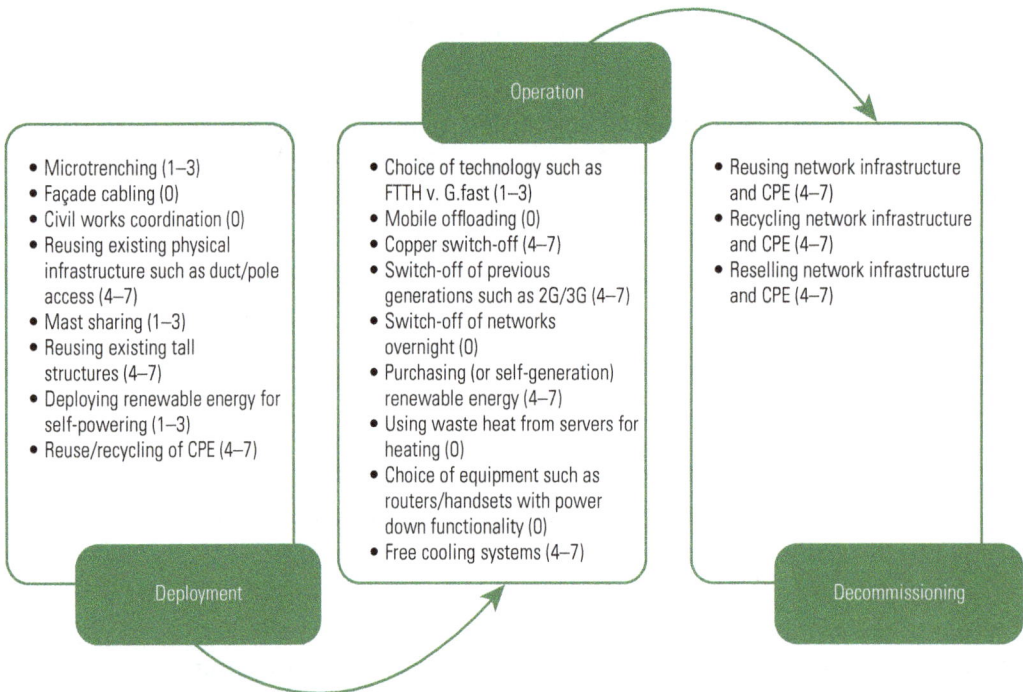

Source: WIK-Consult and Ramboll 2021.

Note: Number of mobile operators mentioning action appears in parentheses. 2G = second generation; 3G = third generation; CPE = customer premise equipment.

would conflict with the principle of technological neutrality. In another, improvements in data transmission quality could also result in additional data consumption, reducing the effects of energy efficiency on emissions. And in another trade-off, actions to reduce energy use could have effects on quality of service if, for example, restrictions are placed on video resolution to restrain bandwidth. Two trade-offs that are very relevant to LMICs are infrastructure sharing versus competition and financial costs versus emissions.

Infrastructure sharing for active and passive elements could help reduce energy use during deployment and operation, but it may clash with the objective of promoting competition between service providers. As a result, it could affect the prices and service bundles offered to consumers and reduce affordability and uptake. In markets where there is limited competition and operators control bottleneck infrastructure such as passive infrastructure and backbone networks, infrastructure sharing can dampen incentives to compete and facilitate coordination. Therefore, the appropriate conditions or regulations would be needed to safeguard competition and facilitate infrastructure sharing at the same time. Independent tower companies could be an option to facilitate sharing and reduce emissions while limiting competition issues, unless tower companies become dominant operators. Helios Towers, which operates in several African countries, estimates that two tenants reduce average emissions per tenant by 41 percent, three tenants by 50 percent, and four tenants by 58 percent (Helios Towers 2021). Estimates indicate that infrastructure sharing of active elements can significantly reduce energy consumption and therefore imply a reduction in emissions (figure 2.16). The baseline carbon emissions for all 4G sites using a wireless backhaul[32] is estimated to be 5.2 kt for 30 gigabytes (GB) per month per user, but the amount can be reduced by 37 percent when using an active sharing approach. A shared infrastructure business model only in rural areas leads to a 19 percent CO_2 reduction (Oughton et al. 2023).

Finally, a very relevant trade-off applies to LMICs, where there are important coverage and usage gaps. Some of the technologies that are more energy-efficient per unit of data are costlier to deploy, but they also lead to more usage and, in turn, more emissions. Adopting more energy-efficient technologies would have direct effects on prices and therefore uptake of digital technologies, especially for the poorest. In countries such as Switzerland, studies find that upgrading to 5G has increased usage even at higher consumer prices, but this finding may not apply to low-income consumers, and it can also be linked to more emissions. In LMICs, simulations reveal that the most cost-efficient alternative for delivering certain capacity at peak time or volume of data per month is a 4G access network with wireless backhaul (although the caveat is that not all users will have more expensive 5G enabled smartphones, leaving some users unconnected). The cost of delivering a 5G access network with a fiber backhaul (for the same capacity and data volume) would be higher. For example, in Colombia, assuming no change in data volumes, the cost of achieving universal broadband access

FIGURE 2.16 **Total Cellular Site CO$_2$ Emissions over 2020–30, by Infrastructure Sharing Strategy and Country Income Group**

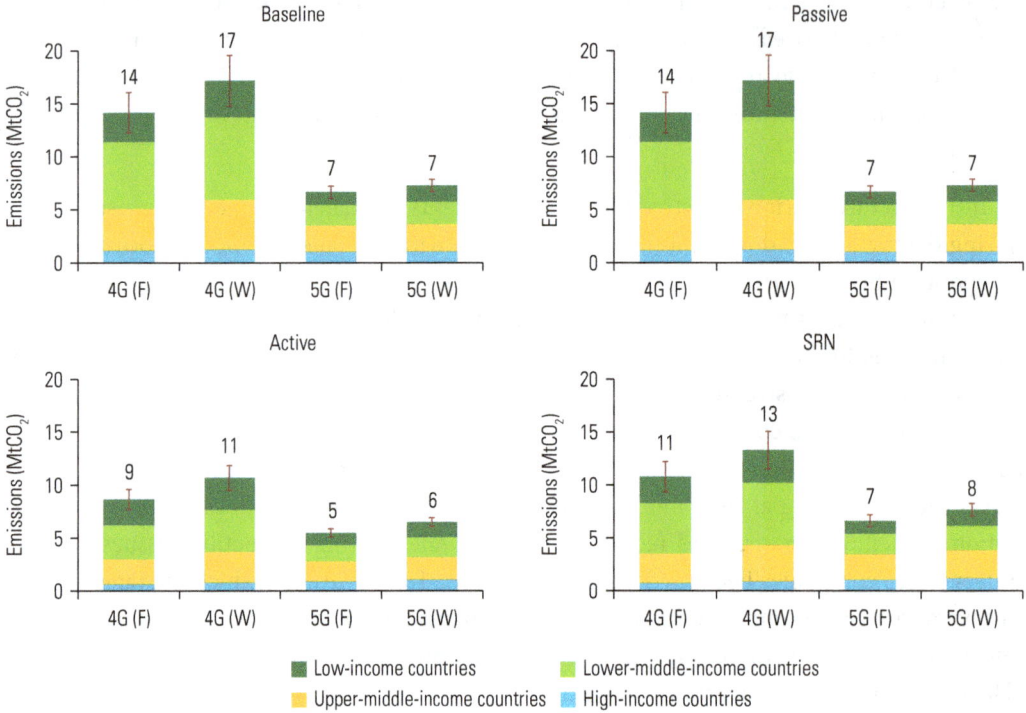

Source: Oughton et al. 2023.

Note: Interval bars reflect low and high adoption scenarios (0.5 percent and 6 percent adoption CAGR [compound annual growth rate] depending on country income group and scenario, respectively) for 30 gigabytes per month of data consumption by subscription. *Active* refers to active radio access network (RAN) sharing. F = fiber backhaul; MtCo$_2$ = megatonnes of carbon dioxide; SRN = single rural network; W = wireless backhaul. The emission effects of deployment and operation of passive infrastructure are not simulated.

would be 18 percent higher using 4G and fiber, than using 4G with wireless backhaul, although CO$_2$ emissions would be lower—24 percent less when deploying 4G with fiber backhaul compared with 4G with wireless backhaul (figures 2.17 and 2.18). However, this could only be achieved if consumers were willing and able to pay for more expensive 5G devices, otherwise this could lead to deepening the digital divide.

Carrying operations with greener electricity are an important option to limit emissions. Various digital infrastructure operators have taken steps to procure more renewable energy or self-generate electricity from renewable sources such as solar and wind. According to the GSMA (2022a), the share of electricity from renewable sources increased from 14 percent in 2020 to 18 percent in 2021. Even for submarine cables, alternatives such as use of onshore electrical grids to power ships while in port for operation and maintenance, installation of solar panels, and use of more fuel-efficient ships are being explored, together with renewable sources of energy for cable landing stations.

FIGURE 2.17 **Financial Cost of Universal Broadband, by Technology, 2023–30**

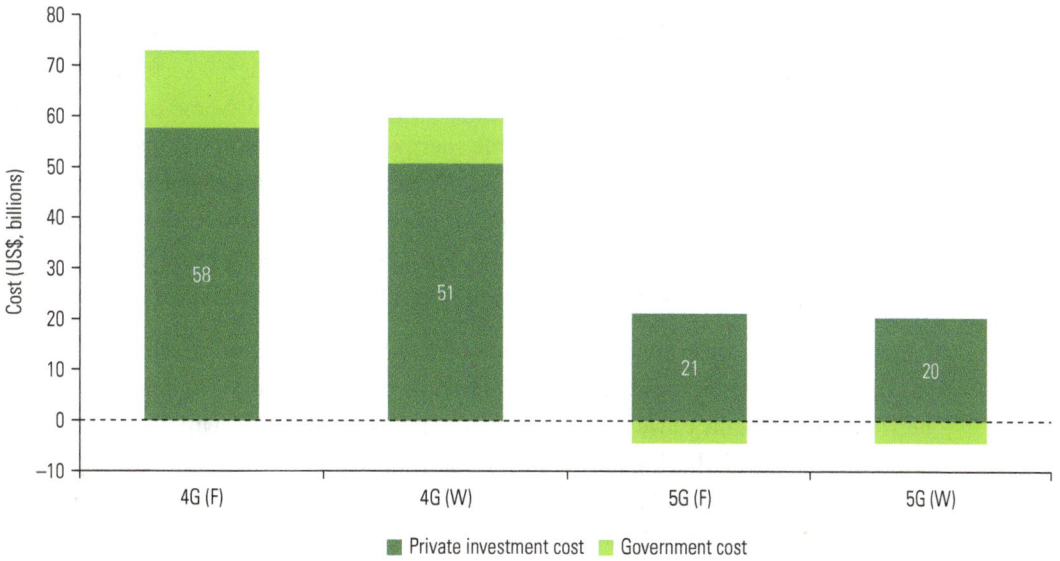

Source: Oughton et al. 2023.

Note: Baseline scenario considering 2 percent adoption CAGR (compound annual growth rate) for 30 gigabytes (GB) per month of data consumption by subscription. 4G = fourth generation; 5G = fifth generation; F = fiber backhaul; W = wireless backhaul.

FIGURE 2.18 **Cumulative Cellular Site Emissions, by Technology, 2023–30**

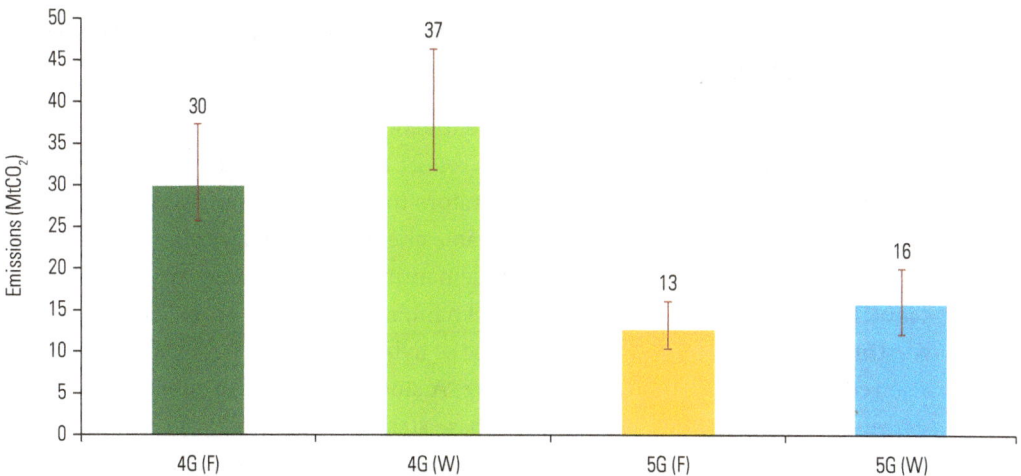

Source: Oughton et al. 2023.

Note: Interval bars reflect low and high adoption scenarios (1 percent and 4 percent adoption CAGR [compound annual growth rate], respectively) for 30 gigabytes (GB) per month of data consumption by subscription. 4G = fourth generation; 5G = fifth generation; F = fiber backhaul; W = wireless backhaul. $MtCO_2$ = megatonnes of carbon dioxide; W = wireless backhaul.

Companies in the ICT sector are working to reduce their operational and sometimes their entire upstream and downstream GHG emissions in various ways. Among other things, they are setting targets for reducing emissions, helping suppliers to reduce emissions and transition to green energy, working with the energy sector to increase renewable options, and funding initiatives for carbon removal. Some operators have committed to specific targets on renewable energy. For example, Vodafone reached the milestone of 100 percent renewable sources of electricity in Europe, and Telefónica can boast about its 100 percent renewable sources of electricity in Europe, Brazil, and Peru. Orange is aiming to use more than 50 percent renewable electricity by 2025. Depending on the energy mix available in a country, these goals are more feasible to achieve.

Opportunities are available to use renewable energy instead of diesel for situations in which the electricity grid is not available or is of poor quality. Digital connectivity networks are typically powered by energy from the electricity grid, with diesel-powered generators serving as backup power or the main source of power in bad grid or off-grid situations, particularly in LMICs. Many electricity networks in LMICs are poor in quality. For example, in Kenya Safaricom reports that average generator use per day rose in 2021 to 3.2 hours (Safaricom 2022). Because of the rising cost of running networks and the emissions from diesel fuel, the use of renewable energy as a source of power for mobile networks has grown over the last few years. The annual CO_2e emissions from diesel-powered generators at off-grid and bad grid towers have been reduced by an estimated 2.2 million tonnes, from 9.2 million tonnes in 2014 to 7 million tonnes in 2020 (GSMA 2020b). The availability of renewable energy from solar and microturbine wind technologies and better power storage through improved batteries are essential to allow for greater use of electricity from renewable sources. Furthermore, new technologies such as fuel cell technology (piloted by Vodacom in Romania) are enlarging the number of fossil fuel alternatives.

Simulations demonstrate the great potential of using renewable energy for mobile network infrastructure. Research for this report explored the sustainability benefits of shifting cellular sites from diesel generators to renewable sources such as photovoltaic and wind power systems. A renewable energy strategy for cellular sites would mitigate emissions (figure 2.19). By implementing a renewable energy strategy for cellular sites with 4G using a wireless backhaul, up to 10 percent net carbon savings is estimated (Oughton et al. 2023). The use of hybrid generators as an alternative can also reduce emissions and be cost-effective. A study looking at the use of hybrid diesel/renewable generators for Safaricom's base stations in Kenya found that, although the initial installation cost of the hybrid system is higher than the installation of a diesel generator, in the long run the cost of operating a hybrid system is lower. Indeed, the operating cost of a hybrid system of solar, wind, and diesel is three times lower than that of a pure diesel generator. The net present cost of the different combinations was estimated at US\$21.8 per megawatt-hour (MWh) for diesel only, \$8.24 per MWh

FIGURE 2.19 **Assessment of the Impacts of Off-Grid Renewable Power Strategies for Universal Broadband Options, by Emissions Type, Colombia**

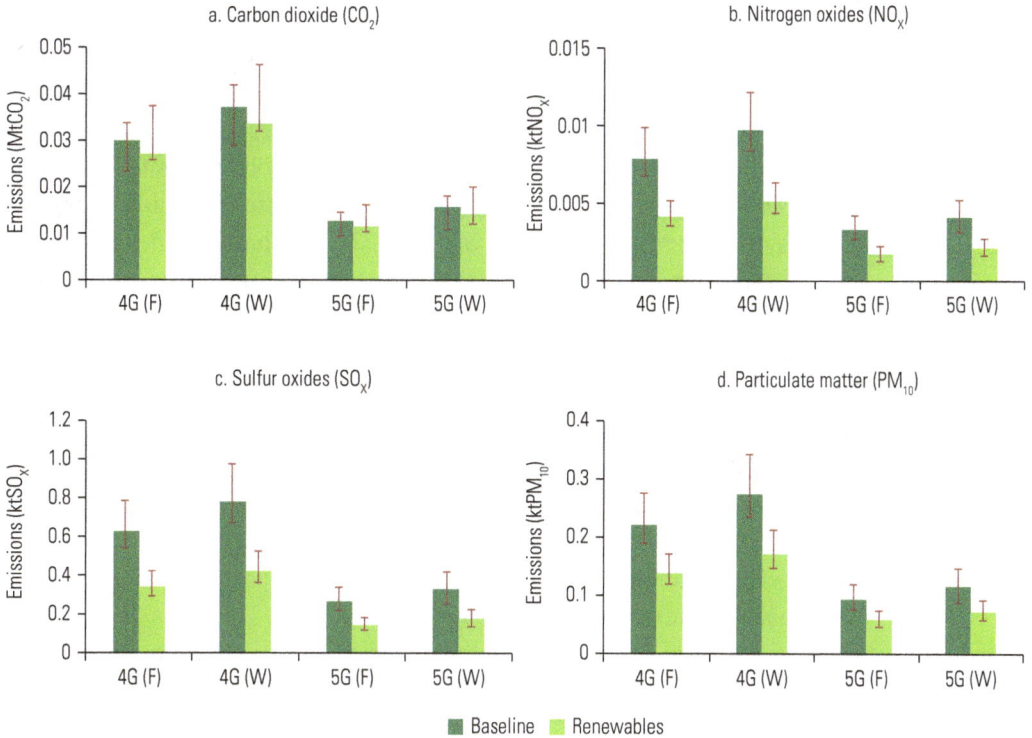

a. Carbon dioxide (CO_2)

b. Nitrogen oxides (NO_x)

c. Sulfur oxides (SO_x)

d. Particulate matter (PM_{10})

■ Baseline ■ Renewables

Source: Oughton et al. 2023.

Note: Graphs indicate the impacts, by emission type, of shifting from off-grid diesel generators to renewable site power. Interval bars reflect low and high adoption scenarios—1 percent and 4 percent adoption CAGR (compound annual growth rate), respectively—for 30 gigabytes (GB) per month of data consumption by subscription. 4G = fourth generation; 5G = fifth generation; F = fiber backhaul; $ktNO_x$ = kilotonnes of nitrogen oxides; $ktPM_{10}$ = kilotonnes of particulate matter; $ktSO_x$ = kilotonnes of sulfur oxides; $MtCO_2$ = megatonnes of carbon dioxide; W = wireless backhaul.

for solar and wind turbine hybrid only, and $6.89 per MWh for solar, wind, and diesel (Owino 2017).

The private sector, by self-regulation, is spearheading efforts to reduce emissions in digital connectivity infrastructure. From collaboration among the Global e-Sustainability Initiative (GeSI), International Telecommunication Union, the GSMA, and the Science Based Targets initiative (SBTi) has emerged a sector-specific decarbonization pathway that allows ICT companies to set targets in line with the latest climate science. Almost 300 tech companies have committed to or have already set science-based targets for reducing emissions, including at least 35 digital infrastructure operators (European Commission 2021). According to the GSMA (2022a), operators that account for half of global revenue of mobile networks committed to net zero carbon emissions by 2050 or earlier.

Governments can also integrate more prominently policies to facilitate deployment and operation of greener digital connectivity infrastructure. The following actions have been either implemented or discussed:

- *Measure to improve.* Limited information is available on emissions, energy consumption, sources of energy, and other environmental sustainability indicators. Operators (mainly multinational) committed to achieving green goals publish information voluntarily, but other operators do not. Mobile operators accounting for 66 percent of global mobile connections disclose their climate impacts using an established methodology (GSMA 2022a). Furthermore, methodologies and indicators are not consistent across operators in a country or across countries, making aggregation, comparisons, and monitoring challenging. Various telecom regulators do not have regulatory mandates to collect and verify this information, including in Europe (BEREC 2022). Meanwhile, other countries have already begun to track certain indicators. In India, a green initiative implemented by the Telecom Regulatory Authority of India (TRAI) tracks the number of diesel-powered and solar-powered mobile towers reported by mobile network operators and tower companies. In France, since January 2022 internet service providers and mobile operators have had to publicly report the quantity of data consumed and the ensuing GHG emissions.

- *Facilitate the use of electricity based on renewable resources.* In countries in which electricity systems have been liberalized, power purchase agreements between digital infrastructure operators and generators are feasible. Digital infrastructure operators can become important off-takers for greenfield renewable energy projects. Direct power purchase agreements with renewable energy generators are critical to making this happen. Group captive models are also emerging to facilitate the access of smaller digital infrastructure players to renewable energy. This model, implemented in India, allows a consumer or group of consumers to contribute to setting up a power plant and to purchase power from the plant for their own consumption. Allowing for the self-provision of electricity or the operation of telecom energy services companies (TESCOs) that can also power minigrids are other alternatives for ensuring the availability of renewable energy for digital infrastructure operators. This is particularly important for off-grid areas, areas where electricity service is poor, and countries in which fossil fuels dominate the electricity system. This is a policy that needs alignment with energy sector institutions.

- *Facilitate infrastructure sharing.* In many countries where (passive or active) infrastructure sharing is desirable, frameworks are still ineffective because practical issues limit sharing, such as technical interoperability or restrictive construction standards. Governments could help revise these frameworks and implement them more proactively. Frameworks to access essential infrastructure controlled by operators with significant market power need to be in place, including publication of reference access offers with maximum cost-oriented access charges when needed, set time periods for processing, and quality of service standards. Systems to allow access to information on the location of current infrastructure, including fiber backbone and towers, such as in France, Poland, and the United Kingdom, and the ongoing open data fiber network platform initiative for Africa, are important to facilitate sharing. Cooperation between operators for joint infrastructure should be facilitated as well under commercial terms with a robust dispute resolution system and appropriate analysis of potential anticompetitive effects. The Netherlands has discussed a possible relaxation of competition analysis to pursue environmental goals, including for such partnerships.

- *Facilitate infrastructure deployment.* Dig-once policies or mutualization rules can be useful to boost efficiency in network deployment, including through cross-sectoral collaboration. However, implementation is important to prevent such measures from acting as a barrier to infrastructure expansion for entrants or smaller players. For fiber network deployment, municipalities can play an important role in allowing more environmentally friendly techniques such as microtrenching, which is encouraged in New York and San Francisco.

- *Consider environmental factors when awarding licenses and granting state aid and for the operation of partial or fully state-owned digital infrastructure operators.* Countries are also considering setting standards for network deployment to ensure energy efficiency and sustainability. In the European Union, proposals have been made to either set certain standards to participate in tenders to access state aid or consider energy efficiency and other sustainability elements as factors that are evaluated favorably. Setting standards for awards under universal service funds would be a way to ensure expansion with greener technologies. Furthermore, through state shareholdings in operators of digital connectivity infrastructure, governments can also infuse change by adopting more mitigation measures.[33] Some countries, such as Ireland, have adopted guidelines for enterprises with state shareholdings to boost mitigation actions.

- *Support more energy-efficient equipment and systems.* Industry standards for energy-efficient equipment as well as experimentation with more energy-efficient technologies would encourage use of the available more efficient technologies and development of more efficient products. In Europe, the European Telecommunications Standards Institute (ETSI) works on standards for transmission and network equipment in line with the European Commission's Ecodesign of Energy Related Products Directive.

- *Increase the transparency of operators' and consumers' carbon footprints.* Increased awareness of consumers' carbon footprints and operators' emissions, as well as energy efficiency and sustainability practices, can allow "green" to become a variable for competition. More sustainable operators could be rewarded by consumers, thereby creating a virtuous cycle of incentives for operators to become more environmentally conscious. Certification and labeling of operators with good green practices could also enhance the information available to consumers. Including information on consumers' carbon footprint in their monthly consumption bills could also restrain rebound effects.

Shrinking the Carbon Footprint of Data Management Infrastructure (Data Centers)

As larger volumes of data are collected, stored, and processed, the capacity and use of data infrastructure are expanding. This trend is expected to continue, turning data infrastructure (data centers and cloud computing) into an important source of emissions in the ICT sector. Nevertheless, more traffic, computation, and storage do not necessarily translate into proportionally higher energy consumption (Center on Regulation in Europe 2021). The twin digital and green transition requires measures to boost energy efficiency and the use of renewables in this segment of the ICT sector.

The GHG emissions from data center operations arise from the energy consumed by ICT hardware and cooling systems. The energy consumption of hardware is directly correlated with its data processing capacity, data servers, data storage devices, and other network components. The electricity consumed in data centers is converted into heat, which is removed by cooling systems. As for the computing part, energy consumption is lowered by greater recourse to energy-efficient servers, storage devices, and other network hardware, and smarter dimensioning of network components in relation to the data center's peak load. As for the cooling part, measures to reduce energy consumption and GHG emissions include (1) using electricity from renewable sources; (2) raising the operating temperature (which reduces energy consumption but shortens the components' life span) and managing it more efficiently, considering weather conditions; (3) using other cooling techniques (free cooling in cold climates and liquid cooling); and (4) recovering heat for use by residential or commercial facilities.

Recognizing the potential for operational cost reductions from energy efficiency and use of more affordable sources of energy, the private sector is showing a strong commitment to reducing the carbon footprint of the sector and achieving policy targets. In January 2021, data center operators and industry associations in Europe launched the Climate Neutral Data Centre Pact. The pact includes a pledge to make data centers climate-neutral by 2030 and has intermediate (2025) targets for power usage effectiveness and carbon-free energy. The 2030 target appears to be in line with the European Commission's digital strategy, which was released in February 2020 and includes a key action on "initiatives to achieve climate-neutral, highly energy-efficient and sustainable data centers by no later than 2030," and the European Green Deal. The European Union (EU) case also illustrates how setting policy targets can provide a reference point to incentivize climate action by the private sector.

Self-regulation and co-regulation are important for the data infrastructure sector. Various initiatives for voluntarily adopting codes of conduct, guidelines, and certification have been implemented across countries. In the European Union, the Voluntary EU Code of Conduct on Data Center Energy Efficiency[34] initiative was launched in 2008 to inform and stimulate data center operators and owners to reduce energy consumption cost-effectively without hampering the critical function of data centers. This initiative provides a platform for stakeholders to discuss and agree on voluntary actions to improve energy efficiency, including best practice guidelines. To date, 345 data centers have requested participant status, and 290 data centers have been approved as participants. Over 120 organizations have at least one data center approved as a participant, with most of the participants having achieved power usage effectiveness of below 1.80.[35] One participant is located outside Europe—eBay, with four data centers. In the Republic of Korea, the Korea Data Center Council established a voluntary green data center certification program. In India, the Indian Green Building Council (IGBC) developed and launched a Green Data Centre rating system in 2016 to offer services to the growing data center industry and to rate energy efficiency.[36] International standards for data centers are also private sector–driven. For example, the Uptime Institute has developed and applied a tier standard for the design, construction, and operation of thousands of facilities, including data centers.[37]

Governments and associations provide guidance for greener data centers and encourage adoption through benchmarking, as well as set mandatory standards. In Hong Kong SAR, China, the government issued a Green Data Centres Practice Guide[38] to provide best practice measures to improve the energy efficiency and environmental performance of its data centers. Both local conditions, including climate and ecosystems, as well as international best practices, are part of the guide, which covers design and construction, procurement, management, operation, and maintenance, as well as disposal. In Denmark, the TIDA project[39] is creating an overview of the sustainability profile of large, medium-size, and small data centers in order to create a common framework for "best practices" and "industry benchmarks" for green data center solutions in Denmark. Other countries have established mandatory standards for data centers. In the Republic of Korea, standards for green data center construction were issued and complemented with self-evaluation guidelines to facilitate compliance. In Malaysia, the Technical Code: Specification for Green Data Centres was developed by the Malaysian Technical Standards Forum Bhd (MTSFB).[40] The technical code was developed to provide minimum requirements for green data centers and outline the best practices that data centers should adopt to achieve a sustainable industry.

On the demand side, governments are using different approaches to green procurement, including for data storage and cloud computing and for climate-friendly management of government facilities. In 2020, the European Commission published the "EU Green Public Procurement (GPP) Criteria for Data Centers, Server Rooms and Cloud Services"[41] as part of the EU Green Public Procurement voluntary initiative to encourage public procurement of sustainable products to enable market transformation. In 2021, the Brazilian government outlined new measures to reduce energy consumption by federal agencies amid energy shortages caused by drought. Among the requirements, the decree states that data processing centers must keep rooms "cooled only to the limit of what is technically necessary"; computers should be programmed to the lowest possible electricity consumption; and agencies should provide access to systems directly from the cloud.[42]

Tech companies operating data centers are large purchasers of renewable energy, thereby helping to scale the market for renewable energy. The ICT sector accounted for 44 percent of renewable power purchases in 2020, and six of the top 10 corporate purchasers of renewable energy in 2020 were tech companies (BloombergNEF 2021). Globally, Amazon is the largest procurer of renewable energy after utility companies themselves.[43] A number of tech companies have committed to expanding the use of renewable energy as part of RE100.

One challenge is that even if tech companies pay for renewable energy, they do not necessarily receive renewable energy because of the energy mix of the grid in the country of location. Google has pioneered the concept of 24/7 carbon-free energy, in which every kilowatt-hour of power consumption is matched by carbon-free electricity production every hour on the grid where the electricity is consumed. The 24/7 Carbon-Free Energy Compact is a movement coordinated by Sustainable Energy for All and the United Nations.[44] The initiative is working to increase the share of matched green power, including using technologies such as AI and renewable storage. Both Google and Microsoft have announced 2030 targets to source and match zero-carbon electricity on a 24/7 basis.

Data centers can be off-takers of renewable energy, but they also feed power to the grid. They typically have a significant amount of backup power, which is used only during power grid incidents to ensure the data center's reliable access to power. Because of the redundancy requirement, the backup power capacity of a data center is typically high, and it may produce a significant amount of electricity for the power grid. Net metering rules would be needed to allow for this occurrence.

Cross-border use of data storage and cloud computing facilities offers low- and middle-income countries opportunities to attract investments in green data infrastructure. Some LMICs are attractive because of the availability of renewable energy resources and renewable electricity. Others may be attractive because of their capacity to use alternative cooling systems, including free cooling. Furthermore, hyperscale data centers provide economies of scale and are more energy-efficient.

Shrinking the Carbon Footprint of End User Devices

The biggest challenge in greening end user devices is the swelling popularity of these products. Responding to the rising performance of end user devices and their new features, users are discarding older devices at a growing pace (IIASA 2019). Although consumers in high-income countries are increasingly keeping their smartphones longer (Freitag et al. 2020), some studies estimate that a phone would have to be used for at least 25 years for the energy efficiency of the new device to offset the emissions generated from production of the previous one (EEB 2019).

The main technical areas in which the GHG emissions of end user devices could be reduced are (1) energy efficiency and the use of renewable energy during manufacturing, which is the point at which most of the GHG emissions released over the life cycle of devices occur (Freitag et al. 2020); (2) reusability (including ease of repair); and (3) recycling of components and materials (including the possibility of recycling individual components before recycling the entire device). Energy-efficient product design could reduce consumption in standby/sleep mode by, for example, installing automatic sleep mode for devices not being used. Reuse and remanufacturing build on the concepts of ecodesign or design-for-recyclability/circularity. Initiatives for labeling and standards based on energy efficiency, ecodesign, and repairability are options for increasing consumer awareness of the impacts of their product choices on the climate and environment.

Ecodesign and ecolabeling measures have been introduced to reduce environmental impacts over the life cycle of end user devices (box 2.2). Under the EU Ecodesign Directive, various regulations were adopted aiming to reduce GHGs via measures with a specific focus on energy efficiency. Regulations have been issued on electronic displays,[45] personal computers,[46] and external power supplies to charge laptops and phones,[47] among other things. Currently, a new regulation on mobile phones and tablets is under preparation. Meanwhile, the EU Digital Product Passport (launched in early 2023) creates a digital twin[48] on the web for every individual product throughout its life cycle (including manufacturing, transportation, disposal, and recycling). It is accessible by consumers, supply chains, and other stakeholders.

Efficient recycling of e-waste can greatly reduce the demand for virgin raw materials, device emissions, and adverse environmental effects.[49] The ITU has been helping countries track e-waste and the adoption of e-waste laws and policies. Although 78 countries had adopted e-waste policies, laws, or regulations by 2019, enforcement is weak, and collection and management are poor (box 2.3). Appropriate facilities are also needed to refurbish equipment and extract valuable materials.

> **BOX 2.2**   **Ecoratings and Ecolabeling of Devices**
>
> Various mobile telecom operators have begun to develop public *ecoratings* to measure the sustainability and environmental performance of mobile handsets. These ratings are then used to inform the public of that performance and communicate the sustainability and environmental performance of the products. Usually such efforts measure sustainability and environmental performance at the corporate, supply chain, or device level. Criteria used for labeling include (1) sustainability of the handset manufacturer based on GHG emissions, environmental policies, and other related factors; (2) sustainability of the supply chain elements based on factors such as contract manufacturing, transportation distances, and mineral sourcing; and (3) actual performance of a handset based on factors such as the components used, energy consumption, recyclability, and packaging. An ecorating highlights five key aspects of mobile device sustainability: durability, repairability, recyclability, climate efficiency, and resource efficiency.
>
> Operators applying ecoratings include AT&T, Orange, Sprint, Telefónica, UL, and Vodafone. Ecoratings are already applied to more than 200 mobile phone models from 16 manufacturers.
>
> *Ecolabeling* is another effort to inform consumers about the environmental performance of a product. It is a voluntary approach to environmental performance certification that identifies a product that meets a specified performance criteria or standard. Different types of organizations, including governments, nonprofits, and for-profit organizations, have developed ecolabeling programs, which address different issues. For example, ENERGY STAR focuses on energy use during equipment operation, while other ecolabels address life-cycle environmental concerns or cover ergonomic and worker health and safety issues.
>
> Today, several types of environmental labeling exist, including those that are grouped and classified by the International Organization for Standardization. Currently, 456 ecolabels are used worldwide in 199 countries. Of those, 72 ecolabels are used on electronics.
>
> An issue associated with ecolabeling is label trust. Consumers may worry that fake ecolabels are being used to greenwash them. Another issue is that international trade obstacles to ecolabels act as nontariff trade barriers. This issue stems from the growing use of ecolabels and the diverse labeling requirements. That brings up the problem of adjusting to the production standards of different markets abroad, which may entail significant cost, information, and technical expertise. Labeling programs also tend to be based on the domestic environmental priorities and technologies of the importing country, and so often they lack relevance to the exporting country's environment and local conditions.
>
> *Sources:* CIEL (2005); Ecoabel Index, https://www.ecolabelindex.com/ecolabels/?st=category,electronics; EPA (2012); ITU (2012); Telefónica (2022).

Measures to facilitate circularity in the use of devices and equipment are now in place in some countries. In France, the anti-waste law for a circular economy adopted in February 2020 requires manufacturers to provide consumers with more information on the environmental impact, life cycle, and repairability of products. This law also introduces regulations on the repairability of electronics. They are intended to provide consumers with more information in support of their purchase decisions and to encourage producers to make their products more repairable. A repairability index has

| BOX 2.3 | **E-waste Management in Low- and Middle-Income Countries** |

As of 2019, 53.6 million tonnes (Mt) of e-waste were produced and discarded globally (Forti et al. 2020). If not managed efficiently, this waste is expected to grow to 74.7 Mt by 2030, or almost double the 2014 amount (Forti et al. 2020). The discarded waste includes toxic and hazardous materials, including batteries, plugs, mercury, brominated flame retardants, and chlorofluorocarbons, which are harmful to human and environmental health.

E-waste management is especially important in low- and middle-income countries (LMICs). Transboundary flows of e-waste have become a major concern over the years. Some reports have suggested that the lack of data on e-waste production in the global North implies that the waste produced is managed outside the official collection systems and is transported to LMICs, further exacerbating the issue (ITU 2022).

The issue of transboundary movements of e-waste raises valid concerns about both environmental health and human health because of the lack of management and infrastructure in the destination countries. Consequently, the waste generated is managed inefficiently, leading to risks to health and environment. For example, most LMICs manage e-waste by open-air burning or acid baths to recover materials from electronic waste (Forti et al. 2020). Such activities expose workers and the environment to the harmful fumes, leading to irreversible health degradation. In addition, in most LMICs activities associated with e-waste management is carried out by members of the informal sector. They buy, collect, and recycle e-waste in an unregulated manner, thereby exposing them to the harm arising from burning, melting, or recycling e-waste.

LMICs are also far behind in deploying and regulating legislation governing e-waste management (figure B2.3.1). As of October 2019, 78 countries had an e-waste management policy, legislation, or regulation in place (ITU 2020). However, in many LMICs policies are not legally binding, which makes it hard to regulate e-waste. For example, across Asia and Africa only 19 countries have legally binding legislation on e-waste. Five countries have a nonlegally binding e-waste policy, and 31 countries have some form of policy in place.

FIGURE B2.3.1 E-waste Management, by Region

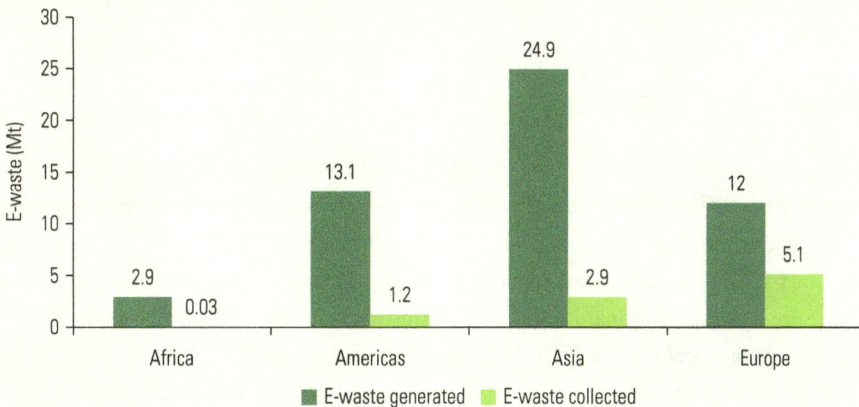

Source: ITU 2022.
Note: Mt = megatonnes.

been in place since January 2021 to rate electronics for their ease of repair and life span on a scale of 1 to 10. A durability index will be introduced in 2024. In the European Union, the 2021 New Circular Economy Action Plan[50] includes a circular electronics initiative that would promote longer product lifetimes. It includes regulatory measures for electronics and ICT, including mobile phones, tablets, and laptops under the Ecodesign Directive; implementation of the "right to repair," including a right to update obsolete software; regulatory measures for chargers for mobile phones and similar devices (including the introduction of a common charger); improvement of the collection and treatment of waste electrical and electronic equipment; and review of EU rules on restrictions of hazardous substances in electrical and electronic equipment.

In low- and middle-income countries, purchasing second-hand devices or refurbishing devices can be an option for accessing digital technologies while also supporting reuse of devices. However, only 11 percent of smartphones sold globally are refurbished (Persistence Market Research 2022). Furthermore, efficient recycling and refurbishing require a value chain approach that integrates producers, telecommunications companies, waste management operators, repair service providers, and second-hand market players, and relies on a better understanding of consumer incentives to use refurbished and ecofriendly devices. Take-back schemes involving the industry, harmonized labeling for devices, and accreditation standards for recycling are examples of initiatives to complement national e-waste frameworks.[51]

Conclusion

Strategies to decarbonize the digital sector include implementation of energy efficiency plans, a switch to renewable or low-carbon electricity supplies, and encouragement of carbon consciousness among end users. At the technical level, providers of digital connectivity and data infrastructure can undertake various actions to reduce emissions (figure 2.20).

A Comprehensive Sectoral Approach

In summary, an integral policy involving the public and private sectors is needed to green the entire ICT sector. However, few regions or countries have specific policies for the sector. Among the few exceptions are the European Union and the Republic of Korea (box 2.4). The European Union is pursuing initiatives such as product passports to track life-cycle emissions; longer device lifetimes; energy efficiency, including zero emissions for data centers and networks by 2030; and support of the use of digital solutions to enable mitigation in other sectors (European Commission 2020). Setting sectoral policy objectives and targets can be useful to steer the sector toward a more sustainable path and help achieve emissions reductions in line with the Paris Agreement's commitments.

FIGURE 2.20 Technical Strategies to Decarbonize the ICT Sector

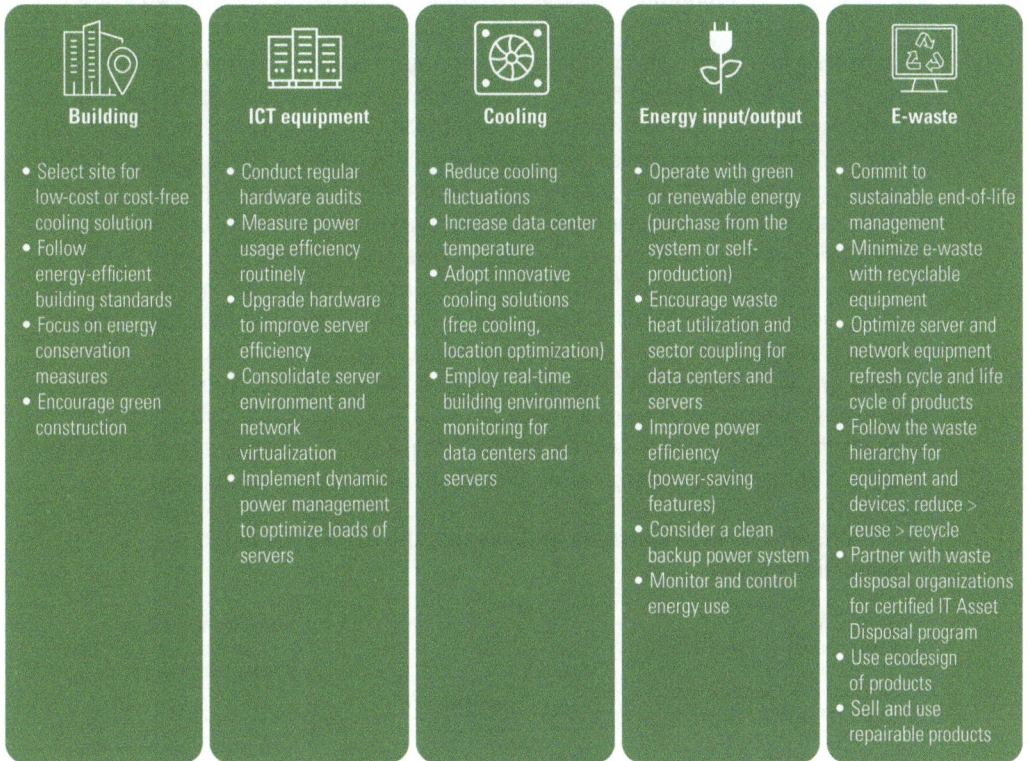

Building	ICT equipment	Cooling	Energy input/output	E-waste
• Select site for low-cost or cost-free cooling solution • Follow energy-efficient building standards • Focus on energy conservation measures • Encourage green construction	• Conduct regular hardware audits • Measure power usage efficiency routinely • Upgrade hardware to improve server efficiency • Consolidate server environment and network virtualization • Implement dynamic power management to optimize loads of servers	• Reduce cooling fluctuations • Increase data center temperature • Adopt innovative cooling solutions (free cooling, location optimization) • Employ real-time building environment monitoring for data centers and servers	• Operate with green or renewable energy (purchase from the system or self-production) • Encourage waste heat utilization and sector coupling for data centers and servers • Improve power efficiency (power-saving features) • Consider a clean backup power system • Monitor and control energy use	• Commit to sustainable end-of-life management • Minimize e-waste with recyclable equipment • Optimize server and network equipment refresh cycle and life cycle of products • Follow the waste hierarchy for equipment and devices: reduce > reuse > recycle • Partner with waste disposal organizations for certified IT Asset Disposal program • Use ecodesign of products • Sell and use repairable products

Source: World Bank team research and ITU (2020).

Note: ICT = information and communication technology; IT = information technology; PUE = power usage effectiveness.

Constraints on and Opportunities for Green Digital in LMICs

Electricity and Renewable Energy

Availability of grid electricity affects the ICT sector. Over 800 million people in LMICs have no access to electricity, and over 1 billion are connected to an unreliable grid.[52] Low-income countries face the biggest access challenge because electricity covers less than half of their populations (42.9 percent), in contrast to the access in lower-middle-income (89.8 percent), upper-middle-income (99.4 percent), and high-income (100 percent) economies.[53]

Unreliable grids are another challenge. These so-called bad grids are subjected to power outages for more than six hours a day on average.[54] They require the use of backup generators, and, if renewables are not available, they are likely powered by diesel.

BOX 2.4 **The Republic of Korea's Multipronged Approach to Green Digital**

Addressing the carbon footprint of the information and communication technology (ICT) sector was one of the priorities of the Korean government's green transition, as illustrated by its announcement of the Green IT National Strategy (2009). Since the announcement of that strategy, the government has introduced various measures to green the ICT sector (figure B2.4.1), including a green certification program (2010), standardization of green data center guidelines (2012), and a number of government-funded research and development (R&D) projects for green data centers and communication network technologies. Since President Moon Jae-In took office in May 2017, the greening ICT has been incorporated into and backed by a long-term vision and strong political commitment (2050 Carbon Neutral Strategy), large-scale infrastructure projects (the Korean New Deal), R&D for innovative technologies (Carbon Neutral Tech Innovation Strategy), and a robust legal framework to support the implementation of green initiatives (Carbon Neutrality Act). Although the government is a lead facilitator for several tools to decarbonize the ICT sector, such as laws and economic instruments, the private sector is also contributing to the national efforts to green the ICT sector by adopting voluntary measures.

FIGURE B2.4.1 **Key Measures for Greening the ICT Sector in the Republic of Korea**

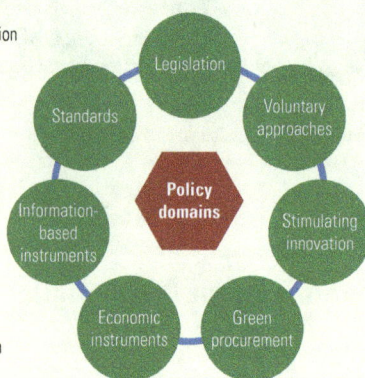

Legislation
- The Framework Act on Low Carbon Green Growth
- The Act on the Allocation and Trading of Greenhouse-Gas Emission Permits
- The Framework Act on Carbon Neutrality and Green Growth to Respond to Climate Crisis (passed August 2021)

Standards
- Standards for green data center construction and self-evaluation guidelines

Information-based instruments
- Regulation on standby power reduction program
- Environmental product declaration (EPD)
- Carbon footprint of products (CFP) labeling certification

Economic instruments
- K-ETS (emissions trading scheme)

Voluntary approaches
- Green data center certification program by the Korea data center council
- RE100 initiative

Stimulating innovation (R&D)
- Energy harvesting technology and intelligent/autonomous Internet of Things
- Super performance/low-power communication equipment technology
- Intelligent and autonomous power usage efficiency (PUE) management technology for green data centers

Green procurement
- Public organizations are required to purchase green products among available options when (1) direct purchasing; (2) purchasing through subcontractoers; (3) purchasing construction materials through construction companies

Source: World Bank 2022.

Apart from access to and reliability of the grid, the mixture of power on the electricity grid has an impact on ICT sector emissions. The ICT sector in countries with dirty grids will emit more emissions than those with relatively green grids. The available data suggest that grids in East Asian LMICs are dirtier than those in Latin America (figure 2.21).

FIGURE 2.21 Access to Electricity Compared with Grid Emissions Factor, Selected Low- and Middle-Income Countries, 2020

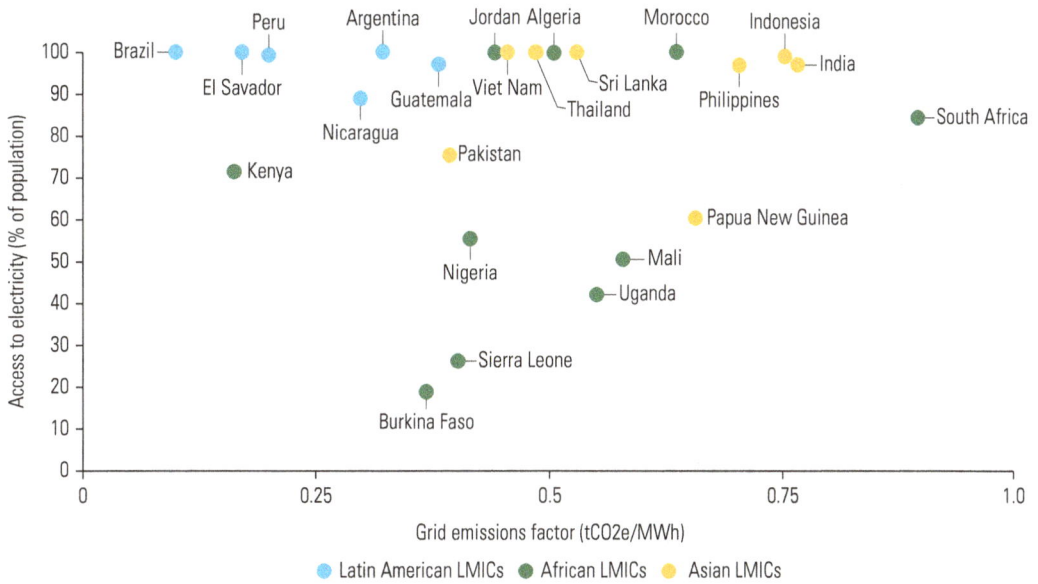

Sources: World Bank and Institute for Global Environmental Strategies.

Note: tCO2e/MWh = tonnes of carbon dioxide equivalent per megawatt-hour. LMICs = low- and middle-income countries.

Because of the significant energy heterogeneity in LMICs, countries could be categorized to identify relevant strategies for a green ICT sector based on country characteristics. For example, an LMIC with high coverage and a clean grid will have a different outlook than one with low coverage and a dirty grid. The former would be attractive to multinationals as a location for data and cloud centers, whereas the latter might benefit from strategic advice on opening its energy market to renewable power suppliers. The latter might also consider commercially viable off-grid pay-as-you-go (PAYG) solar. PAYG solar could help mobile operators enhance use and help tech companies seeking projects for carbon offsets.

Governments have a leading role to play in liberalizing the environment for clean energy. A considerable effort is needed in this area because LMICs lag high-income countries in clean energy policies and regulation. OECD countries have a score of 81 out of 100 on the Renewable Energy pillar of the Regulatory Indicators for Sustainable Energy (RISE),[55] compared with 57 for the MENA region and 41 for the EAP region (figure 2.22, panel a). There are also huge gaps in the renewable energy performances of LMICs. For example, Rwanda scores 90 out of 100 on the Renewable Energy pillar, whereas Turkmenistan scores 7 (figure 2.22, panel b).

As countries continue to improve the functioning of their electricity markets, access to renewable energy for greening the ICT sector will be easier. South Africa is an example of how government policy can influence green energy markets. The country ranks

FIGURE 2.22 RISE Renewable Energy Pillar Scores, 2019

a. Renewable energy
score by region

b. Renewable energy score by low- and
middle-income country, top and bottom 10

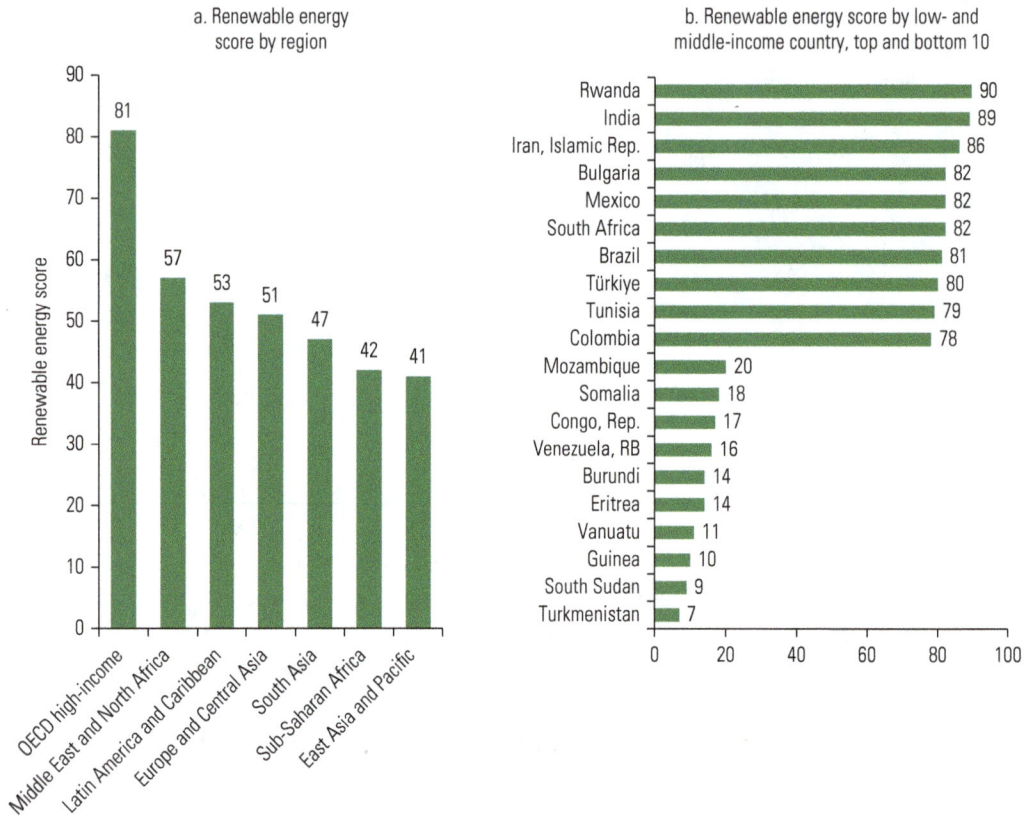

Source: Regulatory Indicators for Sustainable Energy (RISE), https://rise.esmap.org/indicators.

Note: Seven indicators are assessed for the RISE renewable energy pillar: (1) legal framework for renewable energy; (2) planning for renewable energy expansion; (3) incentives and regulatory support for renewable energy; (4) attributes of financial and regulatory incentives; (5) network connection and use; (6) counterparty risk; and (7) carbon pricing and monitoring. OECD = Organisation for Economic Co-operation and Development.

sixth among low- and middle-income countries in the RISE renewable energy indicator. In June 2021, the government announced new regulations exempting power projects of up to 100 megawatts (MW) from having to apply for a license from the energy regulator (Merten 2021). Independent power producers will also be able to upload their surplus energy onto the grid. This step is linked to the requirement that Eskom, the national energy utility, unbundle the grid (Eskom 2022). All these steps are expected to help green the grid—in 2019, over 80 percent of the mix was coal (Department of Energy 2022)—as well as mitigate recurring electricity outages.

Access to energy in Senegal poses a challenge. Thirty-five percent of the population does not have access to electricity, while 90 percent of those on the grid are using electricity mostly powered by oil and coal.[56] In May 2020, the government of Senegal granted a value added tax (VAT) exemption for 22 renewable energy products.[57] The move was driven by the goal of facilitating access to energy, particularly in rural areas. More examples from LMICs are offered in box 2.5.

GHG Emissions Inventory

Emissions and energy data for the ICT sector are needed to inform policy making. Global or regional estimates are not relevant to the design of tailored country policies. The relevant data include breakdowns by ICT industry[58] as well as operational emissions (Scopes 1 and 2) and upstream and downstream emissions (Scope 3).[59] Emissions data and energy use are critical to ascertain the scale of ICT sector emissions compared with those of the economy as a whole, as well as trends over time. Environmental data are becoming increasingly important to environmental, social, and governance (ESG)

BOX 2.5   **Examples of Government and Corporate Efforts to Expand the Use of Renewable Electricity**

- *Jordan.* Orange has a wheeling agreement with Kawar Energy using three solar farms. In 2020, the farms provided over 60 percent of the company's energy needs and reduced carbon dioxide (CO_2) emissions by 50 percent. The four solar farms of mobile network operator Umniah generate 50 percent of its required power. In 2019, Umniah's solar farms avoided 11.5 kilotonnes in CO_2 emissions.
- *South Africa.* Amazon commissioned the SOLA Group to develop a 10-megawatt (MW) solar farm. In the country's first such agreement, 28 gigawatt-hours (GWh) of solar energy will be wheeled via Eskom's grid (the state-owned power utility) to Amazon's facilities each year. The project is one of Amazon's 26 global "utility scale" wind and solar projects. Meanwhile, Vodacom is piloting a new solution to source 100 percent of its electricity demand from renewable independent power producers. It will then power over 15,000 distributed low-voltage sites in 168 municipalities across the country. Eskom will provide transmission infrastructure and services under an alternative solution to standard wheeling.
- *Bangladesh.* Robi, the second-largest mobile network operator in Bangladesh, is installing tower-mounted solar panels to power its base stations. As of August 2022, more than 1,600 stations were being powered by solar generators with an output of 8.4 MW (Robi 2022), lowering pressure on the grid and allowing Robi to sell excess solar power through the country's net metering scheme (CRESL 2018). Robi estimates it could provide the grid with 4.8 million kilowatt-hours of renewable electricity each year (Robi 2021).
- *Brazil.* The new legal framework for distributed microgeneration and minigeneration encourages distributed generation in small renewable plants producing up to 5 MW from alternative sources. Currently, Telefónica has several distributed generation agreements that will enable 83 new renewable energy plants to supply 700 GWh per year (avoiding almost 95,000 tonnes of carbon dioxide per year) and will cover almost half of the electricity consumption of Telefónica's networks in the country.

investors, and so lack of data may discourage them from providing funding in markets where this information is not available. As one report puts it: "Quite apart from the risks of screening out markets most in need of capital for development, markets may simply find themselves 'uninvestable' because investors cannot find the ESG data needed and therefore default those markets out of the investable universe. Both environmental and social data are problematic" (MOBILIST 2022, 58).

Private Sector Participation

Multinational digital companies can provide a positive contribution to addressing climate action because they often have considerable expertise on reducing emissions and their subsidiaries in low- and middle-income countries would fall under the umbrella of the parent company's emissions reduction targets. Local and regional ICT companies can also have significant market influence on energy markets. For example, seven of the top 10 largest procurers of renewable energy are tech firms. This factor provides scale to develop renewable energy sources. Tech companies can also be a valuable source of emissions data through their ESG reports.

Tech companies can have a strong influence on sector climate policies, particularly in LMICs with a weak government capacity. Indeed, targets established by tech companies can drive emissions reductions (box 2.6). For example, the MTN Group, which has its headquarters in South Africa, is a mobile operator with a portfolio in 22 countries in Africa and the Middle East. MTN has set science-based targets to achieve a 47 percent average reduction in operational emissions by 2030 (from a 2019 baseline) and has pledged to achieve net zero emissions by 2040. MTN also aims to power 1,330 rural sites using solar. MTN is a member of the GSMA Climate Action Taskforce, which is seeking to move mobile operators to zero emissions before 2050.[60] Approximately 80 percent of the MTN carbon footprint is from operations in Cameroon, Ghana, the Islamic Republic of Iran, Nigeria, South Africa, and Sudan. Energy sources in these countries are predominantly diesel, and national grids are mainly powered by fossil fuel sources. The MTN Project Zero initiative includes energy management solutions, monitoring, and measurements, and it focuses on reducing carbon emissions.[61]

Companies with headquarters in high-income countries and with subsidiaries in middle-income countries are also working to increase renewable energy options. Orange Middle East and Africa (OMEA) subsidiaries are rolling out several renewable energy production programs in the 18 countries in which they operate. Many sites are not connected to the electricity grid, and when they are, the quality of the grid requires backup solutions such as generators run on fossil fuels. To reduce GHG emissions, OMEA is equipping telecommunication sites with photovoltaic solar panels, and as of 2021, 5,400 base stations had been equipped (Orange 2021). In addition, Orange joined

<table>
<tr><td>BOX 2.6</td><td>**The Private Sector: Moving to Meet Its Climate Change Goals**</td></tr>
</table>

The private sector plays a huge role in the production and consumption of energy. Acting on their commitment to consuming renewable energy and reducing greenhouse gas (GHG) emissions, digital companies are contributing to reducing harmful emissions from industry, transport, energy production, and other activities. Some of the leading digital companies are investing intensely in purchasing renewable energy, issuing green bonds, and other measures to reduce their climate footprint, thereby contributing to the green digital transition.

The report *Greening Digital Companies: Monitoring Emissions and Climate Commitments* notes that 38 of the world's 150 leading tech (ICT/digital) companies are committed to becoming carbon-neutral by 2030, with many of them aiming to be carbon-negative soon (ITU and WBA 2022). If digital companies follow their lead in carbon neutrality, the ICT sector could become one of the greenest sectors of the global economy, as noted in the report.

The GHG emissions of the 150 leading tech companies amounted to 239 million tonnes in 2020, which is 0.8 percent of the world total. These companies can and must play an important role in reducing their GHG emissions and improve their energy efficiency across all areas of operation. Some of the notable efforts include the following:

- Digital companies are seven of the top 10 largest companies that purchased renewable energy in 2020.
- Half of the renewables purchased globally in 2020 were made by digital companies.
- One-third of the total energy (425 terawatt-hours) consumed by the 150 digital companies was renewable energy.
- Companies have also invested in purchasing voluntary offsets to make up for unavoidable emissions. These offsets have supported solar and wind projects, largely in developing countries.
- Digital companies have also partnered with energy buyers, suppliers, governments, investors, and other organizations to accelerate the decarbonization of electricity grids by advancing 24/7 carbon-free energy wherein every kilowatt-hour of electricity consumption is produced with carbon-free sources every day.

forces with Engie, an independent renewable energy provider in West Africa, to convert their main data center, located in Côte d'Ivoire, to solar power. Upon completion, the project will supply the data center with 527 MWh of clean energy per year, supporting the government's plans to use renewables for at least 4 percent of the energy mix by 2030 (Orange 2022). Telenor, a telecommunication operator in Norway, has subsidiaries in four middle-income countries in Asia: Bangladesh, Malaysia, Pakistan, and Thailand. The company is transitioning diesel-powered mobile base stations to solar renewable energy in line with its goal of a 50 percent reduction in carbon emissions for subsidiary operations by 2030. The company has already invested in more than 3,000 solar-based stations and anticipates spending about US$100 million converting diesel to solar to reach its goal.

Financing

Availability of financial resources to fund investments in greener technologies and renewable energy projects may be a constraint. Products for climate financing developed by the private sector are lacking, and government support is needed to facilitate access to financial resources. Because of the limited affordability of digital services and uptake gaps, consumer demand is a limited source of revenue to finance network upgrades and investment in energy-efficient solutions.

Voluntary Offset Market

A number of LMICs are profiting from offsets used by tech companies to account for their unavoidable emissions. The Kyoto Protocol recognized offsets that benefit LMICs through the Clean Development Mechanism (CDM).[62] Offset projects earn Certified Emission Reduction (CER) credits, equivalent to 1 tonne of CO_2, and the emissions reduction must be in addition to what would have otherwise occurred. Many of these offsets are for investment in renewable energy, reforestation (GreenBiz 2021), and related initiatives such as clean cookstoves (Wilson et al. 2016) and PAYG solar (CISION 2022), thereby contributing to sustainable development. A number of ICT companies have been notable purchasers of voluntary offsets. For example, the Belgium telecommunications operator Proximus is the lead backer of the Thermo Electric Generator (TEG) cookstove. In Benin, use of the stove is estimated to avoid 3 tCO_2e per household per year.[63] In Kenya, mobile operator Safaricom invests in emission reduction offsets for reforestation projects in the country. As noted earlier in the financing section, carbon credits have been under scrutiny, and corporate buyers, including ICT companies, are dependent on reliable schemes.

Notes

1. The term *green transition* refers to the shift toward economically sustainable growth and an economy not based on fossil fuels and overconsumption of natural resources.

2. Based on the International Standard Classification of All Economic Activities (ISIC), the ICT sector includes manufacturing of ICT equipment and devices, telecommunications, and information technology (IT) software and services. In this report, analysis of the ICT sector focuses on data management and transmission infrastructure (data centers and telecommunication networks) and ICT equipment and end user devices.

3. In the context of GHG emissions, three scopes are usually covered: Scope 1 emissions are direct emissions from owned or controlled sources; Scope 2 emissions are indirect emissions from the generation of purchased energy; and Scope 3 emissions are all indirect emissions (not included in Scope 2) that occur in the value chain of the firm (including both upstream and downstream emissions from distribution and consumption). See box 2.1 for more details on the methodological approach.

4. ICTFootprint.eu, "ICT Methodologies," https://ictfootprint.eu/en/title-1.

5. Euro-CASE, "Impact of ICT on World Energy Consumption," https://www.euro-case.org/impact-of-ict-on-world-energy-consumption, 2015.

6. Among non-peer-reviewed studies, a study performed by the French IT community GreenIT in 2019 estimated that ICT represents 4.2 percent of total energy consumption and 3.8 percent of total GHG emissions. The recent 2021 update of the Shift project estimated that the ICT currently accounts for 5 percent of the total energy consumption (against 4 percent in 2013), and the ICT contribution to global GHG emissions would be currently at around 3.5 percent (against 2.9 percent in 2013). On its side, the Global e-Sustainability Initiative (GeSI 2015) predicted that the carbon footprint of the ICT sector would reach 1.25 gigatonnes (Gt) of carbon dioxide in 2030, accounting for 1.97 percent of global emissions.

7. ITU estimates for the year 2015 are 740 $MtCO_2e$, including grid electricity supply and losses (International Telecommunication Union, ITU-T-REC-L.1470, Greenhouse Gas Emissions Trajectories for the Information and Communication Technology Sector Compatible with the UNFCCC Paris Agreement, https://www.itu.int/rec/T-REC-L.1470-202001-I, 2020).

8. See ITIF (2020). The ITIF claims to be an independent nonprofit and nonpartisan think tank, although it is funded by several ICT companies and other industries.

9. WBA (2022). The Digital Inclusion Benchmark (DIB) assessed 150 tech companies in 2021 (based on 2020 data), including collection of company emissions, energy use, and climate targets.

10. It is instructive to compare the findings on ICT sector emissions based on company-reported data with estimates from the ITU (2020) for 2020 based on Malmodin and Lundén (2018). Electricity use based on company-reported data is higher than that estimated by the ITU, whereas emissions based on the country-reported data are lower than the ITU estimates. The main reason is that the average grid emissions factors are quite high for the ITU study—834 grams of carbon dioxide per kilowatt-hour (gCO_2/kWh)—compared with the estimate based on company-reported data (504 gCO_2/kWh) and the average carbon intensity reported by the International Energy Agency of 475 gCO^2/kWh.

11. The trajectories, the long-term goal, and the 2015 baseline were derived in accordance with Recommendation ITU-T L.1450 and through complementary methods in support of the 1.5 degrees Celsius objective described by the Intergovernmental Panel on Climate Change.

12. The International Data Corporation (IDC) estimates that 1.35 billion units of smartphones were shipped in 2021—that is, an increase of 5.7 percent over 2020 (IDC 2022b). Gartner estimates this growth to be 6 percent in 2021 (Gartner 2022). However, in 2022, device shipments declined (Garner 2023).

13. Freitag et al. (2020): "Note that Malmodin's estimate of the share of user devices is highest; this is mostly because Malmodin's network and data centre estimates are lower than those of the other studies." The breakdown pattern established by Malmodin and Lundén (2018) is reused by the ITU (2020) study.

14. According to the 2021 *World Development Report*, fiber-optic cable is 85 percent more energy-efficient than vintage copper wires (World Bank 2021).

15. See TowerXchange (dashboard), https://www.towerxchange.com/. The GSMA estimates the number of mobile towers to be 5.2 million in 2021. See Renewable Energy Dashboard, GSMA, https://www.gsma.com/mobilefordevelopment/renewable-energy-dashboard/. However, this chapter relies on the TowerXchange data because they provide regional figures.

16. The CO_2 estimation is based on typical usage of diesel generators at off-grid and bad grid sites and excludes emissions from grid electricity generation.

17. At least 13 international digital companies use only renewable electricity. See Digital Inclusion Benchmark, https://www.worldbenchmarkingalliance.org/publication/digital-inclusion/, 2021, cited in ITU and WBA (2022).

18. DataCenters.com, "And the Title of the Largest Data Center in the World and Largest Data Center in the US Goes to…," June 15, 2018, https://www.datacenters.com/news/and-the-title-of-the -largest-data-center-in-the-world-and-largest-data-center-in.

19. The annualized production energy of the equipment is negligible compared with the energy consumed in operation. For that reason, the contribution of production energy to the annual life-cycle footprint is often ignored in calculations.

20. Cryptocurrency mining is the mechanism by which cryptocurrencies generate new currency and validate new transactions. It entails the use of massive, decentralized networks of computers worldwide that verify and safeguard blockchains, which are virtual ledgers that record transactions.

21. RE100, https://www.there100.org.

22. IEA (2022). According to the IEA, several "data centre operators in particular lead in corporate renewable energy procurement, mainly through power purchase agreements (PPAs). Google (12 TWh in 2019), Apple (1.7 TWh in FY2020) and Facebook (7 TWh in 2020) purchased or generated enough renewable electricity to match 100% of their operational electricity consumption."

23. Sai Industrial, Global and China Data Center Market, https://www.saiindustrial.com/global-and -china-data-center-market/, 2020. No precise definition of a large data center is provided, but it is understood to be an industrial facility (also called a hyperscale data center).

24. GlobalData (2019). The study notes that China, Australia, and Japan represent two-thirds of the Asia region. It states: "By 2023, China will be the largest market accounting for about 36% of the overall market opportunity in APAC [Asia-Pacific], followed by Japan and Australia with 22% and 8.3%, respectively."

25. TeleGeography, Global Bandwidth Forecast Service, Q3 2021. Only country-to-country routes are considered; (intra) national used bandwidth is excluded.

26. The manufacture of devices and equipment has other environmental effects (not covered in this report) related to the depletion of rare earth materials (such as indium, gallium, and germanium) and the use of fossil fuels. See, for example, *Digital Technologies in Europe: An Environmental Life Cycle Approach* (Greens/EFA 2021).

27. Samsung reports that the Galaxy A12 generates 20.5 $kgCO_2e$ of lifetime emissions of which production accounts for 46 percent, resulting in 9.5 $kgCO_2e$. See "LCA results" at https://www .samsung.com/us/aboutsamsung/sustainability/environment/our-commitment/data/). Apple's product use emissions for the iPhone 12 are 58.1 $kgCO_2e$.

28. Multi-SIM refers to the ownership of multiple SIM cards. This phenomenon is a common trend among mobile service users, especially in low- and middle-income countries.

29. For more details on how machine learning affects GHG emissions, see Kaack et al. (2022).

30. Digital infrastructure and services generate other environmental impacts not covered in this report. Actions to address those impacts include waste management to reduce waste, sustainable use of water, and actions to avoid using toxic substances, as well as assessments of the impact of infrastructure deployment on biodiversity.

31. Microtrenching involves digging a narrow trench 1–2 inches wide and up to 2 feet deep to lay fiber. This process is less disruptive of the environment than wider and deeper trenches.

32. Backhaul refers to the use of wireless or fiber-optic communication systems to transport data between subnetworks such as mobile sites and nodes.

33. Only in Africa, 153 fully or majority state-owned enterprises and 46 enterprises with minority state shareholdings operate in 52 countries (World Bank, forthcoming).

34. More information is available on the European Commission's Data Centres Code of Conduct page, https://e3p.jrc.ec.europa.eu/communities/data-centres-code-conduct.

35. A PUE value close to 1 indicates the high effectiveness of the supporting infrastructure, where almost all electricity consumed at the data center is dedicated to IT equipment. This measure

combined with carbon usage effectiveness (CUE) allows analysis of the sustainability of a data center.

36. Indian Green Building Council, IGBC Green Data Center, https://igbc.in/igbc/redirectHtml.htm?redVal=showgreendataenrenosign.

37. Uptime Institute, Tier Certification Overview, https://uptimeinstitute.com/tier-certification.

38. Office of the Government Chief Information Officer, Hong Kong, SAR, China, Green Data Centres Practice Guide, https://www.ogcio.gov.hk/en/our_work/business/tech_promotion/green_computing/green_data_centre.html.

39. TIDA is part of the Danish Datacenter Industry Association.

40. The technical code can be found at https://www.mcmc.gov.my/skmmgovmy/media/General/pdf/MCMC-Green_Data_Centres.pdf.

41. European Commission, Register of Commission Documents (dashboard), https://ec.europa.eu/transparency/documents-register/detail?ref=SWD(2020)55&lang=en.

42. The decree (in Portuguese) can be found at https://www.mcmc.gov.my/skmmgovmy/media/General/pdf/MCMC-Green_Data_Centres.pdf.

43. International Energy Agency, "Top Corporate Off-takers of Renewable Power Purchase Agreements, 2010–2020" (chart). https://www.iea.org/data-and-statistics/charts/top-corporate-off-takers-of-renewable-power-purchase-agreements-2010-2020.

44. 24/7 Carbon-Free Energy Future (dashboard), https://gocarbonfree247.com/.

45. CR (EU) 2019/2021 amended by CR (EU) 2021/341 (https://eur-lex.europa.eu/legal-content/EN/TXT/PDF/?uri=CELEX:32021R0341&rid=18).

46. CR (EU) No. 617/2013 (https://eur-lex.europa.eu/legal-content/EN/TXT/?qid=1521115326014&uri=CELEX:32013R0617).

47. CR (EC) No. 278/2009 (https://eur-lex.europa.eu/LexUriServ/LexUriServ.do?uri=OJ:L:2009:093:0003:0010:en:PDF) and proposed 2018 revisions.

48. A digital twin is a digital representation of a real-world entity or a system that is used to simulate and predict the behavior or performance of the real-world entity or system.

49. Carbon dioxide–equivalent greenhouse gas emissions from recycled metals are usually much lower than those from metals produced from virgin raw materials. For more details on e-waste management, visit https://www.itu.int/en/ITU-D/Environment/Pages/Toolbox/Publications.aspx.

50. To see the plan, visit https://ec.europa.eu/environment/strategy/circular-economy-action-plan_en.

51. For more details about such initiatives, see GSMA (2022b).

52. Lighting Global (dashboard), World Bank Group, https://www.lightingglobal.org/.

53. World Development Indicators (database), World Bank, https://databank.worldbank.org/reports.aspx?source=2&series=EG.ELC.ACCS.ZS&country=.

54. Mobile for Development (dashboard), GMSA, https://www.gsma.com/mobilefordevelopment/renewable-energy-dashboard/.

55. Regulatory Indicators for Sustainable Energy (RISE), https://rise.esmap.org/scoring-system.

56. International Energy Agency, Senegal (dashboard), https://www.iea.org/countries/senegal.

57. See ANER, "L'État du Sénégal a posé un acte fort pour booster le secteur des énergies renouvelables" (The State of Senegal Has Taken a Strong Step to Boost the Renewable Energy Sector), https://www.aner.sn/letat-du-senegal-a-pose-un-acte-fort-pour-booster-le-secteur-des-energies-renouvelables/.

58. See the definition of ICT sector at https://unstats.un.org/unsd/publication/seriesm/seriesm_4rev4e.pdf.

59. Greenhouse Gas Protocol (dashboard), https://ghgprotocol.org.

60. See GSMA, "Climate Action Taskforce," https://www.gsma.com/betterfuture/climate-action/climate-action-taskforce/.

61. See "Project Zero" at https://www.mtn.com/sub-pillar/project-zero/.

62. For a description of the CDM, see https://unfccc.int/process-and-meetings/the-kyoto-protocol/mechanisms-under-the-kyoto-protocol/the-clean-development-mechanism.

63. For a description of the TEG stove, see https://www.tegstove.org.

References

Andrae, Anders S. G., and Tomas Edler. 2015. "On Global Electricity Usage of Communication Technology: Trends to 2030." *Challenges* 6 (1): 117–57. https://doi.org/10.3390/challe6010117.

Beekhuizen, Carl. 2021. "Ethereum's Energy Usage Will Soon Decrease by ~99.95%." *Ethereum Foundation* (blog), May 18, 2021. https://blog.ethereum.org/2021/05/18/country-power-no-more.

Belkhir, L., and A. Elmeligi. 2018. "Assessing ICT Global Emissions Footprint: Trends to 2040 & Recommendations." *Journal of Cleaner Production* 177: 448–63.

BEREC (Body of European Regulators for Electronic Communications). 2022. "BEREC Report on Sustainability Assessing BEREC 's Contribution to Limiting the Impact of the Digital Sector on the Environment." BEREC, Riga, Latvia.

BloombergNEF. 2021. "Corporate Clean Energy Buying Grew 18% in 2020, Despite Mountain of Adversity." Press release, January 26, 2021. https://about.bnef.com/blog/corporate-clean-energy-buying-grew-18-in-2020-despite-mountain-of-adversity/.

BloombergNEF and Facebook. 2018. *Powering Last-Mile Connectivity.* https://data.bloomberglp.com/bnef/sites/14/2018/02/Powering-Last-Mile-Connectivity-BNEF-and-Facebook.pdf.

Center on Regulation in Europe. 2021. "Data Centres and the Grid—Greening ICT in Europe." https://cerre.eu/publications/data-centres-and-the-energy-grid/.

CIEL (Center for International Environmental Law). 2005. "Eco-Label Standards, Green Procurement, and the WTO: Significance for World Bank Borrowers." https://www.ciel.org/reports/eco-labeling-standards-green-procurement-and-the-wto-significance-for-world-bank-borrowers-march-2005-5/.

CISION. 2022. "ENGIE Joins Forces with SOLSTROEM to Issue and Sell Verified and Data-Driven Carbon Credits." https://www.prnewswire.com/news-releases/engie-joins-forces-with-solstroem-to-issue-and-sell-verified-and-data-driven-carbon-credits-301519169.html.

Corcoran, Peter M., and Anders Andrae. 2013. "Emerging Trends in Electricity Consumption for Consumer ICT." Research Repository, National University of Ireland, Galway. https://aran.library.nuigalway.ie/xmlui/handle/10379/3563.

CRESL (Center for Renewable Energy Services Ltd.). 2018. "Net Metering Guidelines—2018." CRESL, Dhaka, Bangladesh. https://policy.asiapacificenergy.org/sites/default/files/Net%20metering%20Guidelines%20-%202018.pdf.

Department of Energy, South Africa. 2022. *The South African Energy Sector Report 2021.* Pretoria: Department of Mineral Resources and Energy. http://www.energy.gov.za/files/media/explained/2021-South-African-Energy-Sector-Report.pdf.

EEB (European Environmental Bureau). 2019. *Cool Products Don't Cost the Earth.* Brussels: EEB. https://eeb.org/library/coolproducts-report/.

EPA (US Environmental Protection Agency). 2012. "Understanding Eco-labels for Electronics." EPA, Washington, DC. https://www.epa.gov/sites/default/files/documents/ecolabel.pdf.

Eskom. 2022. "Update on the Unbundling of Eskom's Transmission Division." Media statement, February 3, 2022. https://www.eskom.co.za/update-on-the-unbundling-of-eskoms-transmission -division.

European Commission. 2020. *Supporting the Green Transition: Shaping Europe's Digital Future.* Directorate-General for Communication. Luxembourg: Publications Office of the European Union. https://data.europa.eu/doi/10.2775/932617.

European Commission. 2021. "Radio Spectrum Policy Group: RSPG Opinion on the Role of Radio Spectrum Policy to Help Combat Climate Change." Directorate-General for Communications Networks, Content and Technology, Brussels. https://radio-spectrum-policy-group.ec.europa .eu/system/files/2023-01/RSPG21-041final-RSPG_Opinion_on_climate_change.pdf.

Federal Ministry for the Environment, Nature Conservation and Nuclear Safety, Germany. 2020. "Video Streaming: Data Transmission Technology Crucial for Climate Footprint." Press release, September 10, 2020. https://www.bmuv.de/en/pressrelease/video-streaming-data-transmission -technology-crucial-for-climate-footprint.

Forti, Vanessa, Cornelis Peter Baldé, Ruediger Kuehr, and Garam Bel. 2020. "The Global E-waste Monitor 2020: Quantities, Flows, and the Circular Economy Potential." United Nations University (UNU)/United Nations Institute for Training and Research (UNITAR), International Telecommunication Union (ITU), and International Solid Waste Association (ISWA), Bonn /Geneva/Rotterdam. https://ewastemonitor.info/wp-content/uploads/2020/11/GEM_2020 _def_july1_low.pdf.

Freitag, Charlotte, Mike Berners-Lee, Kelly Widdicks, Bran Knowles, Gordon S. Blair, and Adrian Friday. 2020. "The Climate Impact of ICT: A Review of Estimates, Trends and Regulations." Lancaster University, Lancaster, UK. https://arxiv.org/pdf/2102.02622.pdf.

Gartner. 2022. "Gartner Says Global Smartphone Sales Grew 6% in 2021." Press release, March 2, 2022. Gartner, Stamford, CT. https://www.gartner.com/en/newsroom/press-releases/2022-03 -01-4q21-smartphone-market-share.

Gartner. 2023. "Gartner Forecasts Worldwide Device Shipments to Decline 4% in 2023." January 31, 2023. Gartner, Stamford, CT. https://www.gartner.com/en/newsroom/press-releases/2023-01 -31-gartner-forecasts-worldwide-device-shipments-to-decline-four-percent-in-2023.

GlobalData. 2019. "APAC to Emerge as Second Largest Data Center and Hosting Market by 2023, Says Global Data." Press release. https://www.globaldata.com/media/technology/apac-to-emerge -as-second-largest-data-center-and-hosting-market-by-2023-says-globaldata/.

GreenBiz. 2021. "Apple, Conservation International Introduce Mangrove Carbon Credit." https:// www.greenbiz.com/article/apple-conservation-international-introduce-mangrove-carbon -credit#:~:text=The%20newest%20carbon%20credit%20on,carbon%20sequestration%20 potential%20of%20mangroves.

Greens/EFA. 2021. *Digital Technologies in Europe: An Environmental Life Cycle Approach.* A study commissioned by the European Parliamentary group. Brussels: Greens/EFA. https://groenlinks .nl/sites/groenlinks/files/2021-12/environmental-impact-technology.pdf.

GSMA. 2019. "Energy Efficiency: An Overview." https://www.gsma.com/futurenetworks/wiki /energy-efficiency-2/.

GSMA. 2020a. *Building a Resilient Industry: How Mobile Network Operators Prepare for and Respond to Natural Disasters: An Interactive Guide for MNOs Based on Experiences with the Humanitarian Connectivity Charter.* London: GSMA. https://www.gsma.com/mobilefordevelopment/wp -content/uploads/2020/03/TWP5861_BuildingAResilientIndustry_v003.pdf.

GSMA. 2020b. "Renewable Energy for Mobile Towers: Opportunities for Low- and Middle-income Countries." https://www.gsma.com/mobilefordevelopment/resources/renewable-energy-for -mobile-towers-opportunities-for-low-and-middle-income-countries/.

GSMA. 2022a. "Mobile Net Zero: State of the Industry on Climate Action 2022." https://www.gsma.com/betterfuture/resources/mobile-net-zero-state-of-the-industry-on-climate-action-2022-report.

GSMA. 2022b. "Strategy Paper for Circular Economy: Mobile Devices." https://www.gsma.com/betterfuture/resources/strategy-paper-for-circular-economy-mobile-devices.

Haut Conseil pour le Climat. 2020. "Controlling the Carbon Impact of 5G." https://www.hautconseilclimat.fr/wp-content/uploads/2020/12/hcc_rapports_5g-en.pdf.

Helios Towers. 2021. "Delivering Mobile Connectivity and Reducing Carbon." https://www.heliostowers.com/media/1993/ht-carbon-reduction-roadmap-presentation.pdf.

Huawei. 2022. "Green Networks: Optimizing Energy Efficiency for Green Development." https://www.huawei.com/en/huaweitech/publication/winwin/40/network-energy-efficiency.

IDC (International Data Corporation). 2022a. "Growth Streak for Traditional PCs Continues During Holiday Quarter of 2021, According to IDC." Press release, January 12, 2022. https://www.idc.com/getdoc.jsp?containerId=prUS48770422.

IDC (International Data Corporation). 2022b. "Smartphone Shipments Declined in the Fourth Quarter But 2021 Was Still a Growth Year with a 5.7% Increase in Shipments, According to IDC." Press release, January 27, 2022. https://www.idc.com/getdoc.jsp?containerId=prUS48830822.

IEA (International Energy Agency). 2020. *Global EV Outlook 2020*. Paris: IEA. https://www.iea.org/reports/global-ev-outlook-2020.

IEA (International Energy Agency). 2022. *Data Centres and Data Transmission Networks*. Paris: IEA. https://www.iea.org/reports/data-centres-and-data-transmission-networks.

IIASA (International Institute for Applied Systems Analysis). 2019. "The World in 2050—The Digital Revolution and Sustainable Development: Opportunities and Challenges." IIASA, Laxenburg, Austria.

ITIF (Information Technology and Innovation Foundation). 2020. "Beyond the Energy Techlash: The Real Climate Impacts of Information Technology." https://itif.org/publications/2020/07/06/beyond-energy-techlash-real-climate-impacts-information-technology/.

ITU (International Telecommunication Union). 2012. *Review of Mobile Handset Eco-rating Schemes*. Geneva: ITU. https://www.itu.int/dms_pub/itu-t/oth/4B/01/T4B010000030001PDFE.pdf.

ITU (International Telecommunication Union). 2018. "Methodologies for the Assessment of the Environmental Impact of the Information and Communication Technology Sector, Recommendation ITU-T L.1450." https://www.itu.int/rec/T-REC-L.1450/en.

ITU (International Telecommunication Union). 2020. "Greenhouse Gas Emissions Trajectories for the Information and Communication Technology Sector Compatible with the UNFCCC Paris Agreement, Recommendation ITU-T L.1470." https://www.itu.int/ITU-T/recommendations/rec.aspx?rec=14084.

ITU (International Telecommunication Union). 2022. *Global e-Waste Monitor*. Geneva: ITU.

ITU (International Telecommunication Union) and WBA (World Benchmarking Alliance). 2022. *Greening Digital Companies: Monitoring Emissions and Climate Commitments*. Geneva: ITU; Amsterdam: WBA. https://www.itu.int/en/ITU-D/Environment/Documents/Publications/2022/Greening-Digital-Companies-22June2022.pdf.

Kaack, Lynn H., Pryia. L. Donti, Emma Strubell, George Kamiya, Felix Creutzig, and David Rolnick. 2022. "Aligning Artificial Intelligence with Climate Change Mitigation." *Nature Climate Change* 12: 518–27. https://doi.org/10.1038/s41558-022-01377-7.

Lundén, Dag, Jens Malmodin, Pernilla Bergmark, and Nina Lövehagen. 2022. "Electricity Consumption and Operational Carbon Emissions of European Telecom Network Operators." *Sustainability* 14 (5): 2637. https://doi.org/10.3390/su14052637.

Malmodin, Jens, and Dag Lundén. 2018. "The Energy and Carbon Footprint of the Global ICT and E&M Sectors 2010–2015." *Sustainability* 10 (9): 3027. https://doi.org/10.3390/su10093027.

Masanet, E., A. Shehabi, N. Lei, S. Smith, and J. Koomey. 2020. "Recalibrating Global Data Center Energy-Use Estimates." *Science* 367 (6481): 984–86. https://www.science.org/doi/10.1126/science.aba3758.

Merten, Marianne. 2021. "Increase to 100 MW Embedded Generation Threshold Will Give 'Oomph' to South African Economy, Says Ramaphosa." *Daily Maverick*, June 10, 2021. https://www.dailymaverick.co.za/article/2021-06-10-increase-to-100mw-embedded-generation-threshold-will-give-oomph-to-south-african-economy-says-ramaphosa/.

Minges, Michael, Shailendra Mudgal, and Xavier Decoster. Forthcoming. "Information and Communication Technology (ICT) and Climate Change. Direct Greenhouse Gas Emissions of the ICT Sector." World Bank, Washington, DC.

MIT Technology Review Insights. 2021. *Decarbonizing Industries with Connectivity and 5G*. Sponsored by Ericsson. https://www.ericsson.com/4a98c2/assets/local/about-ericsson/sustainability-and-corporate-responsibility/environment/mit-technology-review-decarbonizing-industries-with-connectivity-and-5g.pdf.

MOBILIST (Mobilising Institutional Capital Through Listed Product Structures). 2022. *Drivers of Investment Flows to Emerging and Frontier Markets*. London: UK Foreign, Commonwealth and Development Office.

Observatorio Nacional 5G. 2021. "Operators Increase the Efficiency of Their Networks to Reduce Costs." https://on5g.es/en/las-operadoras-aumentan-la-eficiencia-de-sus-redes-para-reducir-costes/.

Orange. 2021. "Orange Jordan Inaugurates Its Mega Solar Farm Project." Press release, November 25, 2019. https://orange.jo/en/corporate/media-center/news/orange-jordan-inaugurates-its-mega-solar-farm-project.

Orange. 2022. "Orange and Engie Join Forces to Convert the GOS, Orange's Main Data Center in Africa, to Solar Power, Helping to Reduce the Carbon Footprint in Côte d'Ivoire." *News*, January 17, 2022. https://orange.africa-newsroom.com/press/orange-and-engie-join-forces-to-convert-the-gos-oranges-main-data-center-in-africa-to-solar-power-helping-to-reduce-the-carbon-footprint-in-cote-divoire?lang=en.

Oughton, E., Jeongjin Oh, Sara Ballan, and Julius Kusuma. 2023. "Sustainability Assessment of 4G and 5G Universal Broadband Strategies." Policy Research Working Paper, World Bank, Washington, DC. https://doi.org/10.48550/arXiv.2311.05480.

Owino, Patrick. 2017. "Evaluation of the Viability of Solar and Wind Power System Hybridization for Safaricom Off-grid GSM Base Station Sites." Thesis, University of Nairobi. http://erepository.uonbi.ac.ke/handle/11295/101576.

Persistence Market Research. 2022. "Refurbished and Used Mobile Phones Market Outlook (2021–2031)." https://www.persistencemarketresearch.com/market-research/refurbished-and-used-mobile-phones-market.asp.

Polytechnique Insights. 2022. "Will 5G Improve or Worsen Our Digital Carbon Footprint?". https://www.polytechnique-insights.com/en/braincamps/digital/5g-6g/will-5g-improve-or-worsen-our-digital-carbon-footprint/.

Robi. 2021. *Integrated Annual Report for the Year Ended 31 December 2021*. Dhaka, Bangladesh: Robi. https://webapi.robi.com.bd/uploads/files/shares/share-file/Robi-Annual-Report-2021-Full-Final.pdf.

Robi. 2022. "Robi Leans on Green Power to Ease Pressure on National Grid." Press release, August 7, 2022. https://www.robi.com.bd/en/corporate/news-room/press-release/robi-leans-on-green-power-to-ease-pressure-on-national-grid.

Safaricom. 2022. "2021 Sustainable Business Report." https://www.safaricom.co.ke/images/sustainability/Safaricom_2021_Sustainable_Business_Report.pdf.

Telecom Lead. 2020. "5G Mobile Operator Strategies to Cut Their Huge Power Cost." https://www.telecomlead.com/5g/5g-mobile-operator-strategies-to-cut-their-huge-power-cost-94645.

Telefónica. 2022. "Telefónica Implements Eco Rating in All of Its Markets." Press release, February 17, 2022. https://www.telefonica.com/en/communication-room/telefonica-implements-eco-rating-in-all-of-its-markets/.

Vodafone UK News Centre. 2021. "Vodafone's European Network 100% Powered by Renewable Electricity." Press release, June 23, 2021. https://www.vodafone.co.uk/newscentre/press-release/vodafones-european-network-100-powered-by-electricity-from-renewable-sources/.

WBA (World Benchmarking Alliance). 2022. *2021 Digital Inclusion Benchmark Insights Report.* Amsterdam: WBA. https://www.worldbenchmarkingalliance.org/research/2021-digital-inclusion-benchmark-insights-report/.

WIK-Consult and Ramboll. 2021. "Environmental Impacts of Electronic Communications." WIK-Consult, Bad Honnef, Germany.

Wilson, D. L., D. R. Talancon, R. L. Winslow, X. Linares, and A. J. Gadgil. 2016. "Avoided Emissions of a Fuel-Efficient Biomass Cookstove Dwarf Embodied Emissions." *Development Engineering* 1 (June): 45–52. https://doi.org/10.1016/j.deveng.2016.01.001.

World Bank. 2021. *World Development Report 2021: Data for Better Lives.* Washington, DC: World Bank. https://www.worldbank.org/en/publication/wdr2021.

World Bank. 2022. "Greening Digital in Korea: Korea Case Study for Greening the ICT Sector." Korea Office Innovation and Technology Note 6. World Bank, Washington, DC. http://hdl.handle.net/10986/37554.

World Bank. Forthcoming. "Governance of the Digital Economy in Africa: Addressing Old and New Risks to Economic Governance." World Bank, Washington, DC.

WRI (World Resources Institute) and WBCSD (World Business Council for Sustainable Development). 2013. *Technical Guidance for Calculating Scope 3 Emissions (version 1.0): Supplement to the Corporate Value Chain (Scope 3) Accounting and Reporting Standard.* Washington, DC: WRI. https://ghgprotocol.org/sites/default/files/standards/Scope3_Calculation_Guidance_0.pdf.

Zain. 2021. *A Resilient Journey across a Challenging Year: Sustainability Report 2021.* Kuwait: Zain. https://zain.com/SR2021/.

3. Making the Digital Sector More Resilient

Introduction

As economies become more digitalized, their dependency on reliable digital infrastructure increases. Climate change is generating natural hazards that are affecting digital infrastructure. Among these hazards are risks of riverine and coastal flooding, landslides, tsunamis, cyclones (wind and storm), water scarcity, and extreme heat (figure 3.1). Damaged infrastructure can disrupt connectivity and access to the data and digital solutions relying on data centers and (cloud) computing facilities. By investing in the resilience of digital connectivity and data infrastructure, the public and private sectors boost their ability to continue to deliver critical public and private services digitally in the event of natural disasters and as part of adaptation efforts in general. This chapter is an overview of measures to improve the resilience of digital infrastructure, focusing on digital connectivity and data infrastructure.

Protecting Networks

Digital network infrastructure—both linear, such as cables, ducts, and poles, and nodal, such as points of presence (PoPs), aggregation points, network operations centers, and other network sites—are susceptible to damage from climate events. Although the damage may be localized, the impacts may be felt by an entire network. As a result, resilience should be considered along the value chain (first, middle, and last miles), as well as over the geographical distribution of networks.

The estimates of direct economic damage to mobile cellular infrastructure (figure 3.2) from coastal flooding range from US$1.2 billion for an event with a 1 percent annual probability (a 1-in-100-year event) in the 1980 historical baseline up to US$1.8 billion by 2080 in the Intergovernmental Panel on Climate Change's RCP4.5 scenario, or US$2.1 billion in its RCP8.5 scenario,[1] for an increase of 55 percent and 75 percent, respectively (Oughton et al., 2023). The large impacts (greater than US$10 million) take place in these regions (followed by country examples): Western Europe (the Netherlands), East Asia (China and Japan), Southeast Asia (Indonesia), North Africa (Arab Republic of Egypt), and Latin America (Brazil).

FIGURE 3.1   Examples of Natural Hazard Risks to Digital Infrastructure

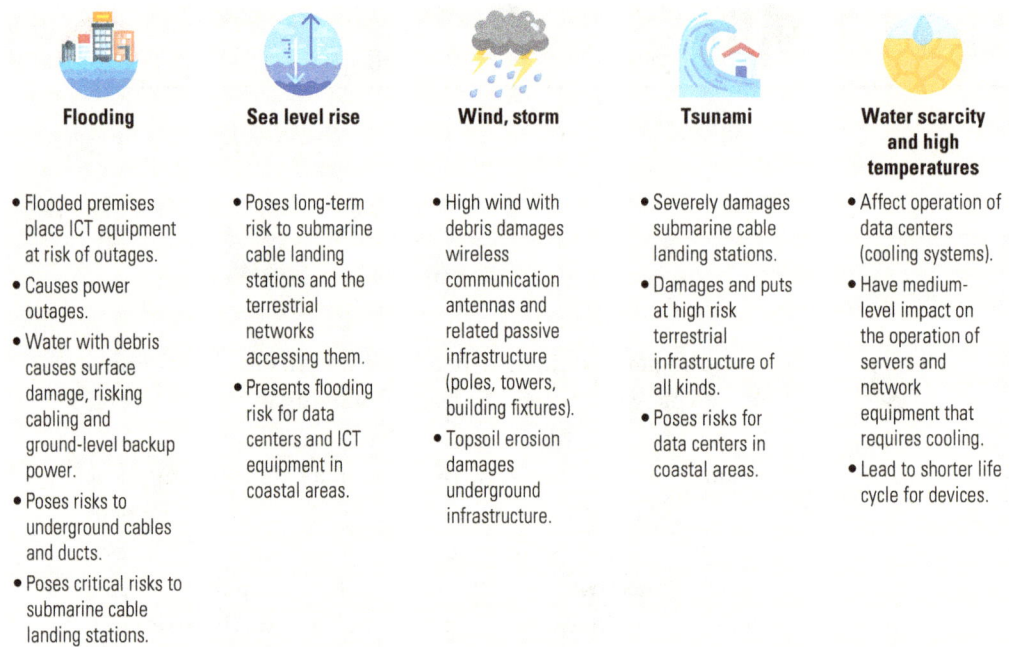

Flooding	Sea level rise	Wind, storm	Tsunami	Water scarcity and high temperatures
• Flooded premises place ICT equipment at risk of outages. • Causes power outages. • Water with debris causes surface damage, risking cabling and ground-level backup power. • Poses risks to underground cables and ducts. • Poses critical risks to submarine cable landing stations.	• Poses long-term risk to submarine cable landing stations and the terrestrial networks accessing them. • Presents flooding risk for data centers and ICT equipment in coastal areas.	• High wind with debris damages wireless communication antennas and related passive infrastructure (poles, towers, building fixtures). • Topsoil erosion damages underground infrastructure.	• Severely damages submarine cable landing stations. • Damages and puts at high risk terrestrial infrastructure of all kinds. • Poses risks for data centers in coastal areas.	• Affect operation of data centers (cooling systems). • Have medium-level impact on the operation of servers and network equipment that requires cooling. • Lead to shorter life cycle for devices.

Sources: Adapted from World Bank (forthcoming a); Sandhu and Raja (2019, table 3).

Note: ICT = information and communication technology.

Similarly, a tropical cyclone has a significant impact on mobile infrastructure (figure 3.3). For tropical cyclone events with a 0.1 percent annual probability (a 1-in-1000-year event), the direct damage estimate ranges from US$400 million in the 1980 historical baseline to US$525 million in 2050 under an RCP8.5 scenario with a model range of US$397–US$653 million (Oughton et al., 2023). The largest impacts take place in these regions (followed by country examples): East Asia (Japan and the Republic of Korea), South Asia (Bangladesh, India, and Pakistan), southern Europe (Portugal and Spain), North Africa (Morocco), and North America and Central America (Dominican Republic, Mexico, the República Bolivariana de Venezuela, and the United States).

Granular geospatial data on the local and climate risks to networks can allow governments and operators to select the appropriate sites for network deployment and estimate the costs of climate shocks. In the case of Ghana, geospatial and big data analysis have identified riverine flooding as the major flooding risk to Ghana's mobile network infrastructure, with coastal flooding being relatively minor (map 3.1). In a worst-case scenario, damage to mobile cellular infrastructure is estimated to be up to US$17 million by 2080 for a large event (such as in the 1-in-1,000-year category) should emissions not be effectively abated over the next decade (based on the Intergovernmental Panel on Climate Change's RCP8.5 business-as-usual climate scenario).

FIGURE 3.2 Mobile Infrastructure Vulnerable to Coastal Flooding

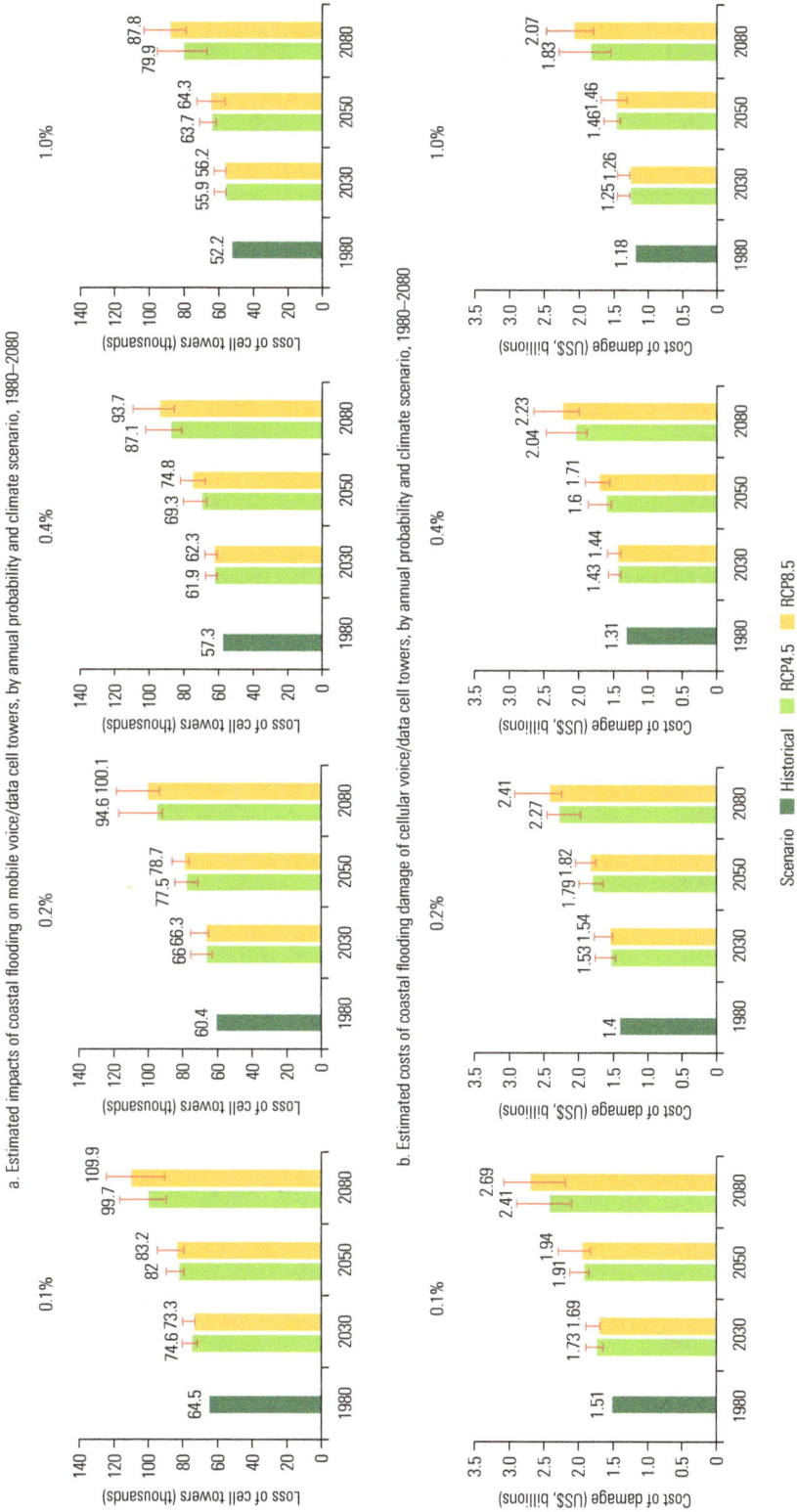

a. Estimated impacts of coastal flooding on mobile voice/data cell towers, by annual probability and climate scenario, 1980–2080

b. Estimated costs of coastal flooding damage of cellular voice/data cell towers, by annual probability and climate scenario, 1980–2080

Scenario: Historical, RCP4.5, RCP8.5

Source: Oughton et al., 2023.

FIGURE 3.3 Mobile Infrastructure Vulnerable to Tropical Cyclones

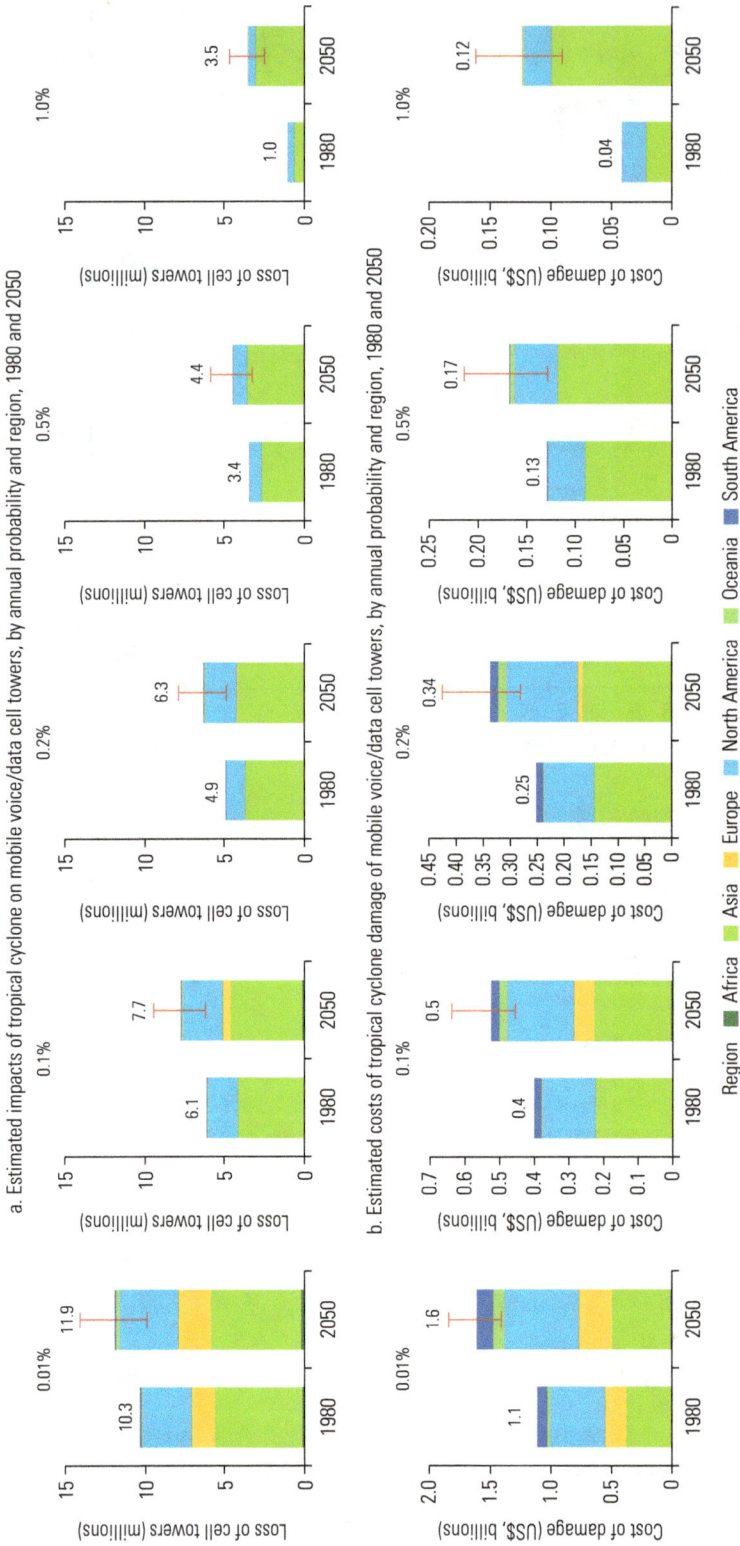

a. Estimated impacts of tropical cyclone on mobile voice/data cell towers, by annual probability and region, 1980 and 2050

b. Estimated costs of tropical cyclone damage of mobile voice/data cell towers, by annual probability and region, 1980 and 2050

Region: Africa, Asia, Europe, North America, Oceania, South America

Source: Oughton et al., 2023.

MAP 3.1   Mobile Infrastructure Assets at Risk in Ghana

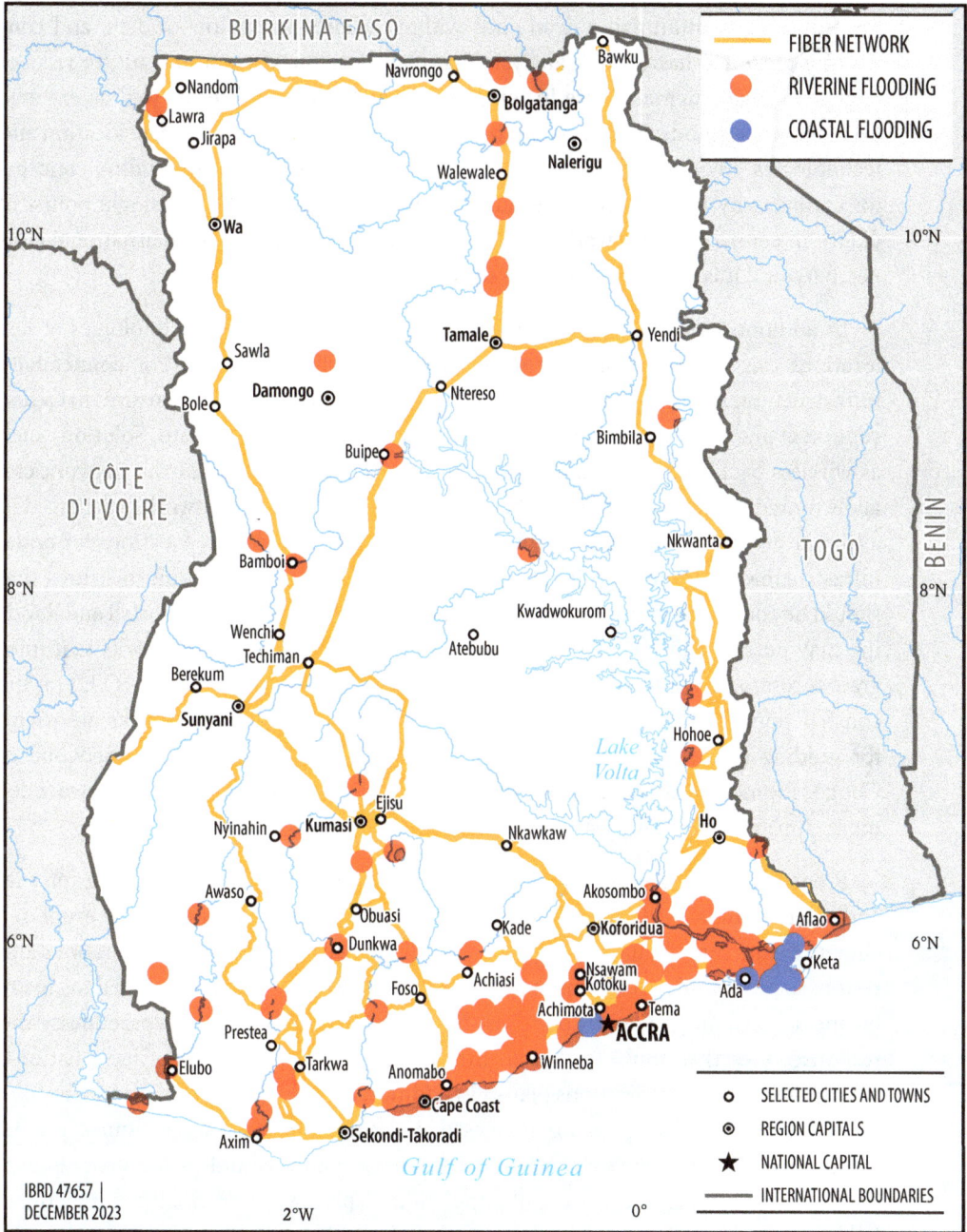

Source: Oughton et al., 2023.

Note: Map is showing the climate hazard risk to mobile infrastructure in Ghana for a 1-in-1,000-year event of riverine and coastal flooding in 2080. This is the Intergovernmental Panel on Climate Change scenario with no carbon abatement (RCP8.5).

Resilience-building measures should be implemented in the early stage of network design and appraisal and throughout deployment. Useful principles include planning for redundancy, minimizing dead ends without bidirectional flow of data, and conducting a climate hazard risk analysis that considers the current and future risks of climate change (such as a rise in temperature and sea level rise) as well as extreme events (such as floods, wildfires, and hurricanes) to select the appropriate location and technologies. Redundancy is one of the most important resilience-building concepts for connectivity infrastructure because it minimizes the number of single points of failure in connectivity networks. This is particularly important for international connectivity, and it is a must for landlocked and sea-locked countries.

In addition to geographical redundancy, the use of multiple technologies at key locations can improve resilience during and after climate events. For connectivity infrastructure, all segments of the network should "close the loop" to ensure that a disruption at one point in the network does not affect others downstream. Solutions such as wireless backhaul between an endpoint and another segment of the network can allow for redundant connectivity when a specific segment of the network is damaged in a climate event. Climate hazard risk analysis is essential to identify locations for nodal infrastructures that need to be at minimal risk, as well as mitigation measures that should be adopted at various sites. For example, locations with heavy rainfall and flooding may pose a higher risk for digital infrastructure. National frameworks that integrate recommendations by the International Telecommunication Union (ITU) on the construction, installation, and protection of telecommunication networks are useful for guiding operators in integrating climate resilience measures. The Republic of Congo, Rwanda, and Sierra Leone are taking steps toward building a framework for more climate-resilient infrastructure.

Preparedness is essential for responding to climate events and managing internal and external impacts.[2] Operators need to plan for business continuity in the event of a climate event. They should designate teams and procedures to continue operations and restore services while protecting staff. Alternative power systems are essential to ensure business continuity. Some countries have specific emergency preparedness and response rules that apply to digital infrastructure operators, or they have national emergency telecommunications plans.[3] In addition to managing a service interruption, operators also need to plan for increased network congestion after climate events, including a medium-term change in consumption patterns and in the geographical distribution of traffic in the event of population displacement or mobility restrictions. In these situations, flexibility in the use of spectrum is advisable (World Bank, forthcoming b). Furthermore, a resilient supply chain will enable accessing the equipment and technical staff needed to address damaged networks and systems.

For infrastructure deployment projects that are fully or partially funded by the government, performance standards can include climate resilience factors. For example, in the Marshall Islands, performance standards—such as capability to meet network resilience, recovery and repair in the aftermath of disasters, and cybersecurity standards—will be integrated into the public-private partnership bidding process for submarine infrastructure. These standards could also be integrated in tenders using universal service funds or other mechanisms that grant state aid to the sector.

Digital tools and advanced analytics can also be used for preparedness and response. As in other sectors, detailed climate risk data and monitoring systems can inform preparedness and response measures. More advanced tools allow for digital twin solutions to simulate the effects of climate disasters and be prepared. Other tools, such as big data analytics of the mobility and consumption patterns of users after a disaster, can also help inform responses by operators. This information can be useful as well for preparing a government response, as discussed in chapter 5 of this report.

Finally, digital devices are equally susceptible to heat, dust, and humidity. Devices in low- and middle-income countries (LMICs) are often more exposed to these factors. In general, users rely on their phones longer in those countries and depend on greater durability. Designing devices in a way that makes them more robust, repairable, and reusable is important to enhance their reliability and extend their useful life.

Protecting Data Infrastructure

Heat, dust, humidity, drought, and flooding can damage data centers, potentially destroying infrastructure and data. Climate change risks are not confined to single sites; they extend to regional infrastructure, partners, and utilities. Climate change can subject countries to higher operating costs, supply chain disruptions, and the migration or relocation of data centers. A data center designed to last 20 years in an area that floods once every 500 years could have a 0.2 percent risk of a flood in any year of its life based on data available in 2010. But this risk may now be once every 100 years, meaning that the risk is now 1 percent, or a 20 percent drop in a data center's planned lifetime. Table 3.1 summarizes the main impacts of extreme weather and climate change–triggered natural disasters.

Several measures can be taken as part of an adaptation strategy that covers diverse aspects: site selection, design, and building, and operation and recovery. Climate change risk management should be part of an economic analysis of the viability of data centers. Although increasing resilience boosts costs, they have to be assessed against the benefits of avoiding service interruptions and data losses. However, public sector oversight may be needed to avoid underinvestment in resilience that can put (personal) data and the business continuity of digital services at risk. The availability of detailed data on climate hazards as a public good can facilitate risk assessment and due diligence for site selection to decrease exposure to natural risks or implement mitigation actions. For existing data centers, it is paramount to upgrade them so they are more resilient to

TABLE 3.1 Extreme Weather or Climate Change Risks to Data Infrastructure

Risk	Site impacts (primary)
Flooding—flash/pluvial	• Damage to equipment, cabling • Electrical risks • Staff and engineer safety and access
Flooding—coastal/tidal	• Damage to equipment, cabling • Electrical risks • Staff and engineer safety and access • Salt damage • Risk of frequent repetition
Flooding—erosion, contamination	• Groundwater contamination • Structural scouring, silt accumulation • Damage to equipment, cabling
High wind, storm	• Damage from flying objects, trees, and so on • Danger to staff • Unstable electricity grid, loss of utility power • Roof collapse due to extreme rain
Drought	• Restricted water for cooling (chilled, evaporative) • Subsidence
Sustained high temperature	• Insufficient economization cooling capacity • Insufficient mechanical cooling capacity • Utility power instability due to very high demand • Health and safety breaches for working temperatures
Sustained high humidity	• Evaporate cooling becomes impractical • Risks to equipment due to insufficient dehumidification
Dry weather or wildfire	• Direct risk of fire in data centers, especially edge • Smoke and particulate contamination reducing use of air economization • Ash entering equipment, clogging fuel filters • Staff unable to access site • Utilities turning off substations or telecommunication towers • Water use restricted

Source: Uptime Institute 2021.

specific climate risks, depending on the specific location and the risks. Measures include using containerized modular data centers to deliver mobility, flexibility, reliability, and scalability at a lower cost; ensuring continuity of power; planning communications and cooling with redundancy built in at every level; and adopting publicly available industry standards for data center design and build, such as the EN50600 series and the equivalent ISO/IEC 22237 series of technical specifications. Furthermore, in a climate shock, it would be essential to establish data backup and recovery systems to prevent data losses. The use of distributed data centers and edge solutions could reduce the risk of data losses.

Climate change will have medium-term effects on data centers. For example, water use will be restricted in many regions, which will likely cause friction between large data center operators and local communities, potentially leading to higher energy consumption affecting emissions (Uptime Institute 2021). Data center locations and additional investments need to be reevaluated more regularly, considering their viability in the face of climate change. Adaptation measures in the sector may increase the speed of migration to public cloud and colocation environments, making the resilience of public cloud and colocation data centers even more important.

Because of the mission-critical role that digital connectivity and data infrastructure play as countries rely increasingly on digital services and solutions, ensuring resilience is in the public interest. Countries have thus designed special frameworks to protect critical infrastructure, including emergency preparedness and response plans. The focus has been on digital connectivity, but because of the growing importance of data infrastructure more specific actions may be needed, at least for certain facilities declared as critical infrastructure. For example, in 2021 the state of New South Wales in Australia issued the *NWS Critical Infrastructure Resilience Strategy Guide,* which addresses the impacts of climate change on critical infrastructure, including digital connectivity (New South Wales 2021). For example, conducting a periodic climate risk assessment of critical digital infrastructure can help identify vulnerabilities and address them. At least 16 Group of Twenty (G20) countries conduct climate risk assessments for various sectors (World Bank 2019).

Policies, laws, and regulations can be put in place to ensure resilience-building measures. They can be embedded in construction codes, land categorization and zoning plans, or specific standards based on ITU recommendations. For public procurement of digital solutions and infrastructure, as well as for government cofunded projects, standards covering resilience aspects should be integrated as well.

Increasing resiliency increases costs, which may present trade-offs, especially in countries where the affordability of digital connectivity and uptake of digital technologies are an issue. Insurance premiums will increase, and investments in climate change adaptation will become a significant operating cost factor in some locations, including in LMICs. Both will require financing instruments and public support to reach socio-economically vulnerable areas. Viability gap funding for investments in resilience would be needed.

It is essential that information on climate risks be available for infrastructure design, and preparedness is essential. Governments have a role to play in ensuring access to this public good, including data sharing across borders because climate events do not respect country borders.

In a climate shock, governments are responsible for coordinating efforts across operators in the ICT sector and other sectors. Preparation for such events is essential. Furthermore, the interconnection between critical infrastructure requires collaboration across sectors. In the case of emergencies, collaboration between competitors should be facilitated.

Notes

1. Representative Concentration Pathway (RCP) 4.5 is a scenario that stabilizes radiative forcing at 4.5 watts per meter squared in the year 2100 without ever exceeding that value. RCP8.5 is the baseline scenario that does not include any specific climate mitigation target, with greenhouse gas emissions and concentrations increasing over time, leading to a radiative forcing of 8.5 watts per meter squared by 2100.

2. See GSMA (2020) for examples of how mobile network operators have prepared for and responded to natural disasters.

3. For the International Telecommunication Union Guidelines to for National Emergency Telecommunication Plans, see https://www.itu.int/en/ITU-D/Emergency-Telecommunications /Pages/Publications/Guidelines-for-NETPs.aspx.

References

GSMA. 2020. *Building a Resilient Industry: How Mobile Network Operators Prepare for and Respond to Natural Disasters: An Interactive Guide for MNOs Based on Experiences with the Humanitarian Connectivity Charter.* London: GSMA. https://www.gsma.com/mobilefordevelopment/wp -content/uploads/2020/03/TWP5861_BuildingAResilientIndustry_v003.pdf.

New South Wales. 2021. *NSW Critical Infrastructure Resilience Strategy Guide: A Focus on Strategy Outcome 1: Improved Infrastructure Resilience.* Sydney: Resilience NSW.

Oughton, E. J., T. Russell, J. Oh, S. Ballan, and J. W. Hall. 2023. "Global Vulnerability Assessment of Mobile Telecommunications Infrastructure to Climate Hazards using Crowdsourced Open Data." Policy Research Working Paper, World Bank, Washington, DC.

Sandhu, H. S., and S. Raja. 2019. "No Broken Link: The Vulnerability of Telecommunication Infrastructure to Natural Hazards." Background paper for Lifelines, World Bank, Washington, DC. http://hdl.handle.net/10986/31912.

Uptime Institute. 2021. "The Gathering Storm: Climate Change and Data Center Resiliency." UI Intelligence Report 41, published November 2, 2020; last updated February 16, 2021. Uptime Institute, New York. https://uptimeinstitute.com/the-gathering-storm-climate-change-and -data-center-resiliency.

World Bank. 2019. *Boosting Financial Resilience to Disaster Shocks: Good Practices and New Frontiers. World Bank Technical Contribution to the 2019 G20 Finance Ministers' and Central Bank Governors' Meeting.* Washington, DC: World Bank. https://documents1.worldbank.org/curated /en/239311559902020973/pdf/Boosting-Financial-Resilience-to-Disaster-Shocks-Good -Practices-and-New-Frontiers-World-Bank-Technical-Contribution-to-the-2019-G20 -Finance-Ministers-and-Central-Bank-Governors-Meeting.pdf.

World Bank. Forthcoming a. "Greening Digital Guidance Note." World Bank, Washington, DC.

World Bank. Forthcoming b. "Spectrum Policy for Resilience." World Bank, Washington, DC.

4. Digital Technologies for Mitigation

Introduction

Digital technologies are creating new opportunities to cut greenhouse gas (GHG) emissions and fight climate change across sectors by means of their direct, enabling, and behavioral effects (World Bank 2021). In energy use, digitalization could facilitate a transition toward more sustainable renewable energy resources across the world. In the transport sector, digital technologies could enable a modal shift, particularly in passenger transportation, entailing the wider provision and use of public transportation, shared mobility options, and the establishment of low-carbon, intermodal transportation systems. In the agrifood sector, precision agriculture based on digital solutions could enhance ways to meet society's nutritional needs while reducing environmental harms. Digital technologies also show great potential in helping cities become climate-smart, such as by advancing intelligent urban planning and land use, as well as monitoring and upgrading the energy efficiency of residential and nonresidential structures.

However, digitalization does not by default reduce sectoral carbon footprints. Some digital solutions may help reduce unit-level emissions, but at the same time enhance overall usage, causing a rebound effect. These effects are not always apparent from the outset, and a better understanding is needed of both the enabling effects on carbon reduction and the rebound effects of digital solutions. In some cases, new policies may reduce the overall rebound effects.

As described in this report, energy, transportation, agrifood systems, and urban centers are high-emitting sectors that show the potential to leverage digital technologies for mitigation of the effects of climate change (figure 4.1). Box 4.1 cites examples of how both mature and evolving technologies are being applied across sectors for mitigation efforts.

Energy

Digital technologies reinforce climate change mitigation in the energy sector by supporting the transition to renewable energy, enhancing energy efficiency, and enabling demand-side flexibility. In fact, the energy sector was an early adopter of digital technologies. Large information technology (IT) systems were deployed to improve energy

FIGURE 4.1   Emissions Profiles of Four Sectors: Energy, Transportation, Agrifood, and Urban Centers

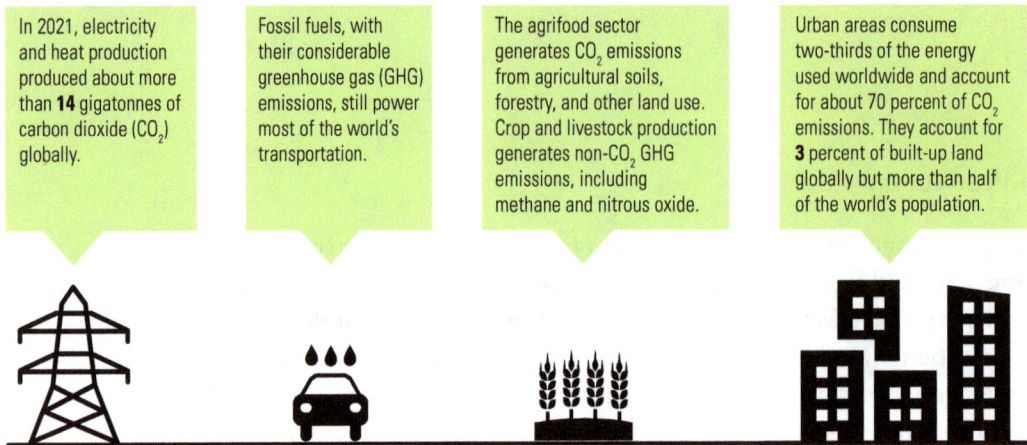

In 2021, electricity and heat production produced about more than **14** gigatonnes of carbon dioxide (CO_2) globally.	Fossil fuels, with their considerable greenhouse gas (GHG) emissions, still power most of the world's transportation.	The agrifood sector generates CO_2 emissions from agricultural soils, forestry, and other land use. Crop and livestock production generates non-CO_2 GHG emissions, including methane and nitrous oxide.	Urban areas consume two-thirds of the energy used worldwide and account for about 70 percent of CO_2 emissions. They account for **3** percent of built-up land globally but more than half of the world's population.

Sources: Climatewatchdata.org; IEA 2022; IPCC 2022; Le Quéré et al. 2018.

BOX 4.1   Contributions of Selected Digital Technologies to Mitigation Efforts

Digital access technologies. These technologies comprise handheld devices (mobile phones), computers, software, and fixed or mobile telecommunication infrastructure that permit connectivity between people and between people and the internet.

- In transportation, mobile phones and apps are used widely to enable shared mobility or establish novel business models linked to "mobility as a service" (MaaS). Telematics can improve route optimization and vehicle efficiency (GSMA 2019).
- In the urban sector, global positioning system (GPS) data from mobile phones have been combined with data on vehicle congestion and air pollution to identify hotspots of urban emissions (see, for example, Dujardin et al. 2020; Gately et al. 2017). Smartphone apps can increase the usability of public infrastructure and urban transportation systems (GSMA 2019).

Internet of Things (IoT). The IoT is a suite of technologies that connect physical objects to the internet and enable communication between physical objects or between physical and digital objects relative to their position, surroundings, and condition, resulting in a network of digital and physical (infra)structures.

- In the energy sector, IoT applications are already being used to control energy supply in smart grids in response to demand (Fraunhofer FOKUS 2016).
- In the transportation sector, the IoT can serve as the basis for the comprehensive reorganization of traffic flows. The vision of the smart city also relies on the IoT by, for example, linking electromobility with energy systems in the context of sector coupling.

(Box continues on the following page)

BOX 4.1 **Contributions of Selected Digital Technologies to Mitigation Efforts *(continued)***

- In the urban sector, the IoT enables networking of both objects and entire public infrastructures. Examples include intelligent power networks and intelligent buildings (Horvath 2012).

Big data and big data analytics. These terms refer to large quantities of machine-readable data, characterized by the three Vs: large data *volume* (data sets with sizes beyond the ability of traditional database structures to capture, manage, and process); *variety* (marked heterogeneity in terms of data types and sources); and *velocity* (high speed of data generation and processing). Big data analytics refers to the techniques for processing data sets that previously were inaccessible owing to their volume or heterogeneity.

- In the energy sector, big data can be applied to increase energy efficiency such as via smart energy management or predictive analytics on building energy consumption (Hassani, Huang, and Silva 2019).
- In the transportation sector, big data analytics can be used for smart mobility such as traffic control systems (Creutzig et al. 2019; Javaid et al. 2018; Taj et al. 2018).
- In the urban sector, big data can be leveraged for smart and sustainable urban and infrastructure planning (Bibri and Krogstie 2017; Hashem et al. 2016).

Artificial intelligence (AI). AI centers on technical systems and applications (software alone or coupled with robotics) that are characterized by an ability to solve problems autonomously and efficiently via machine-based processing, often harnessing big data.

- In the energy sector, methods such as pattern mining and semiautomated artificial neural network clustering have been used to identify patterns in data on building energy consumption in order to improve energy efficiency (Fan and Xiao 2017) and to identify possible energy leakages or outages for greater energy conservation (WBGU 2019).
- In the transportation sector, machine learning can aid in freight consolidation by examining the complex interaction among shipment sizes, modes, service requirements, and origin–destination logistics (Rolnick et al. 2019).
- In the agrifood sector, deep learning algorithms can be used to determine the best crop protection strategy (Wolfert et al. 2017) via predictive analytics based on weather and climate data.
- In the urban sector, machine learning can be used in urban planning to inform policy makers' decisions on infrastructure development or waste logistics (Manyana 2020).

Blockchain. Blockchain technology enables simultaneous access, validation, and recordkeeping across a network.

- In the energy sector, blockchain technology supports the functioning of a decentralized clean energy system by settling and tracking electricity consumption and production at the individual level. Blockchain can also increase the traceability and transparency of renewable energy certificates.
- In the transportation sector, blockchain can automate purchases of renewable energy for electric vehicles and support their maintenance (such as by monitoring battery health).
- In the agrifood sector, blockchain technology can enable the monitoring and traceability of greenhouse gas emissions from farm to table.

management and grid operations as early as the 1970s (IEA 2017, 25). In recent years, the pace of digitalization has increased. Between 2014 and 2016, global investment in digital electricity infrastructure and software grew by more than 20 percent annually (IEA 2017).

Digital technologies could facilitate the shift from a centralized energy system centered on large power plants to a decentralized, renewable energy–based system featuring greatly increased interconnectivity between billions of distributed energy resource devices, energy storage systems, and markets that can accommodate variable electricity supply and flexible demand. Moreover, digital technologies may advance efforts to explore and implement low-carbon energy solutions. For example, satellite-based imagery could help identify suitable places to deploy geothermal or dam-based hydropower plants (Rolnick et al. 2022). Digital energy system solutions, such as digitally supported energy storage systems or energy management systems, could provide the foundation to connect various energy supply facilities based on digital networking and intelligent controlling (Farhangi 2010).

Energy storage systems, specifically battery energy storage systems (BESS), have become critical for the expansion of renewable energy. Digital technologies, such as artificial intelligence (AI), can boost the efficient operation of these systems by optimizing renewable electricity integration (in part by eliminating generation forecast mistakes), minimizing pricing for locally consumed electricity, and maximizing profits for storage system owners.

In low- and middle-income countries (LMICs), where electrification is limited, digital technologies can enable the use of renewable energy solutions. Innovative and affordable pay-as-you-go off-grid solar solutions—such as the Vodacom and Engie partnership in Mozambique and the Safaricom and M-Copa solutions in Kenya—offer individuals and small businesses access to a range of clean and affordable energy systems. Solutions range from entry-level systems powering mobile phones, portable radios, and portable lights to high-end systems powering fans, refrigerators, water pumps, and TVs. Payments are made easily through mobile payment apps.

Enhancing energy efficiency across the entire energy system requires sophisticated monitoring, measuring, and predicting—all of which are enabled or facilitated by digital technologies. Digital technologies such as AI, machine learning, and deep learning can assist energy suppliers in better prediction and balancing of the grid. A range of digital tools have emerged to improve scheduling and dispatching processes, thereby allowing system operators to balance electricity systems and determine how much power every controllable generator should produce (Rolnick et al. 2022). For maintenance and security, big data analytics can also be deployed to monitor failure modes and the cost of outages to develop better replacement and maintenance schedules.

Digital technologies also enable demand-side flexibility, allowing consumption to be adjusted in response to the cost of energy. Adoption of digitally enabled energy-efficient appliances and equipment such as smart meters is an important step toward mitigating climate change from the customer side. Instant information feedback on energy usage and associated saliency is a key predictor of energy-saving behavior (Creutzig et al. 2022; Khanna et al. 2021). Meanwhile, traditional energy consumers can also become energy producers—so-called prosumers. By supplying the grid with unused renewable energy (such as solar power produced in-house), consumers become active participants in the new energy system and help accelerate the growth of the renewable energy contribution to the overall energy system. This is possible on a large scale only with intelligent and connected energy devices. For example, net metering—a billing mechanism that credits renewable energy system owners for the electricity they add to the grid—is in place in some LMICs and under discussion in countries that are reforming their electricity sector, such as South Africa.

Transportation

Digital technologies, now serving as key enablers of many new transportation services, can be useful for mitigating transportation carbon emissions, but this is possible on a large scale only with intelligent and connected energy devices. They can also contribute to the establishment of modern logistic systems that could not exist without the digitalization of orders and the seamless tracking of freight enabled by Internet of Things (IoT)–compatible tags and other devices. Five contributions are described here.

First, digital technologies enable a modal shift, particularly in the context of passenger transportation. "Mobility as a service" (MaaS) is a shift away from personally owned modes of transportation toward the provision of multimodal mobility packages on the basis of a variety of shared mobility services (Flügge 2016; Giesecke, Surakka, and Hakonen 2016; Kamargianni et al. 2016; Nikitas et al. 2017). Digital technologies are essential in MaaS to identify passenger demand and enhance coordination between different transportation modes. For example, data from social media, geographic information system (GIS) data, or mobile phone sensors are used to detect or infer passengers' preferences for travel modes and destinations (Dabiri and Heaslip 2018). Big data analytics can provide travel estimates for various interconnectable transportation modes, thereby facilitating coordination between different modes (WBGU 2019).

The impact of shared services at the country level has, however, shown mixed results in reducing emissions, congestion, and car ownership (Tirachini 2020). It is expected that the reduction in ownership through MaaS will limit the total environmental footprint of the circulating vehicles and contribute to the cobenefit of creating a more livable urban environment. MaaS could reduce GHG emissions by (1) introducing a newer car fleet; (2) increasing the ratio of goods to passenger per vehicle;

(3) shortening journeys; and (4) replacing motorized transport with other active modes such as walking and biking. The impacts of GHG emissions depend on replacement effects (Creutzig 2021). Replacing private cars with car-sharing services, one major component of MaaS, could reduce the vehicle miles traveled (VMT) by an estimated 30–45 percent, and their greenhouse gas emissions by 130–980 kilograms of carbon dioxide ($kgCO_2$) per year (Nordic Council of Ministers 2021). However, some researchers and policy makers argue that if MaaS is based on conventional internal combustion engine (ICE) vehicles, which are common in cities, the VMT could increase, along with GHG emissions. A study of MaaS in Barcelona (ITS4C 2019) noted with justifiable concern that MaaS could push users toward less sustainable modes. However, a similar study in Germany (Best and Hasenheit 2018) and India (Wadud and Namala 2022) found that the MaaS model has clear environmental benefits. Irrespective of the results, it can be argued that to avoid possible adverse outcomes, public transit must remain the backbone of mobility, and Maas should replace private motorized travel.

Second, one area with great mitigation potential is public transportation. Digital technologies could improve the operational efficiency of public transit by enabling automated fare collection systems, advanced transit information systems, and better route planning and scheduling based on actual demand and real-time data (Creutzig et al. 2019). Use of public transit has important mitigating effects and is the default choice for many in LMICs. Public transportation based on zero emission energy would have an even greater effect.

Third, digital technology–enabled smart signaling systems show potential in reducing GHG emissions. Idling vehicles in congested traffic, waiting for signals to change, are big emitters of GHGs. According to the US Department of Energy (DOE 2015), in the United States idling vehicles waste about 6 billion gallons of fuel per year. About half of that amount is attributable to personal vehicles, which generate about 30 million tonnes of carbon dioxide equivalent ($MtCO_2e$) per year. Actuated signal control continuously monitors traffic arriving at an intersection and adjusts the corresponding control parameters to minimize the total delay. In addition, it may also respond to pedestrian needs (for example, by means of push buttons or camera sensors) by adjusting signals to provide safe pedestrian crossing and removing pedestrian phases when no pedestrians are present. When connected, signals along a corridor can also coordinate with one another to keep automobile "platoons" moving to the extent possible, further minimizing stops along the corridor.

Fourth, in the freight system a combination of digital technologies—IoT and blockchain for traceability, global positioning system (GPS) and GIS for positioning, and AI for prediction—increases the utilization and productivity of existing transportation services but also helps to reduce energy consumption and miles traveled. TradeLens, an open platform underpinned by blockchain technology and developed by Mærsk Shipping, one of the world's leaders in shipping, is a case in point. Moreover, multimodal transportation networks integrating cargo ships with freight trains, inland shipping (barges), and trucks are emerging as a cost-neutral solution across Europe thanks to underlying digital networks. Such multimodal networks are more reliable and help save 20 percent of CO_2 emissions.

Finally but not least, digital technologies play a crucial role in increasing the share of electric vehicles (EVs) or non–fossil fuel–based vehicles. For example, predictive maintenance via digital twin–based monitoring of the battery health of electric vehicles can be used to monitor status and performance in real time. Battery design would then be improved, which, in turn, could increase the attractiveness of EVs (TWAICE 2019). Digital technologies might further be conducive to accelerating the uptake of EVs. EV batteries could be linked with energy systems via smart charging and vehicle-to-grid (V2G) technology, which offers opportunities to balance loads in a grid with a higher percentage of intermittent renewables (IEA 2020).

Replacing older fleets of vehicles that have combustion engines with EVs could be an effective strategy for reducing GHG emissions. Electric vehicles are one of the most promising technical pathways for reducing oil use and CO_2 emissions per kilometer. With a moderately clean electric grid, EVs can achieve 50 grams (g) of CO_2 per kilometer, well below today's most efficient cars, which emit between 100 and 150 g of CO_2 per kilometer. For example, by 2017 the Shenzhen Bus Group had converted its entire fleet to electric buses. On average, over its life cycle an electric bus in China produces 37.56 percent lower GHG emissions than its diesel counterpart.

The lack of charging stations is widely recognized as a major obstacle to the rapid adoption of EVs (Dolsak and Prakash 2021; Pevec et al. 2019). A digital strategy for making the real-time availability of the existing charging stations visible and transparent to users could help reduce range anxiety and improve system efficiency. In addition, a study by the US Agency for International Development and the National Renewable Energy Laboratory also pointed out that connecting users with charging infrastructure through such a digital network could foster entrepreneurship and enable creative business models for EV deployment, particularly for LMICs with limited public finance (Aznar et al. 2021).

Agrifood System

Digital technologies can support measures to lower emissions across the entire agrifood system (energy, fertilizer, transportation, processing, and sales) through their direct, enabling, and behavioral effects.

On-farm, the direct effect promotes the best application of natural resources and inputs. New production and distribution processes enabled by digital technologies improve resource efficiency through better production control. GHG emissions are reduced by lowering emissions linked to the production of inputs and to excess nitrogen in the soil.

Precision agricultural practices are gaining attention with their potential to meet society's nutritional needs, while at the same time reducing GHG emissions from agricultural activities and reducing the loss of terrestrial biodiversity (CBD 2014; FAO et al. 2018; IPBES 2019). This approach is related to the digitally enabled precise application of water, seeds, fertilizers, and pesticides based on the needs of plants and soil quality (Gebbers and Adamchuk 2010; Mendes et al. 2020). For example, robots or mobile phones with built-in sensors could collect, analyze, and exchange information on motions, images, environments, or positions (see Mendes et al. 2020, table 2), allowing for targeted pesticide application, mechanical weeding, or vacuuming of pests (Sukkarieh 2017). In Brazil, small farmers were assisted via precision agricultural tools. It was a low-cost and ubiquitous computing environment that supported farmers in inspecting tomato crops and automatically detecting a foliage disease, late blight (da Cruz et al. 2015). Moreover, precision irrigation systems reduce energy use and nitrogen dioxide (NO_2) emissions caused by overwatering, and precision machinery reduces NO_2 soil emissions by curbing the application of nitrogen fertilizer.

Digital technologies used in livestock production can directly benefit the environment. More efficient feeding strategies that stem from digital agricultural technology can cut feed requirements and reduce livestock's large indirect land use. Digital technologies can also address poor animal health, which is estimated to reduce livestock production efficiency by up to 33 percent (Deloitte 2017). Through better monitoring of animal health, digital technologies boost livestock productivity and reduce global GHG emissions per livestock unit (Böttcher et al. 2012). Pastoralist systems also benefit from digital technologies that locate grazing grounds and waterholes and limit overgrazing.[1]

Reductions in GHG emissions also result from dematerializing of products and services on- and off-farm, improved coordination of the agrifood system, and greater customization of production due to better information flows between producers and consumers. Off-farm digital technologies can support the reduction of emissions throughout the value chain and, in particular, the distribution processes, including more efficient transport, storage, and delivery services. For example, digital technologies can optimize transportation and logistics by monitoring fuel usage, speed, and location, thereby making the entire supply chain more efficient. A better connection between supply and demand cuts food loss and waste, as well as the associated carbon footprints, through e-commerce and better coordinated food distribution online (El Bilali and Allahyari 2018). Better traceability of food from farm to fork can also limit food loss throughout the value chain. The World Economic Forum (WEF 2018) estimates that blockchain-enabled traceability could reduce food losses by up to 30 million tonnes annually if blockchain were to monitor information in half of the world's supply chains.

Off-farm, the enabling effect stems from a greater capacity to use information not only to act on preferences but also to create new markets. Digital technologies can strengthen the role of certifications and agreements that aim to promote environmentally friendly production practices and waste management. For example, a new wave of digital services is seeking to better link food supply with downstream demand and throughout the supply chain. Much food waste occurs at the pre-consumer level, and software has been developed to target overproduction, spoilage, and waste in kitchens. For example, Leanpath, an organization targeting frontline food service workers, has proposed an analytics platform that measures waste, values it, and suggests mechanisms for reducing it.[2] Other applications link local food distributors to sustainability-minded consumers who want less food waste in the supply chain. For example, the United Kingdom–based application Too Good to Go uses a daily consumer alert for products on the verge of being reclassified for disposal.[3] So far, the company estimates its service has saved over 36,400,000 meals globally and 91,005 tonnes of CO_2.

Finally, digital technologies can change the attitudes of food consumers and producers and, in doing so, transform the food system. With a greater capacity to monitor, showcase impact, and communicate a farmer's environmental practices, awareness grows among all stakeholders about the effects of their behavior. Awareness can then trigger systemic change. Because interaction among companies, civil society, and regulators is particularly important for lessening environmental impacts, such data will help consumers, regulators, and nongovernmental organizations push for greater sustainability.

Urban Centers

In the urban sector, digital technologies show great potential for mitigating climate change in areas such as buildings, urban planning, and waste management.

The building and construction sector together account for over one-third of total global final energy consumption and almost 40 percent of total direct and indirect CO_2 emissions (IEA 2021). The International Energy Agency (IEA 2017) estimates that by making full use of digitally enabled improvements of buildings' operational efficiency, total energy demand in the building sector could be reduced by about 10 percent, compared with IEA's reference scenario from 2017–40 (IEA 2017). The largest potential savings is in heating, cooling, and lighting as well as smart energy management (IEA 2018, 2021; WBGU 2019). In existing buildings, energy efficiency hinges on the capacity to measure energy consumption and costs. Smart meters can help manage energy consumption, and microgrids can improve operations and optimize energy efficiency. Estimates of potential energy-related emissions reductions are based on the assumption that there are no rebound effects from lower costs and improved quality, full automation, and customized household solutions, and that savings are not offset by the rising standby consumption of newly deployed digital services (IEA 2017).

Another way in which digital technologies can help mitigate GHG emissions in urban areas is by providing information to support urban planning. Urban planning based on real-time data enables a better understanding of the present inefficiencies and problems to be prioritized in tackling climate change. Digital tools can help identify areas where energy demand can be reduced, such as by finding the optimal locations for water features or vegetation to counteract heat islands or reduce the demand for cooling in buildings. Sensors and feedback systems can be deployed in parallel to help quantify the benefits. Advanced spatial energy planning such as GIS and digital twin modeling enables the mapping of potential measures by identifying their benefits and impacts prior to implementation. For example, it can help identify where energy efficiency interventions hold the most value. Demand for heating and cooling can be mapped, combining weather data with demand data, to identify where efficiency interventions are needed. Singapore has invested S$73 million in creating a digital replica of the entire country. Since its launch in 2017, the "Cooling Singapore" project has been tackling the urban heat island effect.

Because urbanization today is characterized by high population density, digital technologies can be employed to effectively and sustainably manage resources and large amounts of waste (Esmaeilian et al. 2018; WBGU 2019). Technologies can identify, analyze, and sort municipal solid waste (Ferrari et al. 2020; Genuino et al. 2017) and construction debris (Bilal et al. 2016), thereby predicting the need for enhanced, location-specific management of large amounts of waste (Adamović et al. 2017). Digital technologies could reduce unrecycled solid waste in cities by 10–20 percent per person (between 30 and 130 kilograms per person), annually. In particular, digital tracking and payment applications for waste disposal could reduce GHG emissions by nearly 1 percent.

Smart applications for optimizing waste collection routes are also emerging. The classic waste collection approach is to empty trash bins once or twice a week in a standard, repetitive fashion that does not account for the level of usage of the bins. Sensor technologies continuously monitor waste bin capacity and provide city planners with that information for a more efficient waste management process. In Newcastle-upon-Tyne in the United Kingdom, IoT sensors in waste receptacles have been connected via wireless digital solutions to a waste management planning system, thereby reducing the number of trucks needed to collect waste by 50 percent and the amount of CO_2 they generate by 49 percent. The use of radio frequency identification (RFID) chips in the Republic of Korea has supported cities in incentivizing households to reduce waste as well as in optimizing waste collection routes. In India, the Mu City Savior application enables citizens to report drainage infrastructure problems in real time to inform maintenance schedules.

Treating and pumping water in cities are estimated to contribute 2–3 percent of global GHG emissions. Only about 20 percent of all wastewater globally is treated. Untreated wastewater released into the environment generates a GHG footprint roughly three times that of the GHG footprint when the same wastewater is treated in a traditional wastewater treatment plant. Digital technology can be leveraged to help ensure the availability and sustainable management of clean water and therefore help improve the accessibility, safety, and usability of water resources. Such digital technologies are typically known as smart water or smart water grids, the internet of water, and smart water management.

Smart water management aims to enable the sustainable use of water resources by relying on digital technologies to provide real-time, automated data to resolve water challenges. Digital technologies can help cities both increase water efficiency and lower GHG emissions. Water consumption tracking applications, which pair advanced metering with digital feedback messages, could reduce water consumption by nearly 15 percent in high-income cities with high water consumption. In low-income cities with very high leakage, or "nonrevenue water," applications for detection and control could reduce water consumption by nearly 25 percent. Although the effects of digital technology on water efficiency are significant, the impact of digital technology on GHG emissions in the water sector is less pronounced.

Challenges to Adoption of Digital Technologies for Climate Change Mitigation

As shown across the four sectors considered here, digital technologies can accelerate mitigation in many ways. Current estimates point to a potential 20 percent reduction in GHG emissions by 2050 in hard-to-abate sectors such as energy, materials, and transportation (WEF 2022, based on Accenture analysis); a 6–12 percent reduction by 2030 in the areas of smart energy, transportation, buildings, and remote work; and an additional 1–4 percent in agriculture (Malmodin and Bergmark 2015). However, research in this area is scant. Further evidence and multistakeholder engagement are needed to reveal the positive and negative effects of digitalization on GHG emissions. The European Green Digital Coalition is an example of such efforts.[4] A better understanding of the magnitude and complexities of decarbonization from digitalization is needed to set priorities, to design enabling policies, and ultimately to implement high-impact solutions on a large scale.

In addition, quality data are needed to understand sector impacts. Digital solutions can enable monitoring and reporting, but methods and data collection need to be more consistent. GHG inventories are largely limited to self-reported data. And most actors that do report data are disproportionately located in the global North, making it difficult to obtain a complete picture of sector impact on the global climate, particularly in view of the growing contribution of the global South actors to GHG emissions.

Meanwhile, GHG emissions are rarely measured directly. They are instead primarily estimated using activity data (such as amount of fuel consumed and vehicle miles traveled), which are inherently problematic because not every activity's impact on climate emissions can be accurately quantified. In addition, because data are self-reported and calculated from activity data, their accuracy and completeness suffer from numerical choices, which can render some things visible but not others. As a result, a GHG inventory does not always provide a complete picture of a sector's impact on climate change (Hsu et al. 2020).

In addition to bridging the methodological and knowledge gap, the wider adoption gaps associated with digital technologies must be overcome. Chief among these are the substantial problems of supply and demand affecting the adoption of digital technologies in LMICs. About 17 percent of the population in the least developed countries still do not even have access to a fixed or mobile broadband network (ITU 2023). On the demand side, the cost of adoption, limited technological sophistication, and insufficient incentives to adopt digital technologies are important barriers. In fact, there is a sizable uptake gap among individuals. For example, only about half of the population in areas of Africa with mobile connectivity actually use the internet. Firms do not make full use digital technologies because of the cost of access to devices and connectivity, poor access to finance, and limited awareness of the productive potential of technologies (World Bank 2023).

For end users, the incentives for adoption of digital technologies are based on assessments of costs and benefits. Many factors beyond the digital technology environment affect adoption. For example, larger farms benefit from economies at scale that lower the unit costs of adopting new digital technologies. Yet for small producers, who together present immense potential for mitigation, additional support is needed, such as matching grants to cofinance equipment purchases or e-vouchers to subsidize rentals of machinery. When the use of digital solutions results in lower energy costs, the incentives for adoption are greater. However, in many countries electricity and fuel costs are subsidized and so do not reflect their true cost. Furthermore, there can be a positive correlation between technological sophistication and the use of energy-efficient technologies, as an analysis of Georgia shows (Cirera, Comin, and Cruz 2022). According to the World Bank's Firm-Level Adoption of Technology survey, lack of demand and uncertainty about demand, lack of finance, poor infrastructure, lack of capabilities, and government regulations are constraints to the adoption of technology by firms in developing economies (Cirera, Comin, and Cruz 2022). On the government side, the adoption of digital technologies such as smart metering of electricity consumption can bring more transparency to the system, thereby reducing the gains for agents that benefit from governance gaps with analog technologies. In summary, factors beyond the digital technology environment affect adoption.

Solutions appropriate for local contexts are needed. A strong innovation and start-up ecosystem for climate solutions and frameworks for allowing access to digital solutions produced internationally would address supply problems. Digital public goods and data sharing frameworks are needed to facilitate the development of digital solutions—for example, for smart agriculture and mobility. Public goods can also drive economies of scale on cloud computing for climate applications across borders. However, appropriate rules on cross-border data flows (for personal and nonpersonal data) are important. Furthermore, the increasing diffusion of digitally enabled technologies across sectors poses risks of data privacy breaches and cybersecurity attacks, threatening the integrity of digital infrastructure. Early consideration of how to increase cyber resilience and the security of the design and management of digitally enabled systems is vital to minimize such risks.

Notes

1. An example is AfriScout in Ethiopia, run by the nongovernmental organization Project Concern International, the World Food Programme, and the Ministry of Agriculture. AfriScout provides pastoralists with satellite-generated images of water and vegetation every 10 days. For more information, visit https://globalcommunities.org/afriscout/.
2. See Leanpath website, https://www.leanpath.com/about/.
3. See Too Good to Go website, https://www.toogoodtogo.com/.
4. See European Green Digital Coalition website, https://www.greendigitalcoalition.eu/.

References

Adamović, V. M., D. Z. Antanasijević, M. Đ. Ristić, A. A. Perić-Grujić, and V. V. Pocajt. 2017. "Prediction of Municipal Solid Waste Generation Using Artificial Neural Network Approach Enhanced by Structural Break Analysis. *Environmental Science and Pollution Research* 24: 299–31. https://doi.org/10.1007/s11356-016-7767-x.

Aznar, Alexandra, Scott Belding, Kaylyn Bopp, Kamyria Coney, Caley Johnson, Caley, and Owen Zinaman. 2021. *Building Blocks of Electric Vehicle Deployment: A Guide for Developing Countries*. Washington, DC: United States Agency for International Development and National Renewable Energy Lab. https://www.nrel.gov/docs/fy21osti/78776.pdf.

Best, Aaron, and Marius Hasenheit. 2018. *Car Sharing in Germany: A Case Study on the Circular Economy*. Berlin: Ecologic Institute. https://www.ecologic.eu/node/16559/printable/print.

Bibri, Simon Elias, and John Krogstie. 2017. "ICT of the New Wave of Computing for Sustainable Urban Forms: Their Big Data and Context-Aware Augmented Typologies and Design Concepts." *Sustainable Cities and Society* 32 (2017): 449–74.

Bilal, Muhammad, L. O. Oyedele, J. Qadir, K. Munir, S. O. Ajayi, O. O. Akinade, H. A. Owolabi, H. A. Alaka, and M. Pasha. 2016. "Big Data in the Construction Industry: A Review of Present Status, Opportunities, and Future Trends." *Advanced Engineering Informatics* 30 (3): 500–21.

Böttcher, Hannes, Pieter Johannes Verkerk, Mykola Gusti, Petr Havlík, and Giacomo Grassi. 2012. "Projection of the Future EU Forest CO_2 Sink as Affected by Recent Bioenergy Policies Using Two Advanced Forest Management Models." *GCB-Bioenergy* 4 (6): 773–83.

CBD (Convention on Biological Diversity). 2014. *Global Bio-diversity Outlook 4. A Mid-Term Assessment of Progress Towards the Implementation of the Strategic Plan for Biodiversity 2011–2020*. Montreal: CBD.

Cirera, Xavier, Diego Comin, and Marcio Cruz. 2022. "Bridging the Technological Divide: Technology Adoption by Firms in Developing Countries." World Bank Productivity Project, World Bank, Washington, DC. https://openknowledge.worldbank.org/handle/10986/.

Creutzig, F. 2021. "Making Smart Mobility Sustainable." Israel Policy Public Institute, Tel Aviv.

Creutzig, F., M. Franzen, R. Moeckel, D. Heinrichs, K. Nagel, S. Nieland, and H. Weisz. 2019. "Leveraging Digitalization for Sustainability in Urban Transport." *Global Sustainability* 2 (e14): 1–6. https://doi.org/10.1017/sus.2019.11.

Creutzig, F., J. Roy, P. Devine-Wright, J. Diaz-José, F. W. Geels, A. Grubler, N. Mäizi, E. Masanet, Y. Mulugetta, C. D. Onyige, P. E. Perkins, A. Sanches-Pereira, and E. U. Weber. 2022. "Demand, Services and Social Aspects of Mitigation." In *Climate Change 2022: Mitigation of Climate Change. Contribution of Working Group III to the Sixth Assessment Report of the Intergovernmental Panel on Climate Change*. Cambridge, UK: Cambridge University Press.

Dabiri, Sina, and Kevin Heaslip. 2018. "Inferring Transportation Modes from GPS Trajectories Using a Convolutional Neural Network." *Transportation Research Part C: Emerging Technologies* 86 (January): 360–71. https://doi.org/10.1016/j.trc.2017.11.021.

da Cruz, Sergio Manuel Serra, Ana Cláudia de Macedo Vieira, and Marden Manuel Marques. 2015. "Technological Management of Small Crops through Mobile Apps and Precision Agriculture." *Proceedings of the XI Brazilian Symposium on Information Systems (SBSI 2015)*. 51.

Deloitte. 2017. "Smart Livestock Farming: Potential of Digitalization for Global Meat Supply." Discussion paper. https://www2.deloitte.com/content/dam/Deloitte/de/Documents/operations/Smart-livestock-farming_Deloitte.pdf.

DOE (US Department of Energy). 2015. "Idling Reduction for Personal Vehicles." DOE, Washington, DC. https://afdc.energy.gov/files/u/publication/idling_personal_vehicles.pdf.

Dolsak, Nives, and Aseem Prakash. 2021. "The Lack of EV Charging Stations Could Limit EV Growth." *Forbes*, May 5, 2021. https://www.forbes.com/sites/prakashdolsak/2021/05/05/the-lack-of-ev-charging-stations-could-limit-ev-growth/?sh=3b8ab57c6a13.

Dujardin, Sébastien, Damien Jacques, Jessica Steele, and Catherine Linard. 2020. "Mobile Phone Data for Urban Climate Change Adaptation: Reviewing Applications, Opportunities and Key Challenges." *Sustainability* 12 (4): 1501. https://doi.org/10.3390/su12041501.

El Bilali, Hamid, and Mohammad Sadegh Allahyari. 2018. "Transition towards Sustainability in Agriculture and Food Systems: Role of Information and Communication Technologies." *Information Processing in Agriculture* 5 (4): 456–64. https://www.sciencedirect.com/science/article/pii/S2214317318301367.

Esmaeilian, B., B. Wang, K. Lewis, F. Duarte, C. Ratti, and S. Behdad. 2018. "The Future of Waste Management in Smart and Sustainable Cities: A Review and Concept Paper." *Waste Management* 81: 177–95. https://doi.org/10.1016/j.wasman.2018.09.047.

Fan, Cheng, and Fu Xiao. 2017. "Assessment of Building Operational Performance Using Data Mining Techniques: A Case Study. *Energy Procedia* 111 (2017): 1070–78. https://www.sciencedirect.com/science/article/pii/S187661021730303X.

FAO (Food and Agriculture Organization), IFAD (International Fund for Agricultural Development), UNICEF (United Nations Children's Fund), WFP (World Food Programme), and WHO (World Health Organization). 2018. *The State of Food Security and Nutrition in the World 2018. Building Climate Resilience for Food Security and Nutrition*. Rome: FAO.

Farhangi, H. 2010. "The Path of the Smart Grid." *IEEE Power and Energy Magazine* 8 (1): 18–28. https://doi.org/10.1109/MPE.2009.934876.

Ferrari, Francesca, Raffaella Striani, Stefania Minosi, Roberto De Fazio, Paolo Visconti, Luigi Patrono, Luca Catarinucci, et al. 2020. "An Innovative IoT-Oriented Prototype Platform for the Management and Valorisation of the Organic Fraction of Municipal Solid Waste." *Journal of Cleaner Production* 247: 119618. https://www.sciencedirect.com/science/article/abs/pii/S0959652619344889.

Flügge, Barbara. 2016. *Smart Mobility*. Wiesbaden, Germany: Springer Fachmedien. https://doi.org/10.1007/978-3-658-14371-8.

Fraunhofer FOKUS. 2016. *Public IoT—Das Internet der Dinge im öffentlichen Raum*. Berlin: Fraunhofer FOKUS.

Gately, Conor K., Lucy R. Hutyra, Scott Peterson, and Ian Sue Wing. 2017. "Urban Emissions Hotspots: Quantifying Vehicle Congestion and Air Pollution Using Mobile Phone GPS Data." *Environmental Pollution* 229: 496–504. https://www.sciencedirect.com/science/article/abs/pii/S0269749117304001.

Gebbers, R., and V. I. Adamchuk. 2010. "Precision Agriculture and Food Security." *Science* 327 (5967): 828–31. https://doi.org/10.1126/science.1183899.

Genuino, Divine Angela D., Butch G. Bataller, Sergio C. Capareda, and Mark Daniel G. De Luna. 2017. "Application of Artificial Neural Network in the Modeling and Optimization of Humic Acid Extraction from Municipal Solid Waste Biochar." *Journal of Environmental Chemical Engineering* 5 (4): 4101–07. https://doi.org/10.1016/j.jece.2017.07.071.

Giesecke, Raphael, Teemu Surakka, and Marko Hakonen. 2016. "Conceptualising Mobility as a Service." In *2016 Eleventh International Conference on Ecological Vehicles and Renewable Energies (EVER)*. IEEE *Xplore*. https://ieeexplore.ieee.org/abstract/document/7476443.

GSMA. 2019. "The Enablement Effect: The Impact of Mobile Communications Technologies on Carbon Emissions Reductions." https://www.gsma.com/betterfuture/enablement-effect.

Hashem, Ibrahim Abaker Targio, Victor Chang, Nor Badrul Anuar, Kayode Adewole, Ibrar Yaqoob, Abdullah Gani, Ejaz Ahmed, and Haruna Chiroma. 2016. "The Role of Big Data in Smart City." *International Journal of Information Management* 36 (5): 748–58. https://www.sciencedirect.com/science/article/abs/pii/S0268401216302778.

Hassani, Hossein, Xu Huang, and Emmanuel Silva. 2019. "Big Data and Climate Change." *Big Data and Cognitive Computing* 3 (1): 12. https://www.mdpi.com/2504-2289/3/1/12.

Horvath, S. 2012. "Aktueller Begriff." In *Internet der Dinge*. Berlin: Deutscher Bundestag.

Hsu, A., W. Khoo, N. Goyal, and M. Wainstein. 2020. "Next-Generation Digital Ecosystem for Climate Data Mining and Knowledge Discovery: A Review of Digital Data Collection Technologies." *Frontiers in Big Data* 3 (September 10).

IEA (International Energy Agency). 2017. "Digitalization and Energy—Analysis." IEA, Paris.

IEA (International Energy Agency). 2018. "Energy Efficiency 2018. Analysis and Outlooks to 2040." IEA, Paris. https://iea.blob.core.windows.net/assets/d0f81f5f-8f87-487e-a56b-8e0167d18c56/Market_Report_Series_Energy_Efficiency_2018.pdf.

IEA (International Energy Agency). 2020. *Global EV Outlook 2020*. Paris: IEA. https://www.iea.org/reports/global-ev-outlook-2020.

IEA (International Energy Agency). 2021. "Tracking Clean Energy Progress 2021." IEA, Paris. https://www.iea.org/topics/tracking-clean-energy-progress.

IEA (International Energy Agency). 2022. "Global Energy Review: CO_2 Emissions in 2021." IEA, Paris. https://www.iea.org/reports/global-energy-review-co2-emissions-in-2021-2.

IPBES (Intergovernmental Science-Policy Platform on Biodiversity and Ecosystem Services). 2019. "Summary for Policymakers of the Global Assessment Report on Biodiversity and Ecosystem Services of the Intergovernmental Science-Policy Platform on Biodiversity and Ecosystem Services." https://ipbes.net/sites/default/files/inline/files/ipbes_global_assessment_report_summary_for_policymakers.pdf.

IPCC (Intergovernmental Panel on Climate Change). 2022. "Summary for Policymakers." In *Climate Change 2022: Mitigation of Climate Change. Contribution of Working Group III to the Sixth Assessment Report of the Intergovernmental Panel on Climate Change,* edited by P.R. Shukla, J. Skea, R. Slade, A. Al Khourdajie, R. van Diemen, D. McCollum, M. Pathak, et al. Cambridge, UK, and New York: Cambridge University Press. https://doi.org/10.1017/9781009157926.001.

ITS4C. 2019. "Mobility as a Service for Climate (MaaS4C)." https://its4climate.eu/wp-content/uploads/briefing-papers_topic5.pdf.

ITU (International Telecommunication Union). 2023. *Measuring Digital Development: Facts and Figures: Focus on Least Developed Countries.* Geneva: ITU.

Javaid, Sabeen, Ali Sufian, Saima Pervaiz, and Mehak Tanveer. 2018. "Smart Traffic Management System Using Internet of Things." In *2018 20th International Conference on Advanced Communication Technology (ICACT),* 393–98. IEEE *Xplore.* https://ieeexplore.ieee.org/abstract/document/8323770.

Kamargianni, Maria, Weibo Li, Melinda Matyas, and Andreas Schäfer. 2016. "A Critical Review of New Mobility Services for Urban Transport." *Transportation Research Procedia,* Transport Research Arena TRA2016 14 (January 1): 3294–3303.

Khanna, Tarun M., G. Baiocchi, M. Callaghan, F. Creutzig, H. Guiias, N. R. Haddaway, L. Hirth, et al. 2021. "A Multi-country Meta-analysis on the Role of Behavioural Change in Reducing Energy Consumption and CO_2 Emissions in Residential Buildings." *Nature Energy* 6: 925–32. https://doi.org/10.1038/s41560-021-00866-x.

Le Quéré, Corinne, Robbie M. Andrew, Pierre Friedlingstein, Stephen Sitch, Judith Hauck, Julia Pongratz, Penelope A. Pickers, et al. 2018. "Global Carbon Budget 2018." *Earth System Science Data* 10 (4): 2141–94. https://doi.org/10.5194/essd-10-2141-2018.

Malmodin, Jens, and Pernilla Bergmark. 2015. "Exploring the Effect of ICT Solutions on GHG Emissions in 2030." *Proceedings of EnviroInfo and ICT for Sustainability 2015.* Dordrecht, The Netherlands: Atlantis Press. https://www.atlantis-press.com/proceedings/ict4s-env-15/25836149.

Manyana, Nombulelo. 2020. "Using AI-Based Solutions to Improve Waste Logistics." *ReSource* 22 (3): 10–11. https://journals.co.za/doi/abs/10.10520/EJC-1f8d7566cf.

Mendes, Jorge, Tatiana M. Pinho, Filipe Neves dos Santos, Joaquim J. Sousa, Emanuel Peres, José Boaventura-Cunha, Mário Cunha, et al. 2020. "Smartphone Applications Targeting Precision Agriculture Practices—A Systematic Review." *Agronomy* 10 (6): 855. https://doi.org/10.3390/agronomy10060855.

Nikitas, Alexandros, Ioannis Kougias, Elena Alyavina, and Eric Njoya Tchouamou. 2017. "How Can Autonomous and Connected Vehicles, Electromobility, BRT, Hyperloop, Shared Use Mobility and Mobility-As-A-Service Shape Transport Futures for the Context of Smart Cities?" *Urban Science* 1 (4): 36. https://doi.org/10.3390/urbansci1040036.

Nordic Council of Ministers. 2021. *Enabling the Digital Green Transition: A Study of Potentials, Challenges, and Strengths in the Nordic-Baltic Region.* Copenhagen: Nordic Council of Ministers. https://pub.norden.org/nord2021-044/.

Pevec, Dario, Jurica Babic, Arthur Carvalho, Yashar Ghiassi-Farrokhfal, Wolfgang Ketter, and Vedran Podobnik. 2019. "Electric Vehicle Range Anxiety: An Obstacle for the Personal Transportation (R) Evolution?" In *2019 4th International Conference on Smart and Sustainable Technologies (Splitech),* 1–8. IEEE *Xplore.* https://ieeexplore.ieee.org/abstract/document/8783178.

Rolnick, D., P. L. Donti, L. H. Kaack, K. Kochanski, A. Lacoste, K. Sankaran, and A. S. Ross. 2022. "Tackling Climate Change with Machine Learning." *ACM Computing Surveys (CSUR)* 55 (2): 1–96.

Sukkarieh, Salah. 2017. "Mobile On-farm Digital Technology for Smallholder Farmers." In *2017: Transforming Lives and Livelihoods: The Digital Revolution in Agriculture.* Barton, Australian Capital Territory: Crawford Fund.

Taj, Frahim Wadud, Abdul Kadar Muhammad Masum, S. M. Taslim Reza, Md. Kalim Amzad Chy, and Iftekhar Mahbub. 2018. "Automatic Accident Detection and Human Rescue System: Assistance through Communication Technologies." In *2018 International Conference on Innovations in Science, Engineering and Technology (ICISET)*, 496–500. IEEE *xPlore*. https://ieeexplore.ieee.org/xpl/conhome/8736112/proceeding.

Tirachini, A. 2020. "Ride-Hailing, Travel Behaviour and Sustainable Mobility: An International Review." *Transportation* 47: 2011–47.

TWAICE. 2019. "EV Market Dynamics." https://www.twaice.com/article/ev-market-dynamics.

Wadud, Zia, and Jeevan Namala. 2022. "The Effects of Ridesourcing Services on Vehicle Ownership in Large Indian Cities." *Transportation Research Interdisciplinary Perspectives* 15. https://doi.org/10.1016/j.trip.2022.100631.

WBGU (German Advisory Council on Global Change). 2019. "Towards our Common Digital Future. Summary." WBGU, Berlin.

WEF (World Economic Forum). 2018. "Innovation with a Purpose: Improving Traceability in Food Value Chains through Technology Innovations." WEF, Cologny, Switzerland. https://www3.weforum.org/docs/WEF_Traceability_in_food_value_chains_Digital.pdf.

WEF (World Economic Forum). 2022. *Fostering Effective Energy Transition 2022 Edition*. Insight Report May 2022. Cologny, Switzerland: WEF. https://www3.weforum.org/docs/WEF_Energy_Transition_Index_2022.pdf.

Wolfert, Sjaak, Lan Ge, Cor Verdouw, and Marc-Jeroen Bogaardt. 2017. "Big Data in Smart Farming–A Review." *Agricultural Systems* 153: 69–80. https://www.sciencedirect.com/science/article/pii/S0308521X16303754.

World Bank. 2021. *World Development Report 2021: Data for Better Lives*. Washington, DC: World Bank. https://www.worldbank.org/en/publication/wdr2021.

World Bank. 2023. "Digital Africa: Technological Transformation for Jobs." World Bank, Washington, DC.

5. Digital Technologies for Resilience

Introduction

Globally, rising temperatures are already affecting the environment. Human society will have to adapt to their effects, which include more frequent extreme weather events, weather-related disasters, and rising sea levels. In 2021, the economic costs of weather- and climate-related events worldwide totaled US$329 billion, the third-highest annual total on record (after adjusting for inflation), trailing only 2017 and 2005.

329 billion

Low- and middle-income countries (LMICs) are particularly vulnerable to the effects of climate change. Eight of the 10 countries most affected by extreme weather events in 2019 were classified as low- and middle-income. Half were the least-developed countries (Reliefweb 2021). Geographically, many LMICs are exposed to the direct effects of rising temperatures and flooding because they lie at low elevations and have densely populated coastlines. Meanwhile, they have relatively weak physical infrastructure, which is vulnerable to disasters; their social services are ill-prepared to deal with extreme weather events; and many households lack the financial capacity to cope with the impacts of such events.

In recognition that some climate impacts are now unavoidable, countries have recently placed a greater emphasis on scaling adaptation efforts. Recovery initiatives designed to kickstart economies in the wake of the COVID-19 pandemic offer a unique opportunity to secure a green recovery by mainstreaming adaptation into public policy initiatives. Although early evidence suggests that progress on the development of national adaptation plans (NAPs) has been delayed by the pandemic, particularly among the least developed countries, there is ongoing progress on national adaptation planning agendas. About 79 percent of all countries have adopted at least one national-level adaptation planning instrument (such as a plan, strategy, policy, or law), which represents a 7 percent increase since 2020 (UNEP 2021). Progress in national-level adaptation planning must, however, be scaled up to avoid falling behind climate risks. In addition, the focus needs to be shifted from mainly corrective measures to prevention.

TABLE 5.1 Examples of Links between Digitalization and Adaptation

	Impact	Enabler
Long-term climate risks	*Household resilience.* Digitalization to reduce poverty and strengthen socioeconomic resilience	Scalable applications for • Public monitoring, reporting, decision-making • Sectors • Disaster risk management • Citizen engagement
	Sector adaptation. Digital solutions that help sectors adapt to climate change	
	Macroresilience. Digitalization to strengthen or diversify economies in response to climate change	
Climate shocks	*Disaster preparedness.* Digital solutions that build resilience to shocks or monitor weather	Digital skills
	Disaster management. Digitally enabled disaster risk management and early warning systems during climate shocks; continuity of business and services	Connectivity and data infrastructure
	Disaster recovery. Social protection enabled by digital identification; digital cash transfer after climate shocks	Digital governance and safeguards

Source: World Bank.

Low- and middle-income countries are vulnerable to both the long-term climate risks and short-term *climate shocks*. Digital technologies can be part of the solution to both sets of problems, as profiled in table 5.1 and discussed in the rest of this chapter.

Enhancing the Capacity to Adapt to Gradual Climate Impacts

Effects of Climate Change on Economies at the Household, Sector, and Macro Levels

At the household level, poverty is a core risk factor that increases vulnerability to climate change. Digital connectivity can contribute to equity through poverty reduction and higher household consumption. Across Africa, third-generation (3G) coverage has been linked to a 10 percent reduction in extreme poverty in Senegal (Masaki et al. 2020) and a 4.3 percent reduction in extreme poverty in Nigeria (Bahia et al. 2020). Digital development can also support socioeconomic development more widely by providing access to education, health care, financial services, and information, which are fundamental to socioeconomic resilience.

Within sectors, digital technologies are being applied to efforts to mitigate income erosion. In agriculture, for example, erratic weather and extreme climate events weaken farmers' livelihoods through loss of productive assets. Digital applications can enable smallholders to better manage the impacts of climate change through the provision of vital information and financial services. Data-driven agriculture services, for example, draw on remote sensing, weather, and farm-level data to monitor agricultural activity and enable evidence-based decision-making.

Agricultural digital financial services enable access to improved, climate-adapted technologies and serve as a safety net against income losses stemming from climate-induced weather patterns. Weather index insurance is an evolving adaptation instrument in this area. Agricultural insurance normally relies on direct measurement of the damage that each farmer suffers. However, field loss assessment is costly and time-consuming, especially when a large number of dispersed farmers cannot afford the inevitable delay in payments. Index-based insurance provides a promising alternative because payouts are triggered not by observed crop losses, but rather when an index—such as rainfall or average yield—rises above or falls below a prespecified threshold (box 5.1). Insurers can automate payouts and make them quickly. This process lowers administrative costs and premiums, compared with those associated with conventional crop insurance.

For many countries, sector adaptation is not enough. Diversification of economies toward more climate-resilient sectors is needed as well. The digital sector can diversify the economy and reduce dependence on sectors such as agriculture. The arrival of fast-speed internet, for example, is having a significant impact on firm productivity, exports, and job creation. When fast-speed internet becomes available, the probability that an individual is employed increases by up to 13.2 percent, total employment per firm increases by up to 22 percent, and firm exports nearly quadruple (Hjort and Poulsen 2019).

LMICs also need to generate and free up resources for climate change adaptation. Agriculture, infrastructure, water, and disaster risk management account for 75 percent of quantified adaptation finance needs (UNEP 2021). Katz and Callorda (2018) estimate that a 10 percent increase in mobile broadband penetration is associated with a 1.8 percent increase in gross domestic product (GDP) in middle-income countries and a 2 percent increase in GDP in low-income countries. In addition, a 1 percentage point increase in adoption of digital technologies is associated with growth in labor productivity of 1–2 percent, on average, in several African countries (Cirera, Comin, and Cruz 2022).

BOX 5.1   **East Africa's Index-Based Insurance**

The Agriculture and Climate Risk Enterprise (ACRE) is the largest index insurance program in the developing world and the largest agricultural insurance program in Sub-Saharan Africa. Farmers pay a market premium, and ACRE acts as their intermediary with insurance companies, reinsurers, and distribution channels/aggregators (such as microfinance institutions, agribusinesses, and agricultural input suppliers). The insurance premium is incorporated into the price of a bag of maize seed.

Each farm is monitored using satellite imagery for 21 days. If the index is triggered, farmers are automatically paid via the M-Pesa mobile phone platform. The indexes used by ACRE for its insurance projects are based on several data sources, including solar-powered automated weather stations, satellite rainfall measurements, and government area yield statistics. ACRE has 200,000 farmer clients in Kenya, Rwanda, and Tanzania. Insured farmers have invested 19 percent more in farm productivity than their uninsured neighbors, resulting in earnings 16 percent higher than those of the uninsured.

Source: Dinesh et al. 2017.

Although digitalization is linked to economic resilience and adaptation capacity, economic development can exacerbate vulnerability by, for example, driving environmental degradation or deepening inequality. In addition, there is an inherent trade-off among economic development, increasing production, and emissions that can exacerbate the need for adaptation.

Reporting and Decision-Making

Digital technologies can also help policy makers by providing tools and data to sharpen predictions and enhance decision-making. Scientific observations and evidence are essential for understanding the scale, urgency, and complexity of climate change, as well as assessing the prevailing uncertainties, which, in turn, are the indispensable basis for informed and evidence-based policy making (IPCC 2018). For example, data on weather and climate, precipitation, pollution, atmospheric composition, ocean parameters, natural resources, typhoons, and other natural disasters are allowing researchers and policy makers to better understand the causes of climate change and how it has unfolded over time.

Sensors mounted in cameras, drones, and satellites are used for real-time observation of natural environments and human and animal populations at the local, national, and global levels. Digital technologies deployed in radar- and radio-based meteorological systems and Earth observation satellites make it possible to study climate change and its effects at the micro and macro levels. Examples include spotting local hurricanes and tracking changes in sea level (ITU 2019; WBGU 2019). Satellite data provide authoritative information on more than half of the 50 crucial climate change variables, including atmospheric chemical composition and greenhouse gas emissions. Satellites are essential for systematic monitoring of changes in ice sheet volumes, sea level rise, and pollution and support recovery from major disasters (WBGU 2019; World Bank Group, GFDRR, EU, UNDP, and CEOS 2019). Currently, some 162 orbiting satellites are measuring indicators related to climate change (Chaturvedi 2020). Digital operators are also supporting initiatives, such as Argo, to build a real-time, high-resolution monitoring system for the world's oceans.

Measurement and monitoring endeavors increase the demand for analysis of large amounts of rapidly generated diverse data. Artificial intelligence (AI) and big data innovations are used to analyze, extract, and handle data from data sets that are too large or complex for the traditional data processing application software. Thus AI and these innovations are critical to understanding the causes of climate change and enabling predictive models and adaptation solutions. Although the data and models needed to understand climate change have greatly advanced (IPCC 1990), more fine-grained data are needed to assess efforts to adapt to the impacts of climate change. Estimates of anthropogenic-induced emissions and drivers are primarily based on climate models, which rely on global Earth observation data derived from ground-based and satellite measurements. More fine-grained data are also needed to evaluate policy and program performance (Hsu et al. 2020). Using satellites and AI can lower costs significantly and expand access to high resolution hazard maps. AI is, for example, enabling more affordable data on secondary and tertiary cities on issues such as flood risk and heat stress (GFDRR, Deltares, and the University of Toronto 2021).

Access to even basic climate and water data monitored by national, state, and local agencies is a major constraint in improving climate resilience around the world. In recent years, there has been an evolution in the ability for data sharing facilitated by flexible open copyright arrangements (World Bank 2023). Open application programming interfaces (APIs) and geospatial services using formats such as those developed by the Open Geospatial Consortium[1] have been important for this development.

Many countries, such as the United States and Australia, have facilitated in situ monitoring data access for hydrometeorological aspects (ranging from weather and flow monitors to reservoir water levels) that have helped spawn a plethora of public apps, research, applications, and collaboration. Austria and ESA have developed a Green Transition Information Factory that makes earth observation data available for diverse climate-related use cases.[2] However, in most of the countries (including those most vulnerable to climate challenges), well-organized open data services are lacking. The situation is even worse in transboundary river basins with a poor history of cooperation or constrained institutional capacity. Some of the modern innovative Earth observation and global analytics tools are helping interested stakeholders transcend this gap, but the quality of these services is often held hostage to the availability of critical in situ monitored data for calibration/training/validation. Collaboration among stakeholders and innovative business models are needed to overcome historical paradigms of data management and facilitate and finance public access models. The Digital Public Goods Alliance is one of several efforts to identify open data models for climate data (DPGA, ITU, and WMO 2022).[3]

Managing Climate Shocks with Digital Technologies

Digital infrastructure and applications can build adaptive capacity before, during, and after climate shocks.

Disaster Preparedness

Before climate shocks, digital financial and insurance services can serve to identify climate vulnerable communities and provide a safety net against income loss. For example, in Bangladesh, using a combination of early flood warnings and mobile money, the UN World Food Programme was able to provide households with US$53 in advance of peak flooding in 2020. The program demonstrated that households that received cash ahead of a crisis had better childhood food security and were more likely to evacuate and take on less debt. Similarly, the government of the Democratic Republic of Congo used satellite imagery of flood-prone areas to identify poor neighborhoods so it could roll out mobile payment account registration for cash transfers.

Digital technologies also play an important role in disaster preparedness. Geographic information systems (GIS) and, more recently, digital twins (virtual models) generate near real-time data that can support advanced flood modeling and simulations to enable cities to prepare for climate hazards.

Many big data applications introduced for use in early detection rely on data passively collected from digital services. Cities are leveraging digital technologies to move toward becoming "smart cities" that monitor the condition of their critical infrastructure—including roads, communications, power, and buildings—to optimize resources and monitor and prevent urban hazards. To better adapt to these types of events, resilient cities are using multisource data integration to generate actionable insights. Computer-aided design (CAD), building information modeling (BIM), geographic information systems, and more recently digital twins generate near-real-time data that can be streamlined into comprehensive workflows that generate actionable insights.

A digital twin is a virtual representation that serves as the real-time digital counterpart of a physical object or process. By using digital twins, cities receive advanced flood modeling and simulation that enable them to better prepare for flood risks. Through the integration of technologies such as artificial intelligence, machine learning, and software analytics with data, a digital twin creates a simulation model that can update alongside or in lieu of a physical counterpart. Digital twins provide comprehensive and actionable insights into flood risk assessment and mitigation. Lisbon, Portugal, created a digital twin for urban flood simulation that enabled the city to comprehensively model alternative scenarios and develop a plan for several return periods (box 5.2). This feature will help Lisbon better manage or even avoid 20 major floods over the next century.

Disaster Management

During climate shocks, early warning solutions can be critical to protecting vulnerable populations. In 2022, the United Nations set a five-year goal of ensuring that citizens worldwide are protected by digital early warning systems against extreme weather and climate change. Other digital technologies facilitate access to and sharing of data and analytics related to weather and disaster information (Aréstegui 2018). Digital platforms or mobile applications may facilitate cooperation between communities and decision-makers when responding to and acting on disasters such as floods (box 5.3) by disseminating timely warnings of risks such as via mobile devices or social media platforms (Balogun et al. 2019; Brink and Wamsler 2019; Cools, Innocenti, and O'Brien 2016). Digital systems also allow the continuity of business operations and public service delivery when physical connections are disrupted.

BOX 5.2   **Lisbon's Digital Twin for Flood Resilience**

Rising sea levels and frequent extreme rainfall events have increased Lisbon's flood risk. Between 1900 and 2006, Lisbon registered 84 inundations, whereas it had already registered 15 between 2008 and 2014. The region around Lisbon has been urbanizing rapidly, leading to soil imperviousness and more flooding in the region, but the city's infrastructure has not been adequate enough to ensure efficient drainage during extreme storm events.

In response, Lisbon created a city-scale digital twin for urban flood resilience. The digital twin helped the Lisbon city government create a drainage master plan for several return periods to better adapt to changing climate conditions and urbanization. It also implemented suitable flood protection measures. The plan has enabled the city to shift its strategy from a reactive to a proactive approach. This project will enhance the drainage capacity of existing stormwater systems, resulting in a new adaptation strategy that will help better manage floods over 100 years and save hundreds of millions of euros.

Source: Losier et al. 2019.

BOX 5.3   **Digitally Enhanced Flood Management**

Floods are the most common of all natural disasters and one of the most damaging to people, livelihoods, and infrastructure (AON 2021). New high-resolution flood hazard and population map analytics have revealed that about 1.47 billion people globally (almost one in every five persons) may be directly exposed to the risk of intense flooding, mostly (92.5 percent) in South and East Asia and mostly (89 percent) in low- and middle-income countries. However, of the 132 million estimated to live in extreme poverty (that is, on less than US$1.90 a day) *and* in high flood risk areas, 55 percent are in Sub-Saharan Africa (Rentschler and Salhab 2020). Digital technologies have also enabled a range of in situ hydrometeorological monitoring sensors, such as for water levels and discharges. To digest this type of complex information, cloud analytics have been leveraged to develop operational products for weather and flood inundation estimates. Finally, to communicate and crowdsource information, early warning solutions are leveraging digital applications and social media.

Disaster Recovery

After a climate shock, the availability of digital identification (ID) systems and digital financial services can allow rapid, targeted, and effective outreach to affected populations through cash transfers and information. Associated with a well-functioning data governance framework, ID systems can facilitate the safe exchange of data about a person across different databases such as social registries (World Bank 2021). Digital identification systems allow people to access services and perform transactions remotely and securely, without a face-to-face presence, which is especially needed during an emergency when physical interaction is inconvenient or impossible. Thus ID and associated foundational systems are critical for efficient social protection efforts after climate events. Other digital systems and applications have also shown to support recovery efforts through mobilization of resources and revitalization of affected sectors.

Challenges to Adoption of Digital Solutions for Climate Change Adaptation

Digital technologies offer opportunities for advancing adaptation, but they are not without challenges. The complexity of climate adaptation strategies requires an interdisciplinary approach that integrates a systematization of scientific knowledge measures across sectors. Data collection for tracking climate adaptation progress suffers from several overarching challenges.

Low-income countries are data scarce relative to industrialized countries. This can lead to poor return on investment from development financing. When resilience efforts, for example, rely on outdated or incomplete data, the most vulnerable beneficiaries might not be identified. Oftentimes, projects overlook recent informal developments that are generally the most climate vulnerable. Empowering local communities with tools for citizen science addresses two key issues: access to scarce data and mobilization of local communities. Digital tools can empower, formalize, and accelerate the work of citizen science and local advocacy groups. In South Africa, communities helped document climate-induced heat stress in informal settlements, which informed interventions (Jones, Gwata, and Akoon 2022).

Measuring the performance of adaptation initiatives is difficult because of a lack of benchmarks for assessing progress. Monitoring progress on climate action commitments is even more challenging because there is a lack of consistent definitions of adaptation activities, baselines, or benchmarks by which to assess progress, coupled with the lack of systematic reporting on adaptation progress and insufficiently large-scale data by which to assess progress. Establishing a common standard for comparing and measuring adaptation efforts is also difficult because of the different challenges and resources that different countries, cities, regions, and companies encounter.

Leveraging Earth observation (EO) and IoT data collection for climate change adaptation will further require technological innovations to store, process, interact, and analyze data. Because of the computational complexity of "Big Earth data," new models are required for how users interact and produce information from these new data. These models include new storage, processing, and retrieval approaches in order to leverage the full information power of the new data that these technologies can generate, thereby broadening the data uptake among users and supporting decision-makers with the evidence they require. Interoperability among EO and IoT systems, data types, and standards (which currently do not exist) is another challenge that must be overcome to effectively make use of the growing pool of EO and IoT data to assess climate change outcomes.

The lack of interoperability and standardization of IoT platforms jeopardizes not only the potential for mass data collection but also increases security vulnerabilities. Today, more than 300 IoT platforms are on the market, including platforms developed by major corporations such as Amazon, Cisco, IBM, Apple, Google, and Microsoft. Differences in each platform's IoT infrastructure, standards, proprietary protocols, and formats create closed ecosystems in which the IoT technology and services of platforms are incompatible. The problem of data heterogeneity in climate data is therefore not resolved with IoT alone. In addition, the lack of interoperability and standardization jeopardizes security because malicious actors can use these software vulnerabilities to reverse engineer techniques to control a device. Recently, the European Union tried to address the interoperability of IoT technology by proposing policies that attempt to standardize IoT technologies.

Finally, limited digital connectivity is an obstacle to the use of digital technologies for adaptation, especially for early warning systems and relief. Most poor populations live in rural and sparsely populated areas that lack connectivity. And some of these areas are more prone to climate shocks. A recent study of the landslide and riverine flooding hazards in Malawi and Ghana, respectively, found that the areas that are home to people in the bottom 40 percent of the wealth index are not covered by even second-generation (2G) mobile networks (Chi et al. 2022).[4] In Malawi, important portions of areas occupied by the bottom 40 percent and subject to cyclones, riverine flooding, and landslide hazards are not digitally connected (map 5.1). In Ghana (map 5.2), limited fourth-generation (4G) long-term evolution (LTE) coverage and lack of fifth-generation (5G) coverage could prevent the adoption of more data-intensive monitoring and early warning and relief systems targeting the most vulnerable populations. Investments that close the digital divide (connectivity, devices, and applications) are critical for this purpose. It is however important to plan beyond one-time investments. Oftentimes, projects fail because recurring costs such as operations and maintenance, skills, and human capital are not considered and financed, or because the technology is too complex. The default should be projects that leverage open standards, locally available devices, and engage local communities in solution development. The Global Facility for Disaster Reduction and Recovery (GFDRR) has supported many countries and extracted good practices for effective use of technology. However, more knowledge is needed to ensure digital development investments systematically support resilience efforts.

MAP 5.1 **Landslide Hazard Areas of Malawi Not Covered by 2G and 3G Mobile Networks and Occupied by Bottom 40 Percent of Wealth Index**

a. 2G GSM Uncovered Bottom 40%

b. 3G UMTS Uncovered Bottom 40%

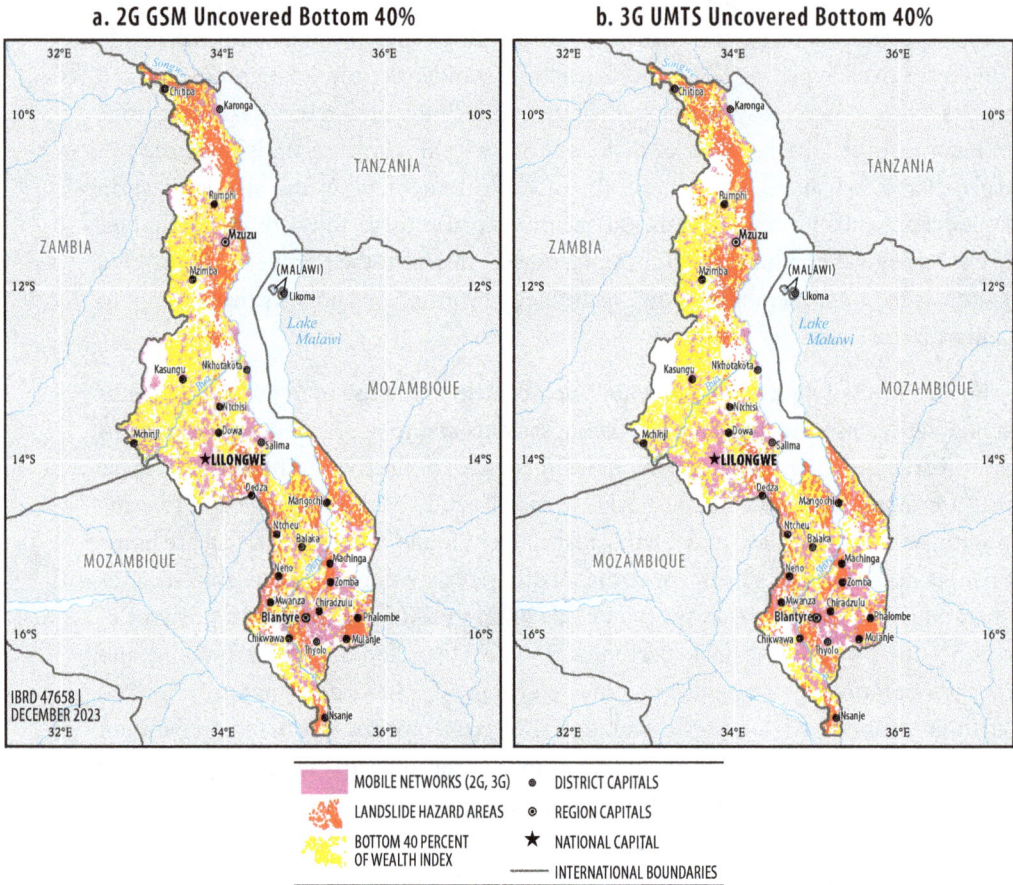

Legend:

- MOBILE NETWORKS (2G, 3G)
- LANDSLIDE HAZARD AREAS
- BOTTOM 40 PERCENT OF WEALTH INDEX
- ● DISTRICT CAPITALS
- ◎ REGION CAPITALS
- ★ NATIONAL CAPITAL
- —— INTERNATIONAL BOUNDARIES

Source: Oughton et al., 2023.

Note: Red indicates the uncovered bottom 40 percent of the population; black indicates areas with landslide risks. For more information, see the GFDRR website, https://www.gfdrr.org/en.

MAP 5.2 **Riverine Flooding Areas of Ghana Not Covered by 2G and 4G Mobile Networks and Occupied by Bottom 40 Percent of Wealth Index**

a. 2G GSM Uncovered Bottom 40%

b. 3G UMTS Uncovered Bottom 40%

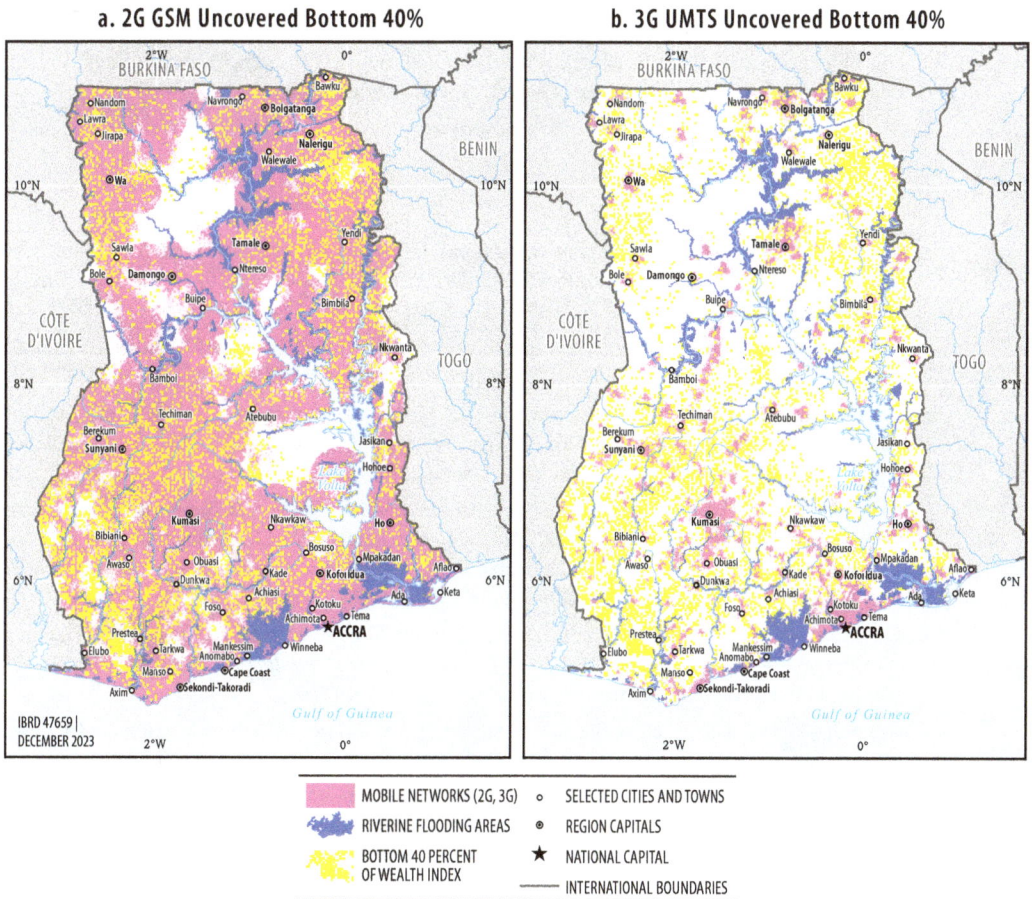

MOBILE NETWORKS (2G, 3G)

RIVERINE FLOODING AREAS

BOTTOM 40 PERCENT OF WEALTH INDEX

○ SELECTED CITIES AND TOWNS

◉ REGION CAPITALS

★ NATIONAL CAPITAL

― INTERNATIONAL BOUNDARIES

Source: Oughton et al., 2023.

Note: For more information, see the GFDRR website, https://www.gfdrr.org/en.

Notes

1. Open Geospatial Consortium website, https://www.ogc.org/.
2. Green Transition Information Factory, https://gtif.esa.int/.
3. For more information, also see the World Bank Group's *"Disrupting" HydroInformatics, An Interactive E-book.* https://spatialagent.org/HydroInformaticsEbook/.
4. Also see Global Poverty Map, http://www.povertymaps.net/.

References

AON. 2021. *2021 Weather, Climate and Catastrophe Insight.* London: AON. https://www.aon.com/getmedia/1b516e4d-c5fa-4086-9393-5e6afb0eeded/20220125-2021-weather-climate-catastrophe-insight.pdf.aspx.

Aréstegui, Miguel. 2018. "Intermediate Climate Information Systems for Early Warning Systems." Practical Action. https://infohub.practicalaction.org/handle/11283/620977.

Bahia, Kalvin, Pau Castells, Genaro Cruz, Takaaki Masaki, Xavier Pedrós, Tobias Pfutze, Carlos Rodríguez Castelán, et al. 2020. "The Welfare Effects of Mobile Broadband Internet: Evidence from Nigeria." Policy Research Working Paper 9230, World Bank, Washington, DC.

Balogun, Abdul-Lateef, Danny Marks, Richa Sharma, Himanshu Shekhar, Chiden Balmes, Dikman Maheng, Adnan Arshad, et al. 2019. "Assessing the Potentials of Digitalization as a Tool for Climate Change Adaptation and Sustainable Development in Urban Centres." *Sustainable Cities and Society* 58: 1–12. https://collections.unu.edu/view/UNU:7499.

Brink, E., and C. Wamsler. 2019. "Citizen Engagement in Climate Adaptation Surveyed: The Role of Values, Worldviews, Gender and Place." *Journal of Cleaner Production* 209: 1342–53. https://www.sciencedirect.com/science/article/pii/S0959652618331810.

Chaturvedi, Aditya. 2020. "How Satellite Imagery Is Crucial for Monitoring Climate Change." *Geospatial World* (blog). https://www.geospatialworld.net/blogs/satellites-for-monitoring-climate-change/.

Chi, Guanghau, Han Fang, Souray Chatterjee, and Joshua E. Blumenstock. 2022. "Microestimates of Wealth for All Low- and Middle-Income Countries." *PNAS* 119 (3): e2113658119. https://doi.org/10.1073/pnas.2113658119.

Cirera, Xavier, Diego Comin, and Mario Cruz. 2022. "Bridging the Technological Divide: Technology Adoption by Firms in Developing Countries." World Bank Productivity Project, World Bank, Washington, DC. https://openknowledge.worldbank.org/handle/10986/37527.

Cools, J., D. Innocenti, and S. O'Brien. 2016. "Lessons from Flood Early Warning Systems." *Environmental Science and Policy* 58: 117–22. https://www.sciencedirect.com/science/article/abs/pii/S1462901116300065.

Dinesh, Dhanush, Bruce M. Campell, Osana Bonilla-Findji, and Meryl Richards, eds. 2017. "10 Best Bet Innovations for Adaptation in Agriculture: A Supplement to the UNFCCC NAP Technical Guidelines." CCAFS Working Paper No. 215, CGIAR Research Program on Climate, Wageningen, The Netherlands.

DPGA (Digital Public Goods Alliance), ITU (International Telecommunication Union), and WMO (World Meteorological Organization). 2022. *Call for Weather, Climate, and Hydrological Information Datasets to Be Made Open and Freely Available as Digital Public Goods.* https://digitalpublicgoods.net/DPGA-Climate_Change_Adaptation_Report.pdf.

GFDRR (Global Facility for Disaster Reduction and Recovery), Deltares, and the University of Toronto. 2021. "Responsible Artificial Intelligence for Disaster Risk Management." Working Group Summary.

GTIF (Green Transition Information Factory/European Space Agency). https://gtif.esa.int/.

Hjort, Jonas, and Jonas Poulsen. 2019. "The Arrival of Fast Internet and Employment in Africa." *American Economic Review* 109 (3): 1032–79. https://www.aeaweb.org/articles?id=10.1257/aer .20161385.

Hsu, A., W. Khoo, N. Goyal, and M. Wainstein. 2020. "Next-Generation Digital Ecosystem for Climate Data Mining and Knowledge Discovery: A Review of Digital Data Collection Technologies." *Frontiers in Big Data* 3 (September 10).

IPCC (Intergovernmental Panel on Climate Change). 1990. *Climate Change. The IPCC Scientific Assessment.* Cambridge, UK; New York: Cambridge University Press.

IPPC (Intergovernmental Panel on Climate Change). 2018. "Special Report. Global Warming of 1.5°C." https://www.ipcc.ch/sr15/.

ITU (International Telecommunication Union). 2019. "2019—Report on Turning Digital Technology Innovation into Climate Action." ITU, Geneva. https://www.itu.int/en/publications/Pages /publications.aspx?lang=es&media=paper&parent=T-TUT-ICT-2019.

Jones, Nick, Mzukisi Gwata, and Is'haaq Akoon. 2022. "Beating the Heat in South African Cities: Lessons from a Citizen Science Assessment." Sustainable Cities (blog), November 17. https:// blogs.worldbank.org/sustainablecities/beating-heat-south-african-cities-lessons-citizen -science-assessment.

Katz, R., and F. Callorda. 2018. "The Economic Contribution of Broadband, Digitization and ICT Regulation." International Telecommunication Union, Geneva.

Losier, Louis-Martin, Fernandes Rodrigo, Palo Tabarro, and Frank Branschweig. 2019. "The Importance of Digital Twins for Resilient Infrastructure." A Bently White Paper. https://cdn2 .webdamdb.com/md_A6HafPVAhHf0.jpg.pdf.

Masaki, Takaaki, Rogelio Granguillhome Ochoa, and Carlos Rodríguez-Castelán. 2020. "Broadband Internet and Household Welfare in Senegal." Policy Research Working Paper 9386, World Bank, Washington, DC.

Oughton, E. J., J. Oh, S. Ballan, and K. Kusuma. 2023. "Sustainability Assessment of 4G and 5G Universal Mobile Broadband Strategies." Policy Research Working Paper, World Bank, Washington, DC. https://doi.org/10.48550/arXiv.2311.05480.

Reliefweb. 2021. *Global Climate Risk Index 2021: Who Suffers Most from Extreme Weather Events? Weather-Related Loss Events in 2019 and 2000–2019.* New York: United Nations Office for the Coordination of Humanitarian Affairs. https://reliefweb.int/report/world/global-climate-risk-index-2021.

Rentschler, Jun, and Melda Salhab. 2020. "People in Harm's Way: Flood Exposure and Poverty in 189 Countries." Policy Research Working Paper 9447, World Bank, Washington, DC. https:// openknowledge.worldbank.org/entities/publication/04ad161e-7144-5984-8b85-91710f2900b4.

UNEP (United Nations Environment Programme). 2021. *Adaptation Gap Report 2021. The Gathering Storm: Adapting to Climate Change in a Post-Pandemic World.* Nairobi, Kenya: UNEP. https:// www.unep.org/resources/adaptation-gap-report-2021.

WBGU (German Advisory Council on Global Change). 2019. "Towards our Common Digital Future. Summary." WBGU, Berlin.

World Bank. 2021. *World Development Report 2021: Data for Better Lives.* Washington, DC: World Bank. https://www.worldbank.org/en/publication/wdr2021.

World Bank. 2023. "Digital Public Goods for Disaster Risk Reduction in a Changing Climate." World Bank, Washington, DC.

World Bank Group, GFDRR (Global Facility for Disaster Reduction and Recovery), EU (European Union), UNDP (United Nations Development Program), and CEOS (Committee on Earth Observation Satellites). 2019. "Use of EO Satellites in Support of Recovery from Major Disasters: Taking Stock and Moving Forward." https://www.gfdrr.org/sites/default/files/publication/Use _of_EO_Satellites_012322020_D_LOW-RES.pdf.

6. Policy Recommendations: Coordinated Action for Green Digitalization

The Key Principles of Green Digitalization

Governments have a stake in enabling and encouraging the information and communication technology (ICT) sector and other actors to use the full power of digital technology to advance the mitigation of and adaptation to climate change, while mitigating the impacts of increased digitalization on the climate. However, governments are not alone in pursuing these goals and should coordinate their efforts with the private sector, nongovernmental organizations (NGOs), international development organizations, financial institutions, and the public at large. The key principles that should inform green digitalization strategies are described in the following sections.

Consider Context

- *Consider risk and emissions profiles.* Priorities and the scope of feasible government policy interventions vary by country. A country's climate risk profile and carbon footprint should guide green digitalization priorities. Low- and middle-income countries (LMICs) are particularly exposed to climate change and so need to identify cost-effective ways to adapt through digital and other means. All countries need to reduce global greenhouse gas (GHG) emissions, especially high-emitting countries. And they all should include the ICT sector in their mitigation strategies by both reducing emissions from the sector and leveraging digital technologies for mitigation.
- *Calculate costs and benefits in a local context.* Most but not all energy efficiency measures and green technology choices are cost-effective. Costs and benefits should be assessed considering a country's development profile and weighed against other development priorities, such as digital inclusion.
- *Remember that climate tech does not have to be high tech.* For artificial intelligence (AI) and other emerging technologies, the rate of technological climate innovation is accelerating. However, there is a risk that investments in advanced solutions might fail in countries with low digital maturity. As noted in this report, simple solutions based on phone messaging services may be the more

effective short-term solution while digital foundations are being strengthened. At the same time, high-tech and high-performing solutions should be tailored to the needs of LMICs—a process that could also be the source of global inspiration. A durable phone should be both affordable and climate-friendly for citizens globally.

Build Foundations for Scale

- *Invest in digital enablers and foundations.* Promising climate applications are emerging and being piloted, but many fail to scale. Often, digital enablers and risks are not factored into project plans. To support a green transition, digital enablers need to be considered at the project level and digital foundations at the national level. Areas for investment include connectivity, digital skills, and safeguards, as well as global and local investments in digital public goods requiring data access, management, and governance.

- *Ensure the resilience of critical digital infrastructure.* Climate events inevitably have an impact on digital infrastructure. Nevertheless, governments can improve its resilience by incentivizing the adoption of resilient technology choices, requiring consideration of climate risks in design/deployment/upgrade processes, and ensuring adequate redundancy while maximizing infrastructure sharing. Meanwhile, the digital sector is connected with other utility or infrastructure sectors such as water, transportation, and energy. Disruptions of the internet are likely to affect real-time traffic management, while power supply is essential for the functioning of the telecommunications network. Therefore, a holistic, systemwide view that takes into account the resilience of critical infrastructure of all kinds is needed in policy design and implementation.

- *Reach rural populations to enhance resilience.* A key concern is whether digital solutions and digital investments reach the people, regions, and countries most vulnerable to hazards arising from climate change. Rural areas are a particular challenge because population density and connectivity costs reduce commercial viability. Often, climate vulnerability is correlated with other development stressors. Strategies to close the digital divide should target population groups vulnerable to climate change alongside other priorities.

Disrupt the Trajectory

- *Decouple digitalization from emissions.* Because nearly 3 billion people remain offline across the globe, fostering digital inclusion is of great importance. Investing in digital infrastructure and addressing constraints in accessing and using a fast, reliable, safe, and affordable internet provide opportunities for countries to accelerate economic growth. The impacts of climate change cannot be neglected during digital transformation. As noted in this report, emissions from the sector need to be halved by 2030, calling for both deeper and wider mitigation efforts. For example, effective measures need to be mainstreamed across countries and stakeholders. All countries should accelerate their adoption of smarter, more energy-efficient equipment, devices, and processes; expand the use of renewable energy in the ICT sector; and apply digital technologies effectively to reduce GHG emissions from other sectors. Policies are needed across the digital value chain, covering networks and devices, data infrastructure, and data use for digital applications (see section "Greening along the Digital Value Chain"). Meanwhile, new, transformative measures are needed to keep up with digital growth. Significant investments in research and innovation are needed to rethink digital power sources, durability, battery life, and other mitigation drivers.

- *Leverage position in the value chain.* Because of the global nature of the ICT sector, emissions from some parts of the value chain are concentrated in a few countries, such as those with digital manufacturing or large data centers. This factor naturally shapes the sphere of influence for global stakeholders. Governments can influence their own private sector and engage internationally to set standards and apply them at home.

Develop a Twin Transition Policy

- *Break policy silos.* Green digitalization calls for whole-of-government approaches. Digital policies need to be "greened," and climate policies need to be digitalized. Digital ministries must consider national climate risks and ambitions and support the ICT sector in contributing positively. Climate entities and sector ministries should engage digital stakeholders to ensure that digital foundations are adequate for climate applications. They may also require capacity building on how to apply digital technologies effectively and to recognize digital risks.
- *Apply agile regulation principles.* The green–digital nexus is uncharted territory for most governments. Agile policy principles can help governments create a responsive enabling environment for green digitalization. So-called regulatory sandboxes and support for innovation test beds can enable novel approaches to data use and testing of climate-friendly digital technologies.
- *Improve data for decision-making.* Energy consumption and emissions data from the ICT sector are needed to inform policy making. The relevant data include breakdowns by different segments and types of emissions to ascertain the scale of sector emissions compared with those of the economy, as well as trends over time. Efforts to define standard methodologies, obtain data, and create confidence in reporting and monitoring have not been as strong in the ICT sector as in other sectors, but different standards and initiatives are under way, such as those led by the International Telecommunication Union (ITU). At the country level, public institutions in some countries (such as France,

Rwanda, and Singapore) are beginning to build the frameworks and capacity needed to collect this data.

Change Together

- *Engage the private sector.* As described in this report, emissions from the ICT sector are found across the digital value chain. Thus the full global digital value chain—from manufacturing to connectivity to production of digital services—needs to be engaged. Companies play a key role in green digitalization. Multinational digital companies can make a positive climate contribution because they have not only a big carbon footprint but also considerable expertise in and resources for reducing emissions. Moreover, they have a natural interest in reducing energy consumption and associated costs, as demonstrated by changes in the telecommunication value chain and data center industry. Many companies are partnering in initiatives such as the UN 24/7 Carbon-free Energy Compact, Circular Electronics Partnership, and European Green Digital Coalition. Standards, certification programs, and measurement practices developed by the private sector could inform the design of government interventions for climate action in the ICT sector. Digital companies can potentially have a say in spurring development of the renewable energy industry in markets where their purchases of clean energy can initiate a virtuous circle. Furthermore, voluntary offsets of carbon—backed up by data-driven verification solutions—can generate funding for renewable energy projects, reforestation, clean cookstoves, and pay-as-you-go solar, thereby contributing to sustainable development. Governments should engage and motivate the private sector by means of policies, enabling infrastructure, and investments in skills, research, and innovation.
- *Engage across sectors. The* greatest promise of digitalization lies in its decarbonizing potential within and across sectors. But links among sectors also create complex interdependencies. The digital–energy nexus is a case in point. Greening the ICT sector requires access to renewable energy, which depends on national energy policies and actions. At the same time, the ICT sector is pioneering the use of renewables and can drive demand. Governments play an important role through their renewable energy policies and investments and by enabling direct power purchase agreements by firms.
- *Engage academia and civil society.* In influencing government and the private sector and harnessing the power of communities, NGOs and civil society represent the interests of the general public as it faces the challenges of climate change. Academic institutions can play a key role in helping public and private firms understand climate change and the role of digital technologies. However, digital technologies are not a panacea. As described in this report, some solutions may reduce unit-level emissions while boosting overall usage, producing a rebound effect. Because these effects are not always foreseeable at the outset, constant

attention should be paid to measuring and balancing the climate-friendly effects of a given innovation and the possible rebound effects. Substantial research will be needed to clarify these relationships and guide climate action.

- *Engage citizens.* The public has many roles. People are consumers of climate-friendly products and services. They support climate action initiatives through daily practice or political leverage. To the extent that they understand the overall challenges and options of climate change, they can take the opportunity at work and in other areas of daily life to use green digital tools to advance climate goals. Digital platforms are an important avenue for educating and engaging citizens in climate action and for enhancing accountability and trust in government climate action. Citizens also need to be engaged in reducing the carbon footprint of the ICT sector. Data centers and AI algorithms can be energy-intensive, but the same is also true of the millions of emails, video calls, and bytes of stored data—and of the production of the millions of devices used every day globally. Greening digital requires big and small actions across multiple stakeholders, including individual users. Sensitization and incentives will be needed from government, as well as adequate infrastructure to support more climate-friendly behavior.

Greening along the Digital Value Chain

Along the digital value chain, telecom networks, digital devices, and data centers each contribute to about a third of the carbon footprint of the telecom sector. Nevertheless, they possess different characteristics and challenges, requiring targeted policy interventions.

Telecom Networks

To decarbonize telecom networks, governments can create an enabling environment for access to renewable energy and boost energy efficiency through incentives, standards, and monitoring. Telecom networks also need to be protected from climate risks. Specifically:

- Governments have an important role to play in eliminating barriers to the use of renewable energy by telecom operators. This role includes enabling power purchase agreements and allowing the self-provision of electricity. Operation of telecom energy services companies (TESCOs) that can also power minigrids is another alternative. This is particularly important for off-grid areas and where fossil fuels dominate the electricity system.
- Governments can also establish mechanisms to incentivize energy efficiency and efficient network deployment. In many countries where (passive or active) infrastructure sharing is desirable, frameworks are still ineffective. Governments could help revise these frameworks and implement them more proactively. Dig-once policies and mutualization rules can be useful to boost efficiency in network deployment,

including through collaboration across sectors. For both mechanisms, competition should be considered to, for example, avoid barriers to new entrants.

- Consideration of climate and environmental factors is an option when awarding licenses and granting state aid and for the operation of partially or fully state-owned digital infrastructure. Countries are also considering setting standards for network deployment to ensure energy efficiency and sustainability. Supporting the inclusion of green considerations in universal service funds is a cost-effective way to ensure greener network expansion. Governments could also ensure that requirements for low-carbon and resilient connectivity are embedded in public-private partnerships. In areas with poor or no grid connectivity, governments could support the use of off-grid renewable energy.

- In countries exposed to climate hazards, governments should support the deployment of resilient infrastructure to connect areas at risk and provide redundancy. They could also set up funds to plug gaps in investments in ensuring redundancy for resilience. Moreover, emergency and preparedness plans are needed for critical digital infrastructure to enable quick recovery of services and prioritization of critical communications and services in the wake of a climate event. Advanced technologies such as artificial intelligence can be leveraged to monitor, prepare for, and respond to climate shocks that can affect digital infrastructure. The use of basic digital connectivity (such as 2G+ mobile networks for early warning systems and mobility data analysis) should be integrated into disaster risk management plans. In the European Union, operators are mandated by law to push emergency warnings through telecom networks. Governments could also update spectrum management to allow for reliable postdisaster connectivity and emergency communications.

Data Infrastructure

As the use of digital applications expands, the capacity and energy consumption of data centers are expected to grow. To decouple data infrastructure from energy consumption and emissions, wider use of renewable energy, greater energy efficiency, and lower energy consumption from data center cooling are all essential. Specifically:

- Global players in the data center realm have committed to important emissions targets, in some cases making access to renewable energy a precondition for investment. Reporting methods and purchase of carbon credits to offset emissions have, however, been subject to discussion. Governments should enable and incentivize carbon reductions within the corporate value chain and encourage not only global companies but also small and large local players to participate.

- Standards and certification schemes that fit local needs need to be developed and supported, and they can engage the private sector. As noted in this report, a growing number of countries are already doing this. Governments can use international standards as a benchmark for the development of data infrastructure and adjust them to local conditions.

- The government, as a user and regulator of data infrastructure, also has a role in considering emissions and resilience in public procurement, choosing green options when feasible for data storage and computing.
- Data centers should be considered critical infrastructure and the appropriate measures taken to mitigate climate risks. Adaptation strategies can cover site selection, design and building construction, operation, risk management, and recovery. The additional capital costs of integrating resilience must be weighed against the benefits of avoiding service interruption and data losses. Public sector oversight may be needed to avoid underinvestment in resilience that may lead to interruptions in service that affect individuals who are not protected by stringent service agreements. The availability of detailed data on climate hazards as a public good can facilitate risk assessment and due diligence for both the public and private sector.

Digital Devices

A range of policy instruments could be conducive to minimizing carbon dioxide emissions linked to the manufacture, use, and disposal of digital devices, targeting both the supply and demand sides. Specifically:

- On the supply side, governments can promote the manufacture of durable and repairable devices, e-waste management, energy efficiency, and ecodesign. Examples include imposing mandatory standards on higher recycling rates for digital devices. Research and development on the increased modularity, repairability, and recyclability of technological components can also help prolong the lifetime of digital devices. Labels and certificates could promote responsible and sustainable design. The manufacture of digital devices tends to be concentrated in a few countries. Adoption of global green standards for manufacturing should be encouraged in those countries.
- On the demand side, for users of digital devices it is important to increase the transparency of individual users' digital carbon footprints to mitigate a rebound effect. Information campaigns to promote shifts from a throwaway mentality to a recycling mentality among public and private sector consumers have been found to be effective. Extended producer responsibility and clean information technology labels for sustainable ICT products may also allow for more informed consumer choices.

Data and Applications

A sound data ecosystem is needed to support digital applications for climate action. Appropriate investments and regulations will enable good use of data for informed policy decisions and monitoring, innovation to address local climate challenges, and adoption of pro-climate digital technologies across sectors. Examples include the following:

- A commitment to open-access climate data is among the first steps to making informed policy decisions and developing digital solutions to combat climate change. Weather, climate, and hydrological data, as well as outputs from climate modeling, should be made available to all countries on a free, unrestricted basis whenever possible, building on public-private partnerships. Governments can adopt open-data laws to establish ex ante responsibility for the disclosure of public data and standards to facilitate use and accessibility. Adoption of an open licensing regime, such as a Creative Commons License, maximizes the benefits of making data available. For the private sector, voluntary licensing on fair, reasonable, and nondiscriminatory terms helps promote data sharing by encouraging companies and patent holders to share technology and data. Access to data to develop new digital solutions, train algorithms, and test products is central to generating a green digital innovation ecosystem.
- Data interoperability is essential in facilitating the use of data among stakeholders at the local, regional, and global levels. Data sharing within ecosystems is critical for solutions such as efficient logistics chains, urban transportation systems, and smart grids.
- Safeguards are important. A secure, trusted environment is needed so that countries are able to apply advanced digital technology to address climate change, while also avoiding the risks associated with digital technologies. A lack of cybersecurity may deter people and enterprises from using digital technologies. Cybersecurity risks expand exponentially with the use of IoT, putting whole industries at risk. A robust data governance framework that enables data use and reuse while safeguarding the rights and personal information of data subjects promotes trust in digital solutions.
- Efficient data governance across digital solutions and platforms cannot be realized without enhanced digital literacy and skills among the public. The situation may be worse in LMICs where literacy rates are low. Better digital skills are also needed within businesses and government institutions to make informed decisions about leveraging digital solutions for climate action.

Governments, private companies, the broad community of nongovernment and scientific organizations, and the public at large share the burden and challenge of climate action. Emissions from the ICT sector value chain are concentrated in countries where digital manufacturing takes place or large data centers operate. This naturally shapes the sphere of influence for global stakeholders. Governments can influence their private sector and engage internationally to set standards, and the private sector can shape its value chain (table 6.1).

TABLE 6.1 Actions to Be Pursued by Stakeholders along the Digital Value Chain

	Digital connectivity	Data infrastructure	Data use for digital applications	Devices
International	Devise energy efficiency and ecodesign standards for devices and equipment. Develop a methodology and indicators to calculate digital emissions and energy efficiency.	Converge standards and definitions of climate-friendly data infrastructure. Create certification programs for green data centers.	Enable trusted cross-border data flows to support data sharing, including interoperability of data protection frameworks for global and regional digital solutions. Establish global platforms to share climate data.	Establish global standards to promote the manufacture of durable and repairable devices, e-waste management, energy efficiency, and ecodesign.
National	Set policy targets at the country level and provide methodological guidance for measurement. Facilitate access to renewable energy and integration of renewable energy into the digital value chain.			
	Draft rules for infrastructure sharing; pro-climate spectrum management; public-private partnerships and public investments with green requirements; and mechanisms for e-waste management, recycling, and repairability of devices.	Provide guidance on standards and certification mechanisms and transparency. Promote green procurement of data center equipment and cloud services.	Draft rules for data protection, data sharing, and cybersecurity. Provide incentives for the adoption of digital technology across sectors. Pursue policies to boost green digital innovation. Establish artificial intelligence (AI) principles and rules. Create data-sharing platforms to facilitate the exchange of climate information for monitoring, preparedness, and responses.	Draft standards for higher recycling rates for digital devices. Provide research and development support for increased modularity, repairability, and recyclability of technological components.
Digital companies	Adopt net zero commitments to energy-efficient equipment, renewable energy, and carbon offsets; the repurposing and reuse of decommissioned infrastructure; and the circular economy approach for devices. Adopt transparency on emissions for governments, investors, and consumers. Adopt climate-resilient infrastructure to ensure fulfillment of service-level agreements, including for retail markets.	Adopt net zero commitments to energy-efficient equipment and cooling systems, renewable energy, carbon offsets, and appropriate equipment management. Adopt transparency on emissions. Adopt climate-resilient infrastructure to ensure fulfillment of service-level agreements.	Limit spurious data analysis and computational capacity for blockchain and AI. Share essential climate data for compliance, preparedness, and responses.	Extend producer responsibility. Launch information campaigns to enhance customer awareness.

Source: World Bank.

The Way Forward

The global community must undertake important tasks to achieve green digitalization. The ICT sector lags other sectors when it comes to understanding the links with climate change. Despite digitalizing rapidly, few countries are able to report emissions from the ICT sector. Stronger methodologies and country-level capacity are needed. In the data center industry, efforts toward greening are common, but internationally recognized standards are lacking. Examples of country-level or regional codes of conduct are emerging, and these are important for setting a common direction. For cross-sectoral technologies, the focus is moving from uncritical optimism to tough but necessary exploration of the positive and negative drivers of emissions. Multistakeholder partnerships are leading the way, and these will be critical in determining which solutions and approaches deserve to be scaled up through investments.

Financing investments in low-carbon and resilient digital technologies, especially where ability to pay is limited, is a pressing topic. The adoption of digital technologies in climate change strategies will require significant investments in networks, devices, applications, capabilities, and services. An estimated US$428 billion is needed to achieve universal coverage of a minimum level of quality broadband, calling for a new mindset when allocating climate financing. Currently, the ICT sector is largely ignored in climate financing. There is no direct investment in digital infrastructure among multilateral climate funds such as the Green Climate Fund and the Global Environment Facility. Similarly, the power of digital platforms and transparency should be leveraged to improve the climate financing landscape.

The international community, including development banks, has a role to play in facilitating financing resources. Private sector funding is essential in filling in the financing gap. Some of those investments will have to be cofinanced by the public sector through investment in sustainable and resilient infrastructure. Meanwhile, domestic digital ecosystems would benefit from access to venture capital as well as government financing facilities and services (such as incubation and acceleration programs). Approaches must be designed to avoid crowding out private investors and to make public investments effective and efficient.

This report is the first by the World Bank to address the relationship between digitalization and climate change with the aim of providing policy makers in low- and middle-income countries with information about the opportunities and risks digitalization can bring to combating climate change. The World Bank Climate and Digital Business line helps countries translate green digital ambitions into effective policies, investments, and innovations. This includes offering practitioners guidance material related to climate proofing digital infrastructure, greening data infrastructure, and greening telecom networks. However, more action is needed. The World Bank welcomes cross-sectoral collaboration and partnerships to move this important agenda forward.

Appendix. Nationally Determined Contributions

For this report, an analysis was conducted of the Nationally Determined Contributions (NDCs) submitted by 199 countries (tables A.1 and A.2) to the United Nations Framework Convention on Climate Change (UNFCCC 2022). Countries were selected from the Energy and Climate Intelligence Unit's Net Zero Tracker,[1] which is an effort to increase the transparency and accountability of the net zero targets of states and regions, countries, cities, and companies. This analysis covered the general technologies (table A.3) and digital technologies (table A.4) mentioned in both adaptation and mitigation actions in the submitted NDCs. Also covered was an analysis of the sectors that countries have prioritized for climate action.

TABLE A.1 Number of Countries and Economies in Analysis, by Income Level

Income group	Number
Low-income	27
Lower-middle-income	55
Upper-middle-income	56
High-income	59
Unclassified[a]	2
Total	199

Source: World Bank.

a. "Unclassified" refers to Niue and the European Union. European Union countries submitted one Nationally Determined Contribution. The income group classification is based on the World Bank's 2019–20 income group classification (World Bank 2019).

TABLE A.2 Countries and Economies Included in Analysis, by Country or Economy Income Group

Low-income	Lower-middle-income	Upper-middle-income	High-income
Afghanistan	Algeria	Albania	Andorra
Burkina Faso	Angola	American Samoa	Antigua and Barbuda
Burundi	Bangladesh	Argentina	Australia
Central African Republic	Benin	Armenia	Austria
Chad	Bhutan	Azerbaijan	Bahamas, The Bahrain
Congo, Dem. Rep.	Bolivia	Belarus	Barbados

(Table continues on the following page)

TABLE A.2 Countries and Economies Included in Analysis, by Country or Economy Income Group *(continued)*

Low-income	Lower-middle-income	Upper-middle-income	High-income
Congo, Rep.	Cabo Verde	Belize	Belgium
Eritrea	Cambodia	Bosnia and Herzegovina	Bermuda
Ethiopia	Cameroon	Botswana	Brunei
Gambia, The	Comoros	Brazil	Canada
Guinea	Côte d'Ivoire	Bulgaria	Cayman Islands
Guinea-Bissau	Djibouti	China	
Korea, Dem. People's Rep.	Egypt, Arab Rep.	Colombia	
Liberia	El Salvador	Costa Rica	Chile
Madagascar	Eswatini	Cuba	Croatia
			Cyprus
			Czech Republic
Malawi	Ghana	Dominica	Denmark
Mali	Haiti	Dominican Republic	Estonia
Mozambique	Honduras	Ecuador	European Union
Niger	India	Equatorial Guinea	Finland
	Indonesia	Fiji	France
Rwanda	Iran, Islamic Rep.	Gabon	Germany
Sierra Leone	Kenya	Georgia	Greece
Somalia	Kiribati	Grenada	Hungary
South Sudan	Kyrgyz Republic	Guatemala	Iceland
Sudan	Lao PDR	Guyana	Ireland
Syrian Arab Republic	Lebanon	Iraq	Israel
Togo	Lesotho	Jamaica	Italy
Uganda	Mauritania	Jordan	Japan
			Korea, Rep.
Yemen, Rep.	Micronesia, Fed. Sts.	Kazakhstan	Kuwait
Zambia	Mongolia	Kosovo	Liechtenstein
	Morocco	Libya	Lithuania
	Myanmar		Luxembourg
	Nepal	Malaysia	Malta
	Nicaragua	Maldives	Monaco
	Nigeria	Marshall Islands	Nauru
	Pakistan	Mauritius	Netherlands
		Mexico	New Zealand
	Papua New Guinea	Moldova	Norway
	Philippines	Montenegro	Oman
	Samoa	Namibia	Panama
	São Tomé and Príncipe	Niue	Poland

(Table continues on the following page)

TABLE A.2   Countries and Economies Included in Analysis, by Country or Economy Income Group *(continued)*

Low-income	Lower-middle-income	Upper-middle-income	High-income
	Senegal	North Macedonia	Portugal
	Solomon Islands	Palau	Qatar
	Sri Lanka	Paraguay	
	Tajikistan	Peru	Romania
	Tanzania	Russian Federation	
	Timor-Leste	Serbia	San Marino
	Tunisia	South Africa	Saudi Arabia
	Ukraine	St. Lucia	Seychelles
	Uzbekistan	St. Vincent and the Grenadines	Singapore
	Vanuatu	Suriname	Slovak Republic
	Viet Nam	Switzerland	Slovenia
	West Bank and Gaza	Thailand	Spain
			St. Kitts and Nevis
	Zimbabwe	Tonga	Sweden
		Türkiye	
		Turkmenistan	Trinidad and Tobago
		Tuvalu	United Arab Emirates
			United Kingdom

Sources: Nationally Determined Contributions Registry, United Nations, New York, https://unfccc.int/NDCREG, October 2022; Energy and Climate Intelligence Unit, United Kingdom.

TABLE A.3   Classification of General Technologies Considered in Analysis, by Mitigation and Adaptation

Mitigation	Adaptation
Renewable energy	Smart agriculture
Clean energy	Technologies for climate-resilient infrastructure
E-mobility/electric vehicles	Desalination technologies
Energy conversion technologies (waste to energy)	Early warning systems
Digitalization of processes and services	Disruptive technology use for adaptation (artificial intelligence, Internet of Things, drones)
Greenhouse gas emissions monitoring and verification systems	Software for data collection, verification, and monitoring for adaptation
Carbon trading	Capacity building in innovative climate technologies
Zero and low emissions technologies	Nature-based solutions
Energy-efficient technologies	Geographic information systems, remote sensing, satellites for mapping, and so forth
	Smart grids

Source: World Bank.

TABLE A.4 **Classification of Digital Technologies Considered in Analysis, by Adaptation and Mitigation**

Digital mitigation	Digital adaptation
Energy-efficient technologies (smart grids, smart buildings, smart agriculture)	Smart agriculture
Greenhouse gas emissions monitoring and verification systems	Early warning systems
Transport management systems	Databases and systems for collection, verification, and monitoring of forestry, water, coastal zone, and climate change data
Satellite imagery for emissions reduction monitoring	Geographic information systems, satellites for mapping, and so forth
Information and communication technology for mitigation measures	hydrometeorological monitoring systems
	Information and communication technology for adaptation measures

Source: World Bank.

TABLE A.5 **Number of Mentions of Mitigation and Adaptation Technologies (General and Digital) in Nationally Determined Contributions and Percentage of Countries Mentioning Technologies**

Mitigation		Adaptation	
Total mentions of mitigation technologies	165	Total mentions of adaptation technologies	124
Percent of countries mentioning mitigation technologies	83%	Percent of countries mentioning adaptation technologies	62%
Total mentions of digital technologies for mitigation	89	Total mentions of digital technologies for adaptation	105
Percent of countries mentioning digital technologies for mitigation	45%	Percent of countries mentioning digital technologies for adaptation	53%

Source: World Bank.

Of the 199 countries analyzed, 83 percent mentioned mitigation technologies in their NDCs, and 62 percent mentioned adaptation technologies (table A.5). Forty-five percent of countries noted they relied on one or more digital technologies for mitigation, and 53 percent of countries relied on one or more digital technologies for adaptation.

In table A.6, general and digital mitigation and adaptation technologies are broken down by country income group for the 199 countries in the analysis.

Table A.7 shows the priority sectors for mitigation and adaptation in countries in the analysis, classified by income group.

TABLE A.6 General and Digital Mitigation and Adaptation Technologies Mentioned in Nationally Determined Contributions, by Country Income Level

	Low-income	Lower-middle-income	Upper-middle-income	High-income
Mitigation technologies	23	45	46	51
No mitigation technologies	4	10	10	8
Digital technologies for mitigation	14	26	22	27
Adaptation technologies	22	40	38	24
No adaptation technologies	5	15	18	25
Digital technologies for adaptation	20	39	30	15

Source: World Bank.

Note: Table shows the number of countries.

TABLE A.7 Priority Sectors for Mitigation and Adaptation, by Country Income Group

Mitigation

	Energy	Industry	Agriculture	Land use, land use change, and forestry	Waste management	Transport	Cross-cutting	Other
Low-income	28	17	23	25	24	18	6	2
Lower-middle-income	52	40	47	44	46	42	12	14
Upper-middle-income	50	28	36	41	43	39	11	8
High-income	54	46	46	44	45	49	33	7

Adaptation

	Energy	Industrial processes and product use	Agriculture	Land use, land use change, and forestry	Waste management	Transport	Urban	Other
Low-income	22	3	28	23	13	12	6	13
Lower-middle-income	34	9	50	43	26	26	29	44
Upper-middle-income	23	8	38	29	14	19	26	33
High-income	42	43	43	44	41	39	15	9

Source: World Bank.

Note: Table shows the number of countries.

Note

1. Net Zero Tracker (dashboard), Energy and Climate Intelligence Unit (UK), https://zerotracker
    .net/, 2022.

References

UNFCCC (United Nations Framework Convention on Climate Change). 2022. "NDC Registry."
    https://unfccc.int/NDCREG.

World Bank. 2019. "New Country Classifications by Income Level: 2019–2020." Data Blog, July 1,
    2019. https://blogs.worldbank.org/opendata/new-country-classifications-income-level
    -2019-2020.

www.ingramcontent.com/pod-product-compliance
Lightning Source LLC
Chambersburg PA
CBHW080552220326
41599CB00032B/6456